The Mafia of a
Sicilian Village,
1860-1960

The Mafia of a

Sicilian Village, 1860-1960

A Study of Violent Peasant Entrepreneurs

Anton Blok

With a Foreword by Charles Tilly

WAVELAND
PRESS, INC.
Prospect Heights, Illinois

For information about this book, write or call:
    Waveland Press, Inc.
    P.O. Box 400
    Prospect Heights, Illinois 60070
    (312) 634-0081

To Valeria Melissa

Contents

		Page
Foreword		xiii
Preface		xxvii

Part One
THE SETTING

I	*The Argument*	5
II	*The Village*	17
	Physical features of the area	17
	The appearance of the village	20
	Communications	22
	Early history	26
	Demography	29
III	*The Land*	36
	Land Tenure	36
	Agricultural work	42
	Latifondismo and rent capitalism	53
IV	*The Latifondo*	58
	Attempts at reform	68
	Decline	76

Part Two
THE MAFIA

V	*Genesis of Mafia*	89
VI	*Expansion, 1860–1914*	103
	The case of Matteo	103
	Discussion	112
	The sale of church domains	116
	The peasant versus the *gabelloto*	121
	The rise of the Cassinis	127
	A struggle for *gabelle*	131

		Page
VII	*Heyday and Decline, 1914–1943*	141
	The network of *cosche*	142
	Cosche in conflict	161
	The structure of violence	171
	The roundup	182
VIII	*Re-emergence, 1943 and After*	190
	The struggle for land	193
	Excursus on violence	210
	Epilogue	213
	Appendices	231
	Glossary	264
	Bibliography	267
	Index	287

List of Tables

		Page
I	Population of Genuardo: 1548–1966	244
II	Distribution of land in Genuardo (1900)	245
III	Changes in the distribution of landed properties in Genuardo: 1843–1966	245
IV	Changes in the distribution of landed properties larger than 200 hectares	246
V	Patterns of land use in Genuardo from 1852 to 1947	246
VI	Animals belonging to people living in Genuardo (1900–1966)	247
VII	The pattern of landholdings in Genuardo (1930)	247
VIII	Labor force at Baronessa (1902)	248
IX	Flocks herded on the Baronessa estates between September 1920 and August 1921	249
X	Land use and division of labor at Baronessa according to Buttazzoni (1939)	250
XI	Animals employed at Baronessa according to Buttazzoni (1939)	250
XII	Changes in the distribution of landed properties in Genuardo: 1947–1966	251
XIII	Division, sale, and expropriation of the Baronessa estates from 1946 onwards	252
XIV	Elections in Genuardo: 1946–1948	252

List of Diagrams

		Page
1	The Jaconis: *gabelloti* and professionals	253
2	Latifundist kin group Vassallo	254
3	Intermarriage Pizzo/Jaconi	255
4	Inheritance of the Santa Maria del Bosco estates	256
5	Section of the Jaconis	257
6	The Selvinis	258
7	The Cassinis: *gabelloti*	259
8	Composition of the core of the Adernò *mafia*	260
9	Section of the Jaconis (about 1914)	261
10	Section of the Cassinis	262
11	The Olivieris: *gabelloti*	263

List of Plates

Between pages 126 and 127

    I   Agro-town in the Palermo hinterland

   II   *Latifondi* north of Genuardo. By courtesy of Bianca Dony

  III   Guenardo as seen from the North

  IV   Boy plowing with mules

   V   *Masserìa* near the Cascina estate

  VI   *Masserìa* of the Moli estate

 VII   Former *gabelloti* during intermezzo at threshing

VIII   Area south of Baronessa. By courtesy of Bianca Dony

  IX   Grisafi and his companions

   X   Threshing on the commons just above the village

  XI   Area where Alessandro was killed

 XII   *Contadino*

XIII   *Contadino*

(With the exception of plate IX, all photographs were taken during 1965—67. Photographs I, IV, V, VI, VII, XI, XII, and XIII are by the author.)

List of Maps

		Page
1	Map of western Sicily	1
2	Commune of 'Genuardo'	2

The author's and publishers' thanks are due to George Stuber, who designed the maps, and to H. M. van Groos, on whose originals the maps were based.

Foreword

As recently as January 1973, the political connections of Sicily's *mafia* made headlines. One more parliamentary commission had emerged to study "the phenomenon of Mafia in Sicily." Once again observers linked one of the Sicilian members of the commission to *mafia* activities. This time the tempest began when a newly-elected deputy, a lawyer from Palermo, joined the commission. Giovanni Matta had been Palermo's public works commissioner in a time when the city had been renting high-priced classrooms from a reputed *mafioso*, instead of spending the school construction money already earmarked for Palermo by the central government. Two years earlier, Mr. Matta had actually been called to testify before the same commission. "The records show," reports the *New York Times*, "that Mr. Matta, in his testimony before the commission, praised Mr. Vassallo, the developer and alleged *Mafioso*, 'as a builder and also as a benefactor.'" The Sicilian phenomenon of *mafia* was over a century old, and apparently still well-connected.

Anton Blok identifies the crucial connections. He doesn't make them in the usual way; he doesn't dazzle us with a Who's Who of "chiefs" and "families." That way of dealing with the problem is often sensational, but its importance is fleeting; the Sicilian way of doing business has lasted far longer than any particular leader or clique.

Instead, Blok closes in on the circumstances that created *mafia*. He singles out the structures that keep it thriving. He concerns himself with the rural setting in which the phenomenon originated and prospered, rather than with the cities in which it eventually multiplied. There he uses a combination of direct observation, historical reconstruction, and shrewd deduction to display the destructive genius of the system.

The central characteristic of *mafia*, in Blok's view, is the private use of unlicensed violence as a means of control in the public arena. Although real people employ the unlicensed violence, although some people are full-time specialists in its employment, Sicily has never had any single organization one could properly call The Mafia. The Mafia supergang is a simplifying fiction, invented by publicists and by Fascist officials charged with eliminating southern lawlessness. On the other hand, there really are *mafiosi*—men wielding power through the systematic use of private violence. The sum of their actions makes up the phenomenon called *mafia*.

If *mafia* exists, but The Mafia does not, should we conclude that *mafia*'s concentration in Sicily results from some unusual facet of Sicilian attitudes and personalities? At one point Luigi Barzini suggests as much:

> The reason why Sicily is ungovernable is that the inhabitants have long ago learned to distrust and neutralize all written laws (alien laws in particular) and to govern themselves in their own rough homemade fashion, as if official institutions did not exist. This arrangement is highly unsatisfactory (the inhabitants themselves endlessly lament their fate) because it cures no ills, in fact makes them worse, promotes injustice and tyranny, leaves crimes unpunished, does not make use of the Sicilians' best qualities, and has kept the country stagnant and backward in almost every way. It consists of a technique, or art, which is second nature to all Sicilians, both the decent, hard-working, honorable Sicilians, and the criminal minority, which includes the Mafia, that of building up one's personal power, and of acquiring enough power to intimidate or frighten one's competitors, rivals, or enemies, in order to defend one's honor and welfare at all times (Barzini 1972: 75–76).

The actions of the *mafiosi*, however, are not simply the expression of a peculiar Sicilian character; they depend on a peculiar set of economic and political arrangements. If that were not the case, it would be puzzling that *mafia* virtually collapsed for the entire Fascist period, only to spring up refreshed after World War II. Blok explains why. The problem is not to discover who the *mafiosi* were, or even what their character was. It is to locate the connections between the prevalence of private violence and the structure of economic and political life.

In the rural region below Palermo where Anton Blok lived and observed, the fundamental framework of social life was a three-class system. Landless and land-poor laborers inhabiting dense villages worked the fields, and gave up most of the product of their labor to others. Rentiers, many of whom inhabited Palermo and other cities, owned a major part of the land, and lived on its proceeds. Between the laborers and the rentiers were a group of managers running from leaseholders and overseers to the strongarm men hired to protect the landlord's property and to keep unruly tenants and workers in line. The managers assured the landlord's income, and defended his local power; in return they received wide liberty to exploit and coerce the workers for their own ends. The landlords used their private armed forces to ward off rivals, as well as the State, and provided their managers with protection from outside interference.

On hearing of such a place, we are likely to call it "backward" or "feudal" or "underdeveloped," one more proof that Sicily is actually part of the Third World. Certainly most Sicilians are very poor, and are trapped in a web of exploitation. Yet it would be quite wrong to consider Sicily a leftover from traditional Europe. Wrong for more than one reason. Sicily has, at several points in history, been a major center of European civilization. The island's 13th-century Norman court was, for example, one of Europe's most brilliant. Through the 18th century Sicily was a rich supplier of wheat to the rest of the continent. We have to explain, not eternal backwardness, but a decline from greatness.

Furthermore, the Sicilian peasantry—if we mean by peasants agricultural populations organized into households which supply most of their own needs, yield a surplus to outsiders, and have some stable control over the land they work—has long since given way to a population composed essentially of mobile agricultural laborers. The three-class system works on the premise that the land and its products belong to the landlords, that the crops will be marketed for distant consumption, that the workers barter their labor for wages or a share of the crop, and own little or nothing beyond their labor. These are not traditional agrarian conditions; they are the outgrowth of the specific relations Sicilian landlords and managers worked out with modern world markets, the product of the system of productive relations Anton Blok calls rent capitalism.

In these regards, the origins and present circumstances of Sicilian agricultural workers resemble those of former peasant populations at the edge of capitalism throughout the world: in Latin America, in Southeast Asia, and elsewhere. Through mechanisms such as the latifundium, the hacienda, or the plantation we find "rent capitalists" consolidating control over the land, harnessing cheap labor for world markets, and converting semi-autonomous peasants into dependent proletarians.

Other authors have sketched these relationships on an international scale in the midst of broad theories of imperialism and dependency (see, e.g., Cockcroft, Frank and Johnson 1972). Anton Blok shows how they affect the lives of individuals. One important summary runs like this:

> The vast majority of peasants, even those who held small plots of their own, depended for their livelihood on the large estates, working seasonally as sharecroppers, day laborers, herdsmen, plow-servants, pruners, or watchmen. Very often, the peasant performed several of these roles in the course of the agricultural year, and often on several different estates. With the triennial rotation system and the *latifondo*'s requirement of a strong labor force only in the summer and fall, the peasant was compelled to move continuously from place to place in search of work. Moreover, he could rarely obtain a sharecropping contract for a plot on a single *latifondo* sufficient to the needs of himself and his family, and consequently he had to lease additional plots from several other employers on different and

often widely scattered estates. Even the peasant's own small plots were generally dispersed throughout the territory. Therefore, he spent considerable time traveling on foot and muleback between the village and the land, and between the several holdings on which he had to work. This itinerant character of labor, moreover, given the situation of endemic insecurity and the inability of the State to guarantee public order in the countryside, rendered the peasant vulnerable to assault and hence dependent on private power holders capable of providing "protection" in exchange for tribute—all in addition to the burdens of direct exploitation, which in certain periods left the peasant sharecropper with but a quarter of his product.

He documents this summary by describing particular estates and individual peasants.

Why didn't the agricultural workers fight or flee this miserable existence? As a matter of fact, they did both—when they could. The rural populations of Sicily rose *en masse* during the national revolutions of 1848 and 1860, as well as at several other points in the 19th century. In the 1890s, the Sicilian Fasci mounted a large and impressive effort to organize agricultural workers around a program of better wages, improved leases, and reduced taxes; it took a massive military force, dispatched by the central government, to crush the movement. After then, Sicilians migrated elsewhere at an extraordinary rate.

Nevertheless, the rural population was vulnerable. Blok's analysis helps us to understand why. There was enough population pressure to keep wages low and underemployment prevalent. Rural villages were poorly connected with each other. The strategic importance of vertical patron-client ties itself blocked the formation of extensive horizontal ties among workers bearing the same relationship to different managers and landlords. The whole system made it costly, even dangerous, to maintain connections in other villages and other structures of power. So long as emigration was difficult and the protection of the national State uncertain, the rural population remained eminently exploitable.

The particular system of exploitation Anton Blok analyzes came into being in the nineteenth century. Following a line of analysis already proposed for Sicily as a whole by Salvatore Francesco Romano, Blok locates the historical origins of the *mafiosi* in the "liberalization" of land ownership—the dispossession of the Church, breaking up of common lands, abolition of "feudal" modes of landholding, and so on. In that process a few bourgeois joined the old aristocrats in consolidating large estates, in holding down the demands of the peasants who were being dispossessed, and in warding off the unwelcome intervention of the State in favor of centralized administration or of genuine land reform. The *mafiosi* were creatures of the landlords; they began as armed retainers, and ended up as exploiters with considerable autonomy. As Blok says:

> ... *mafiosi* were recruited from the ranks of the peasantry to provide the large estate owners with armed staffs to confront both the impact of the State and the restive peasants, especially in the inland areas of the island where the Bourbon State failed to monopolize the use of physical power.... Thus while on the one hand *mafiosi* heightened class tensions through their control over land, they checked open rebellions and sustained revolts in several ways: by force; by keeping a hold on outside influence; by opening avenues for upwardly mobile peasants; and by turning outlaws and bandits into allies.

Blok follows this theme through the past and present of one Sicilian village—a village he knows, loves, and grieves for. The secret of his work is his blending of real lives, sympathetically observed, with big processes, keenly detected.

There would be no point in my rehearsing his analysis. Anton Blok's book will stand by itself. If *The Mafia of a Sicilian Village* needs commentary at all, it is only to bring out the connections between the local processes he has portrayed so deftly and the concentration of power at the national and international levels. For we have a nice paradox: At first view, the set of social arrangements called *mafia* is the antithesis of strong and orderly government; yet that same *mafia* couldn't exist without great concentration of power in national states. The reason is simple: the *mafioso* can't push ordinary people around without having some claim on the protection of someone wealthier and more powerful than he is, and the great landlords who protect the *mafiosi* can't enjoy their surprising freedom of action unless they have fashioned a sort of non-intervention agreement with the regional and national authorities.

The system rests on patronage without complete control. If the national State collapsed, the ability of the persons higher up in the chain of patronage both to protect and to restrain those below them would dwindle. Relatively stable local systems of power (not necessarily gentler or juster than *mafia*) would tend to emerge. If the national State supplanted the great protectors, on the other hand, the autonomy of their *mafioso* clients would decline. (Whether that would end up being a good thing for the mass of the population, however, would depend on the relative rapacity of the *mafia* and of the State.) Changes in the amount of day-to-day force applied within the system result mainly from changes in the relative autonomy of the different groups involved in it.

The system producing *mafia* is cruel and curious. It parallels government in some respects, and intertwines with government in other respects. Like governments, its operators rely on control of concentrated and effective means of coercion to keep the bulk of the population in line. Like governments, the beneficiaries of the system, directly or indirectly, tax the producers of wealth—the agricultural workers. Like many governments, the system permits each of the operators to scoop some of the proceeds from the flow toward the top. It depends on government to stand far enough away not to interfere with the flow of proceeds, but close enough to assure that neither rivals nor the people at the bottom will block the flow. Unlike most governments, however, the system has no accountability, no visibility, no means of representation for those under its control. So the *mafia* system is more curious and more cruel than government itself. The murders, thefts and mutilations its operators use to maintain their control—

to "make themselves respected"—are only the most lurid manifestations of its evil.

Blok's own approach to government is interesting and subtle. He regards state-formation (including the concentration of control over the use of violence in a single organization) as an immanent, civilizing process. It is immanent in the sense that it has its own momentum and direction; the process is too big and complicated for any particular ruler or regime to control it. It is civilizing in the sense that it incorporates segmented and peripheral populations into a common system of communication and understanding. In this view, the power-holders have blocked the process of state-formation. The multiplicity of power centers testifies to the early stage of the process in which Sicily is still situated. Although *mafia* could not have appeared without a measure of state-formation, *mafia* survives because of state-formation's arrested development.

This analysis helps us to relate *mafia* to banditry. To the extent that they operate on their own, without protection, those who kill and plunder for gain are bandits. There are bandits in Sicily now; at times the island has been infested with bandits. They differ from *mafiosi* in two important regards: (1) they do most of their work through the direct use of force; the *mafiosi* only employ force when someone steps out of line; (2) they do not belong to long, reliable, and protective patron-client chains. To the extent that they are successful, in fact, bandits tend to be drawn into *mafia*. When they begin to build up their own power domains, bandits threaten *mafia*; the operators of *mafia* then coopt them or destroy them. The comparison shows *mafia* to be both more similar to regular government and more dependent on regular government than is banditry. In that regard, one might imagine a continuum running from anarchy to banditry to *mafia* to routine government. The defining feature of that continuum is the extent to which control over the use of force is concentrated in a single organization.

That implicit continuum connects Blok's analysis to phenomena far more general than *mafia* or Sicilian villages. What he calls state-formation, other people have often tried to deal with as "political development." The notion of political development stresses the analogy with the self-sustaining economic growth much desired (but, in fact, little achieved) by today's nations. It suggests a difficult but irreversible break with traditional authority, apathetic citizens, ineffective government. Nothing is easier than to slip into the explanation of Sicily's problems as a consequence of political *under*development. A careless reading of Blok will give the impression that by stressing the incompleteness of state-formation, he is advancing that very view.

He is not. According to his analysis, *mafia* is in no sense a residue of the lawless past. It is an outgrowth of the particular form that the process of state-formation took in Italy. It grew up precisely because national systems of power expanded without obliterating local systems of power—and the connections between the two were few, fragile, and open to monopoly. For a long period the central governments (if they wanted to govern at all) had to work through their rivals, the very landlords and *mafiosi* they had helped to create. In that regard, they resembled the Chinese governments which had little choice but to deal with gentry and warlords, or the Central American governments which reached the people through *caciques*. A splendid dialectic. And one which renders inappropriate any idea of political development as the continuous, self-directed struggle of a particular government over the forces of tradition, corruption, and particularism.

State-formation, then, is a great and powerful process, but it is not immanent in particular governments, is not unidirectional, and is not, in any simple sense of the words, a displacement of the "traditional" by the "modern." The process is international and historically specific. After 1500 national states supplanted churches, clans, empires, cities, federations, tribes, and many other kinds of groupings as the dominant organizations throughout the world. The contemporary system of states grew up in Europe, expanded into Europe's dependencies, and eventually took over the rest of the world. Since the 1940s the United Nations and similar international structures have been engaged in the frenzied mapping of the entire globe into stably-bounded states. The process has continued for hundreds of years with relatively few reversals.

Outside political units have always played a large part in the formation of any particular state; they have acted as rivals, allies or models. Italy and Austria helped create each other—not least by making war. The extent of outside involvement in the formation of particular states has generally risen over time; witness the redrawing of national boundaries at the ends of World Wars I and II, not to mention the international involvement in the recent formation of states throughout Africa and Asia. The greater the intervention of outsiders in the State-building process, the less reasonable it is to represent the process as immanent.

Second, the State-building processes of the last few centuries have not produced individual states, each passing through a standard evolution, so much as whole *sets* of interdependent states. There are sets consisting of a dominant state with its clients, as with the United States and Central America or the Soviet Union and Eastern Europe. There are clusters of approximate equals, all related to each other, as with the Middle East. There are networks linked more subtly by economic and/or military dependency, as with the 16th century symbiosis between the grain-exporting principalities of Eastern Europe and the grain-importing states of Western Europe. If immanence and linear development are operating, they must operate at a larger scale than the single state.

Third, the great European State-building processes involved the building of political units where none had existed before, rather than the straightforward transformation of existing political entities. Most often the rulers of one vital area extended their control to adjacent areas by conquest, alliance, marriage, inheritance, subversion, and every other device at their disposal. Italy grew up around the domains of Savoy, Germany around the territories of Brandenburg-Prussia, Spain around Castile. These cases are particularly telling because in all of them effective unification under a central government came only recently. A single group of managers assumed control over territories and populations which had remained subject to multiple, more or less autonomous, governments into the 19th century. So what unit experienced the State-building process? Prussia? Savoy? Sicily?

Finally, the processes Anton Blok has witnessed in Sicily are, in fact, standard State-building processes: consolidation of control over the use of force, elimination of rivals, formation of coalitions, extension of protection, routinized extraction of resources. If one *mafia* network managed to extend its control over all of Sicily, all concerned would begin to describe its actions as "public" rather than "private," the national government would have to come to terms with it, outsiders and insiders alike would begin to treat its chief as the legitimate authority. It would be a government; it would resemble a state. With outside recognition of its autonomy, plus the development of differentiated and centralized instruments of control, it would *be* a state. (At that point, no doubt, some political scientist would pop up to demonstrate the applicability of a general model of political development to the Sicilian case, and to point out how Sicily's success grew from its 19th-century roots.) The difficulty is simply that Sicily now has many such proto-states. Sicily's problem is not a shortage, but a surfeit, of government.

At first glance, then, Anton Blok is undertaking one more analysis of the politics of backward areas, offering one more brief for modern, effective government. Yet as his analysis unfolds, it bursts the prefabricated boxes into which we try to stuff it. *Mafia* does not fit our categories of lawlessness, disorder, conspiracy, or organized crime; it does not reflect the traditionalism, anarchism, impenetrability, perversity of individual Sicilians or of Sicily as a whole; the process of State-formation helped create it, as it will eventually help destroy it. His observations should make us stop and think every time someone proposes the strengthening and rationalization of government as the solution to crime, corruption, injustice or local tyranny in Brazil, in Vietnam, in Italy ... or, for that matter, in the United States or Great Britain.

Still, Blok's ideas about State-formation are only the context and outgrowth of his book's main concerns. For the most part, he deals with the fates of vulnerable people in the midst of multiple concentrations of power. The fate is not pretty; Blok makes no effort to beautify it. The beauty of his book is in the analysis, in the way he ties everyday routines, ordinary suffering, concrete social relations in one forlorn Sicilian village to structures of power and exploitation which are common throughout the contemporary world.

CHARLES TILLY

University of Michigan

References

Luigi Barzini
1972   *From Caesar to the Mafia.* New York: Bantam Books

James D. Cockcroft, Andre Gunder Frank and Dale L. Johnson
1972   *Dependence and Underdevelopment: Latin America's Political Economy.* Garden City: Doubleday Anchor.

Salvatore Francesco Romano
1959   *Storia dei Fasci Siciliani.* Bari: Laterza.
1963   *Storia della mafia.* Milan: Sugar.

Preface

*Underlying all intended interactions
of human beings is their unintended
interdependence.*

Norbert Elias

This study seeks to account for the rural *mafia* in western Sicily in the 19th and 20th centuries through a detailed examination of the overall social networks *mafiosi* of a particular peasant community formed with other individuals. In this way, it reveals the conditions under which *mafiosi* became a powerful force in the west Sicilian hinterland.

Living in the community of "Genuardo" for two and a half years, I assumed a "village-outward" viewpoint to understand what happened there over the past hundred years. From conversations and impromptu interviews with local people, which were complemented with and checked by work on published material and archival documents, it became gradually clear that the rise and development of the village *mafia*, as well as its temporary decline under Fascism and its rebirth after the last world war, should be considered in a larger social and historical context.

The community, though appropriate as a locus for study, proved hardly adequate as a unit of analysis. Villages like Genuardo are part of larger complex societies. Many of their particular characteristics are dependent upon and a reflex of the larger society and can only be explained with reference to their specific connections with it. This is especially true of *mafiosi*, rural entrepreneurs of sorts, who were until recently an outstanding feature of peasant communities in Sicily's western interior. Recruited from the ranks of peasants and shepherds, and entrusted with tasks of surveillance on the large estates (latifundia) of absentee landlords, they constituted a particular variety of middlemen—individuals who operate in different social realms and who succeed in maintaining a grip on the intrinsic tensions between these spheres. *Mafiosi* managed these tensions by means of physical force. Poised between landowning elite and peasants, between city and countryside, and between central government and the village, they sought to control and monopolize the links between these various groups and segments of society. The argument of this book is that the violent operations of *mafiosi* in the west Sicilian countryside and the general level of socially permitted physical violence remain incomprehensible unless these phenomena are understood in relation to the distinct stage of development reached by Italian society at large—in particular, the degree of stable central control over the means of physical force in its southern periphery. The reader should be forewarned, however, lest he misread the argument of this book as a call for *étatisme*. These pages merely assert an inverse relationship in a given setting between the extent and acceptance of private violence and the level of State control over the means of coercion. The State is ultra-violence incarnate, and such acts of State as the extermination of European Jews, the elimination of the kulaks as a class, and the napalming of unsubmissive peasants in Southeast Asia are well beyond the modest means of the violent individuals and the local cliques portrayed in this volume.

The approach followed in this book involves specific notions of society, social order, and social structure. To discover and understand the factual interdependencies between *mafiosi*, landlords, bandits, peasants, and many other individuals, there is no need to assume that groups, configurations, and societies are something abstracted from the individuals who form them. The second part of this volume, which deals with coalitions and larger networks of which *mafiosi* were part, demonstrates that these configurations are neither more nor less "real" than the individuals who formed them. One way to disencumber onself from the reified abstractions which still loom large in conventional sociological and anthropological analysis is to shift one's focus from a short-term to a long-term perspective. I have not primarily dealt with problems regarding the way the village society worked at a particular point of time, that is, when I lived there in the 1960s. One often gains the impression that such problems proceed from an inadequate conceptualization of what we actually observe and seek to explain. They seem to rise from the question of what society *is* rather than from the question of how society *becomes* or *has become* in the past. Change is a normal characteristic of human beings and societies. Yet when asked to conceptualize social changes adequately, we often find ourselves in a mental cramp. One can see why. To study a particular society in a given state and at a given point of time entails essentially static notions or order, social structure, and society which leave problems of change and development largely unexplored and hence unexplained. If changes in such "social systems" are perceived at all, they are seen as an unstructured flow, as incidental, "historical" changes. In their paradigmatic study of an urban community in the English midlands, Elias and Scotson emphasize

> that sociological problems can hardly ever be adequately framed if they seem to be concerned with social phenomena exclusively at a given point and time—with structures which, to use the language of films, have the form of a "still." They approximate more closely . . . what one can observe, and lead to comprehensive explanations only if they are conceived as problems of phenomena which have the form of processes, which participate in a movement of time. . . . The ruling concept of social structure has a strong tendency to make people perceive structures as "stills," as "steady state structures," while movements of structures in time, whether they have the form of developments or of other types of social changes, are treated as "historical"; and that often means in the sociologists' language as something apart from the structure, not as an indelible property of social structures themselves (1965:11–12).[1]

1. Elsewhere they state: "In community studies as in many other

The central problem here is to discover how and why communities like Genuardo have become what they are, and this requires a shift from a static system model to a dynamic process model. The genesis and development of *mafia* in the village of Genuardo and its recent waning in the rural areas constitute a structured process, which becomes intelligible once we see how *mafiosi* were part of larger configurations of interdependent individuals, and how *mafia* was connected with other aspects of the same long-term development of Sicily and Italian society at large: the growing impact of the market, the increase of population, the proletarianization of large sectors of the peasantry, upward and downward social mobility, urbanization, outward migration, and State-formation. In this study, the concepts of structure and social order refer to these interconnections *over time.* This dynamic conceptualization of society, in which the structure of change moves into focus, enables one to understand such contemporary episodes in the village as, for example, the large-scale migrant labor movement and the growing marginality and obsolescence of peasant farming, since these events proceed from and are structurally related to the processes and configurations explored below. Considering the rural exodus and the decline of peasant farming as mere contemporary phenomena, one can only describe. not explain them.

My task has thus been that of both an anthropologist and a social historian. However invaluable and indispensable, the field work experience alone is insufficient to cope with the events of change in complex societies. To grasp the relationship between peasants and the larger society, data from

> sociological investigations, the exploration of the development of the organisation of people under review is often treated as extraneous to the ′exploration of its structure at a given time. According to the present conventions of thinking, history has no structure and structure no history. . . . The conceptual and methodological separation of enquiries into the structure of human groupings at a given time and enquiries into the structure of the processes in the course of which they became what they were, showed itself . . . as wholly artificial" (Elias and Scotson 1965: 21–22).

field work must be supplemented with historical information. This point is increasingly recognized by anthropologists— yet, apart from a few important exceptions (notably Eric Wolf), more in words than in actual fact. The relationships between part and whole are still poorly conceptualized and hence poorly understood. Peasants and *mafiosi*, the main personages of this book, were not only part of a larger society in the same sense that certain organs form part of a larger organism. They also reflected the larger society, as a microcosm reflects a macrocosm. Their characteristics—their language, their attitudes toward manual labor, their relationship with kinsmen and women, and their relatively low level of revulsion against using and witnessing physical violence— can only be understood as a representative of the larger society they formed with other individuals. At the same time they remained distinct and different from these individuals and the larger whole.

Through his relatively long personal contact with local people, the anthropologist can empathize with their specific problems and thereby discover what particular kind of historical information on the larger society is relevant for a more adequate understanding of these problems. In this way, anthropology and social history are geared to one another and lend a new meaning to the field work experience.

The present book is the outcome of a concern with Sicilian peasant problems that stretches out over the past eleven years. Field research lasted roughly thirty months, spent in the community of Genuardo, situated toward the western interior of the island. A preliminary visit that lasted from June through November 1961 yielded material on settlement patterns and agrarian reform (Blok 1966; 1969a). In April 1965 I returned to the same village and continued field work until June 1967. Alongside teaching anthropology and other commitments, the writing of the present volume took some five years.

During my research in Sicily and the prolonged gestation of this essay I have incurred many debts. To acknowledge them all is hardly possible, and, given the subject, hardly xxxii *Preface*

advisable. There are original debts of gratitude to Professor André J. F. Köbben, who aroused my interests in anthropology and under whose aegis I began field work. He read an earlier version of the manuscript and criticized it constructively. I remain indebted to the Netherlands Organization for the Advancement of Pure Research (Z.W.O.) for grants which supported the field work and for additional financial aid during 1967–68 which enabled me to write up part of the collected material (Blok 1969c; 1973). I gratefully acknowledge the kindness of Dr. E. Meerum Terwogt, who has been very helpful during those years. Professor Eric R. Wolf, whose work is basic to my understanding of peasants and their problems, has been a constant source of inspiration and encouragement. The University of Michigan Mediterranean Study Program generously provided a grant that permitted me to attend two conferences on Mediterranean peasant communities that Professor Wolf and Professor William D. Schorger organized in Aix-en-Provence in 1966 and in Canterbury in 1967. I am indebted to my good friends Jane and Peter Schneider (who studied a neighboring town) for many insights into the problems herein discussed, as well as for their friendship and hospitality. The paradigmatic writings of Professor Norbert Elias have deeply influenced the cast of this book. I wish to thank him for his kindness in giving me valuable advice. Professor Johan Goudsblom and Dick van den Bosch read through the entire manuscript and saved me from some serious errors. I also have to thank Bianca Dony, Anna Eyken, Gerrit Huizer, Pasquale Marchese, Pieter de Meyer, Rudo Niemeyer, and Willem Wolters who helped me in various ways. Mrs. Margaret Jansen and Ms. Barbara Kessler typed two versions of the manuscript with skill and patience, for which they have my warm thanks. My indebtedness to several friends in Sicily is obvious and must be expressed silently.

My major personal and intellectual debt, however, is to my very good friend Professor Jeremy Boissevain, who supervised the preparation of an earlier version of this volume as a doctoral dissertation at the University of Amsterdam. He has carefully and patiently read various drafts of the manu-

script, providing valuable advice, criticism, and encouragement. Finally, I wish to thank my friend Roderick Aya, who,
besides translating the passages from Marx and Vöchting in
Part I, rendered editorial advice on style and substance that
has made this a much better book.

ANTON BLOK

Ann Arbor, Michigan
October, 1972

. . . any simple straightforward truth about political institutions or events is bound to have polemical consequences. It will damage some group interests. In any society the dominant groups are the ones with the most to hide about the way society works. Very often therefore truthful analyses are bound to have a critical ring, to seem like exposures rather than objective statements, as the term is conventionally used. . . . For all students of human society, sympathy with the victims of historical processes and skepticism about the victors' claims provide essential safeguards against being taken in by the dominant mythology. A scholar who tries to be objective needs these feelings as part of his ordinary working equipment.

BARRINGTON MOORE, JR.,
Social Origins of Dictatorship and Democracy: Lord and Peasant in the Making of the Modern World.
Boston: Beacon Press, 1966, pp. 522–23.

WESTERN SICILY
with PROVINCIAL BOUNDARIES

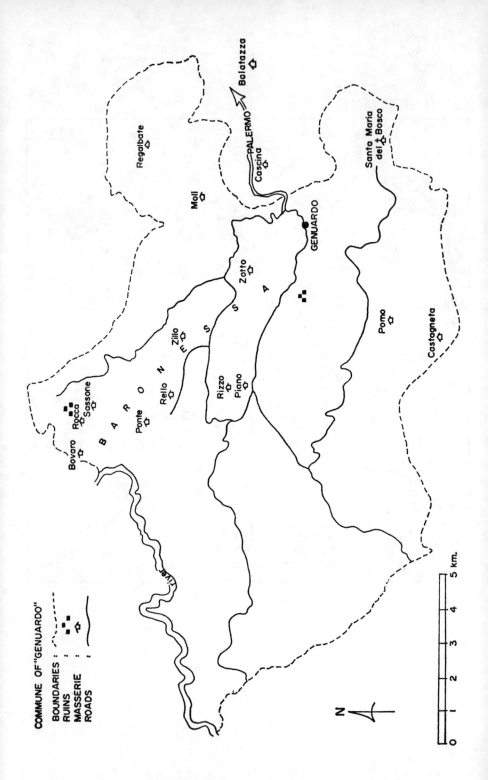

COMMUNE OF "GENUARDO"

BOUNDARIES :
RUINS :
MASSERIE :
ROADS :

PALERMO

Balatazza

Regalbate

Moli

Cascina

Santa Maria
del Bosco

Zotto

GENUARDO

A

Zillo

Pomo

S

Castagneta

S

Rizzo

Piano

Rello

N

Sassone

Rocca

Ponte

O

Bovaro

B   A   R

N

0   1   2   3   4   5 km.

PART ONE
THE SETTING

The specific economic form in which unpaid surplus labor is pumped out of the direct producers determines the relation of domination and servitude, as it grows directly out of production itself and in return reacts upon it as a determinant. Upon this, however, is founded the entire formation of the economic community which grows up out of the production relations themselves and therewith simultaneously its specific political form. It is in each case the direct relation of the owners of the conditions of production to the direct producers—a relation whose prevailing form always by nature corresponds to a definite stage in the development of the kind and mode of labor and therefore of its social productive power—in which we find the innermost secret, the hidden foundation of the entire social construction and therefore also of the political form of the relation of sovereignty and dependence, in short, of the prevailing specific form of the State. This does not hinder [the fact] that the same economic basis— the same as regards its main conditions—can, due to innumerable different empirical circumstances, natural conditions, race relations, external historical influences, etc., show infinite variations and gradations in appearance, which are only to be understood through analysis of these empirically given circumstances.

KARL MARX,
Das Kapital, Vol. III.
Berlin: Dietz Verlag, 1951, pp. 841–842.

I
The Argument

The present study attempts to give an account of the *mafia* of a Sicilian village with special reference to *mafiosi* in their role as political middlemen. The approach is diachronic and covers the period between 1860 and 1960. Genuardo, as this village will henceforth be called,[1] is a peasant community located in the mountainous western interior of the island, the area of the large landed estates in which *mafia* rose and flourished. As was the case with many mountain villages in southern Italy, the population of Genuardo decreased since the unification of Italy in 1861. At that time, it amounted to almost 3,400 inhabitants and was reduced to just 1,900 by the end of World War I. When I lived there (1965–67), Genuardo had roughly 2,600 inhabitants, some 500 absent migrant laborers included. Like most villages and towns in this inland region, Genuardo forms a highly compact settlement, which physically separates the people from the land on which most of them still depend for their living.

Mafia has been defined in various ways, and in a sense we are still trying to come to grips with it: conceptually, empirically, and as a social problem.[2] Since the term gained currency in the mid-19th century, widely different views on *mafia*, in everyday language as well as in scientific idiom, have had their staunch upholders. For some people the *mafia* was a criminal association operating at the margin of Sicilian society. For others it was an appendage of the social order: a corporate structure opposed and detrimental to the State

1. For obvious reasons I have changed the names of certain persons and places.
2. From 1963 to 1972 a Parliamentary Commission investigated its genesis and present spheres of action.

and Italian society. For still others it was a mere fiction, an invention of outsiders who could not or did not want to understand the fabric of Sicilian life. It might be argued that each of these different views makes sense with respect to the social position of those who maintain it. The study of native categories of thought is essential for any understanding of social reality. But in the end the anthropologist must translate the idiom of the culture he investigates into his own conceptual framework. I have tried to do this by considering *mafia* in terms of the private use of violence as a means of control. *Mafia* is a form of unlicensed violence, and those who participate in it are called *mafiosi* (sing.: *mafioso*). *Mafiosi* make decisions that affect the community. Their realm is the public, and this distinguishes them from those who have recourse to violence in other spheres such as, for instance, the home. The relationships between *mafiosi* and formal authorities are strongly ambivalent. On the one hand, *mafiosi* disregard formal law and are able to withstand the impact of the legal and governmental apparatus. On the other, *mafiosi* act in connivance with formal authority, and validate their control through covert and pragmatic relationships with those who hold formal office. This symbiosis distinguishes them from outlaws and bandits, whose power domains are also buttressed by physical force but contrast openly with those of the State.

These provisional definitions suggest that the *mafia* with which I am concerned in this book should be understood with reference to both the village and the larger society in which the village is contained. In the study of complex societies, anthropologists have recognized that the explanation of what goes on in small-scale local communities like Genuardo involves consideration of the outside forces impinging on those communities, as well as the reaction at the grass-roots level to these forces.[3] In fact, *mafia* developed through the 19th and 20th centuries when the modern State superimposed itself on a marginal peasant society which was

3. For the insights derived from this approach we remain indebted to Eric Wolf, who has consistently emphasized this point in his work on peasant societies.

still largely feudal in its basic features. The present essay, which focuses on a particular peasant community, attempts to trace the persistence of Sicilian *mafia* as a *modus vivendi* between the claims of the formal political framework on the one hand, and traditional local demands on the other. A central problem then is to explore the conditions that may account for the development of the gaps in communication between these different levels as well as the processes through which these gaps were bridged and exploited by *mafiosi*. The *mafioso* can therefore be considered as a variety of the political middleman or power broker, since his *raison d'être* is predicated upon his capacity to acquire and maintain control over the paths linking the local infrastructure of the village to the superstructure of the larger society.[4]

In this way the present study is not only of regional relevance. It seeks to contribute to the current discussion among social scientists of the processes through which small-scale communities all over the world are becoming increasingly intertwined with larger structures. In an early and most illuminating essay on this subject, Eric Wolf has demonstrated that we may enlarge our understanding of the ties between social groupings operating on different levels of a society through the study of such power brokers:

> For they stand guard over the crucial junctures or synapses of relationships which connect the local system to the larger whole. Their basic function is to relate community-oriented individuals who want to stabilize or improve their life chances, but who lack economic security and political connections, with nation-oriented individuals who operate primarily in terms of the complex cultural forms standard-

4. As Richard Adams has conceptualized the role of the power broker: "His actual control over either sphere depends upon his success in dealing with the other; his controls in one level of articulation provide a basis for controls in another. . . . He controls one domain only by virtue of having access to derivative power from a larger domain" (1970:320–21). Some authors define these domains in terms of political cultures or political structures, that is, as the sets of patterns and rules by which men in particular societies organize the competition for power (e.g., Friedrich 1968a: 199–204; Bailey 1969:1).

ized as national institutions, but whose success in these operations depends on the size and strength of their personal following. . . . [Brokers] must serve some of the interests of groups operating on both the community and the national level, and they must cope with the conflicts raised by the collision of these interests. They cannot settle them, since by doing so they would abolish their own usefulness to others. They thus often act as buffers between groups, maintaining the tensions which provide the dynamic of their actions (1956: 1075–76).

Given his strong interest and field experience in small-scale communities, the anthropologist has a special license to study the processes of encapsulation—the way in which State societies absorb or integrate these communities. His approach has the advantage of yielding primary data consisting of observable actions of political middlemen as they deal with community-oriented and nation-oriented individuals. The anthropologist's contribution should therefore be wholly complementary to that of the other social sciences which, from different points of view, focus on the same subject.

Mafiosi distinguish themselves from other intermediaries in at least two different respects. First, they exploit the gaps in communication between the peasant village and the larger society rather than closing or destroying them: they thrive upon these interstices and prevent others from making their own connections. Second, *mafiosi* ensure and buttress their intermediate position through the systematic threat and practice of physical violence. It is precisely along these two dimensions that the Sicilian *mafioso* as a broker of a violent type resembles the *cacique* in the Hispano–American area. In fact, *caciquismo* has been described as a form of informal politics that involves partially arbitrary control by a relatively small association of individuals under one leader. Like the *mafioso*, the Mexican Indian *cacique* is poised between incongruent political cultures which provide the setting for brokerage as well as the resources to be exploited in highly self-conscious styles.[5]

5. See Friedrich (1965; 1968a; 1968b). For an instructive discussion

As the title of the present book suggests, I have concentrated the description and analysis on a particular category of individuals. The village, its territory, and the outside world are considered as the setting in which *mafiosi* operated. More specifically, this setting involves landlords and peasants as well as professionals, civil servants, and politicians. Again, it should be appreciated that *mafia* could not have become what it was independently of these other groupings with which *mafiosi* formed specific configurations of interdependent individuals. Let me briefly explain the sense in which the term configuration is here understood.

The concept of configuration emphasizes the changing patterns of interdependencies in which individuals and groups of individuals are involved: both as allies and as opponents. The locus of change is not extraneous to the configuration. Change evolves from the built-in tensions and polarities between the elements that form the configuration. Elias, from whom I borrow this concept, has described the process of political centralization in terms of changing configurations. He demonstrates that the changes which ultimately led to the formation of centralized states in Western Europe can be largely understood from the immanent dynamics of these societies (Elias 1969, II: 123–311). People form configurations with each other, and these configurations have their own structured course through time. This can be envisaged in small groups, such as sport teams or villages, but also in larger units such as nations, or even at the level of inter-State relations. What these configurations have in common are their problems of tensions and of tension control which account for their inherent dynamics.[6] Unfortunately, contemporary sociological theories and most of the current

---

of the role of political middlemen in processes of encapsulation, see Bailey (1969:167–76). Cf. also Bailey (1966); Weingrod (1968); and Tilly (1967:60–61, 64–65, 141–42, 173) 196–97, 279–80).

6. See Elias and Dunning (1971) for a configurational analysis and synopsis of small groups. Frank has attempted a description and explanation of international dependency relationships in his study of capitalist development and underdevelopment (1967).

concepts are inadequate to understand the problems of social development. One reason for this state of affairs is that a long-term perspective has been systematically neglected in social theory since Durkheim. As a consequence, we cannot visualize social change, or any change for that matter, save in terms of a series of static pictures. This can be readily seen, for example, in the ease with which anthropologists indulge in the use of the so-called ethnographic present when dealing with past events. A configurational approach to society may help us break out of this impasse, because it focuses explicitly on the events of change, on structured, historical processes and the way they are interrelated. The insights to be gained from a configurational enquiry will only become clear from the very description of these changing interdependencies. The following synopsis of the processes with which Sicilian *mafia* was intertwined may help to clarify this point.

Mafia emerged in the early 19th century when the Bourbon State tried to curb the power of the traditional land-owning aristocracy and encouraged the emancipation of the peasantry. This initial configuration[7] involved the situation in which the central government claimed the monopoly of physical power on the local level and advocated a radical redistribution of the land. Feudal rights and privileges were abolished by law, and the peasants were offered a prospect of land which had become marketable. This so-called anti-feudal policy touched off tensions between the central government and the landowners, who sought to maintain their control over both the land and the peasants. At the same time, a growing population exacerbated pressure on the land. The rising aspirations of the peasantry on the one hand, and the reaction of the landowning elite on the other, set the course for specific patterns of interdependencies which were formed by these various groupings. The gradual emergence of what came to be known only later on as *"mafia"* can be understood in the context of this development in which the central government, the landlords, and the peasants arranged

7. No "zero-point" is implied here: Bourbon centralization grew out of distinct developments in 18th century Sicily which will be discussed later on.

and rearranged themselves in conflict and accommodation. I have referred above to this pattern as a *modus vivendi*, in which *mafiosi* were recruited from the ranks of the peasantry to provide the large estate owners with armed staffs to confront both the impact of the State and the restive peasants, especially in the inland areas of the island where the Bourbon State failed to monopolize the use of physical power. Discussing Bourbon times, Mack Smith observes:

> Twenty-five Companies at Arms policed the countryside, but altogether there were usually fewer than 350 such policemen for the whole island. Two or three times a year a company of troops would arrive in each village and round up a token number of malefactors, but this would be followed by another few months of complete impunity (1968a:368).

More often than not, these Companies at Arms became identified with the armed retainers of the landlords in whose interests they operated. Thus while on the one hand *mafiosi* heightened class tensions through their control over land, they checked open rebellions and sustained revolts in several ways: by force; by keeping a hold on outside influence; by opening avenues for upwardly mobile peasants; and by turning outlaws and bandits into allies. After the inception of the Italian State in 1861, with its concerted attempt at centralization, these interconnections and collusions became more evident. In the course of time, a new landed gentry partly replaced and partly merged with the traditional landowning aristocracy by acquiring most of the land that came on the market, as well as by enclosing fields to which the peasants had legal rights.[8] It was no mere coincidence, therefore, that from that time onwards the term *"mafia"* became part of the Italian idiom, though the word was and still is used with widely different meanings. This variety of meanings not only reflects the complexity of the phenomenon, but indicates as

---

8. The career of the rich upstart Don Calogero, one of the characters in Di Lampedusa's well-known novel *The Leopard*, exemplifies this process. The reader may take him as a *mafioso avant la lettre*.

well the extent to which it has changed over the past hundred years. What remained relatively constant in this succession of configurations, and what may justify the use of one and the same term when dealing with the phenomenon, was the fact that the Italian State did not succeed in monopolizing the use of physical force in large areas of Sicily. Under Fascism centralization advanced to an unprecedented degree, but *mafiosi* re-emerged shortly after its demise. Even today, local strongmen are able to withstand the impact of the central government, and the very extension of government activities in recent decades has, in certain areas, provided *mafiosi* with increasing leverage.

The present volume deals with a particular instance of the process of encapsulation. It is from the local level that we shall look at this process and try to understand how and why *mafiosi* fulfilled pivotal roles in it. In this way I hope to show that the local and the national level belong together in any analysis of society. Though we have different terms for them and, unfortunately, also different types of analysis to deal with each of them separately (the so-called micro- and macro-sociology), it should be recognized that these terms refer to events which are structurally and historically interconnected. As implied in my brief profile of the Sicilian *mafia* and to be elaborated in the following chapters, the behavior of *mafiosi* should not be separated from the context of configurational development. To consider local events in isolation from the long-term developments of the larger society would deprive us of the possibility of finding out and explaining how and why these events happened at all. Though this point may seem fairly obvious, it is worth noting that anthropologists, for purposes of analysis, have often exclusively concentrated their attention on the local level.[9]

9. E.g., Foster's attempt to account for certain sectors of peasant behavior in terms of a model he calls the "Image of Limited Good" (1965). In his reply to the criticism of Kaplan and Saler (1966), he states: "For purposes of analysis, and at this stage of the argument, I am considering a peasant community to be a closed system. I don't believe peasant communities are closed systems; the definition I follow implies just the opposite. But it is methodologi-

There are still relatively few village studies dealing at length with the links between both levels while, in former days, anthropologists studied tribal people rather than the inter-relations between tribal society and colonial government. It might be argued that the protracted predominance of static equilibrium models over developmental models is far from alien to this tradition and, in fact, has kept it alive.

In the following three chapters I present a narrative de-scription of the village. This part of the book, which deals with the locale of the village of Genuardo, its early history, and the development of land tenure, is highly selective. Its main function is to provide the reader with the necessary information on the setting in which the village *mafia* oper-ated in order to follow the argument in the second part of this volume. Apart from one section in Chapter II, there is no special part in this book dealing with history, for the simple reason that I have tried not to lift any subject herein dis-cussed out of time or space. Since the argument is concerned with the period between 1860 and 1960, I have used the past tense, except where reference is made to contemporary cir-cumstances. This does not imply, however, that all described conditions definitely belong to the past. Far from it: *mafia* is still a going concern.

A final note on references: there exists a vast literature on Sicilian *mafia*. Unfortunately, however, only a few studies contain detailed and systematic empirical data, and a com-prehensive treatise on the subject is still lacking.[10] One reason why Sicilian *mafia* is less well known than might be expected is related to its very nature: secrecy buttressed by violence

---

cally sound to assume, for analytical purposes, a cultural situation that is contrary to fact . . . For analytical purposes, I am making use of an ideal type that nowhere corresponds to reality" (1966: 213–14). The difficulties of this time-honored nominalism need not be discussed any further at this point: they show themselves clearly enough.

10. See, however, Hess' recent study (1970) based on archival material which came to my attention after completing the present book. For an extensive and useful annotated bibliography, see Novacco (1964).

played and still plays an essential role in associations formed by *mafiosi*. Systematic violence and the relative dissociation of *mafia* from the public limelight produce a terrifying effect on communities.[11] Secrecy and fear hamper open discussion as well as research, and the same conditions have helped to insure the persistence of *mafia* over time.[12] Another reason why accurate knowledge about *mafia* is scarce relates to the poor development of the social sciences in Italy. After a promising start in the decades before Fascism teaching and research dwindled. Though a revival has set in recently, participant observation is not part of the stock-in-trade of Italian sociology (cf. Braga 1967). As a consequence, Sicilian *mafia* has been largely studied "at a distance" by people often trained in other disciplines. Prolonged residence in small-scale communities may render information on the minutiae of their social life and the development of the larger society, from which the operations of *mafiosi* and the mechanisms of *mafia* may be understood. As one informant explained in a somewhat patronizing style: "You have to know the people as thoroughly as I do. We all know each other. That's why we understand who has killed whom and why, or who carried off the animals of Tizio, without actually being there to witness these things."[13]

Though few scholars have worked on the village level and immersed themselves in local gossip over a relatively long period of time, some of the more important writings on the *mafia* have been of great aid to me and should be recom-

11. Walter's recent and original analysis of secret societies in West Africa in which he emphasizes the elements of terror and "invisibility" is much to the point here (Walter 1969:87–108).

12. See Mack Smith's Preface in Pantaleone (1966: 17–19); and Pantaleone (1969). In the spring of 1972, after considerable delay, the Anti-*Mafia* Commission published an account of its findings. This report was unavailable to me at the completion of the present study.

13. In the presentation of case material in the second part of this book, I have tried to follow Van Velsen's dictum: "Particularly when several or most of the actors in the author's case material appear again and again in different situations, the inclusion of such data should reduce the chance of cases becoming merely illustrations" (1967:140).

mended to any reader interested in the subject. Four early publications must be mentioned as useful studies (Franchetti 1925; Alongi 1887; Cutrera 1900; and Mosca 1900). Two recent historical books (Novacco 1963; Romano 1966) draw heavily on earlier studies and constitute general surveys. Original data from primary sources are contained in the studies of Mori (1933), Candida (1960), Dolci (1963), Marino (1964), and Pantaleone (1966). Though these studies answer important questions such as, for example, the involvement of *mafia* in national politics and its anti-peasant orientation, they often lack crucial dimensions since they do not discuss particular places and problems over time. Questions bearing on the recruitment of *mafiosi* have hardly been asked, let alone carefully investigated. Accordingly, we must expect that the relations between *mafiosi* and peasants are much more complicated than some writers, who emphasize the element of exploitation, are ready to admit. In this respect, we should distinguish between different kinds of peasants and find out how they pass from one category to another. Likewise, we must ask to what extent the private use of violence is accepted as both normal and proper in this part of the world. As suggested before, it must not be assumed that *mafiosi* have their own independent structure. It is one thing to describe their operations in terms of crimes, but quite another to explain how and why these people could act out of legal bounds with impunity. The task of the anthropologist is not primarily to praise or to blame, since these evaluations are extraneous to his subject matter. Rather, he should address himself to an understanding of human beings in terms of their interdependencies, ways in which human beings are fundamentally dependent upon one another, in various modalities or configurations. Hopefully the present book will contribute to this larger understanding and complement those studies on *mafia* in which certain questions are raised but only partly answered. The following example may illustrate more clearly what I am after. It deals with the elimination of a peasant leader, a man called Placido, in one of the neighboring towns of Genuardo in 1944. As one of his friends recalled after taking their last evening stroll:

When we reached my house, I went in. It never occurred to me to think that anything could happen; there were people everywhere. The others turned round and went back down to the square. From there they were followed by two men who were waiting in a café, and who stuck their pistols into his back. He halted and asked them what they wanted. They were standing in the middle of the square. It was in March when the days are already long. There'd been no rain and there were quite a few people about. All of a sudden, the people disappeared from the square. There wasn't a soul to be seen. One or two open doors were closed. He couldn't do anything but accept their invitation to walk on; perhaps they told him that it was only to have a discussion. The people in the streets had seen what was happening, scores of them. Besides, where were the police? You may well ask. Everyone turned a blind eye. There were two others waiting for him at the point where the steps lead down from Corso Bentivegna to Via Santo Rocco. He understood his danger at once, and tried to escape up the steps to the right. At the top he was met by two others who threw a blanket over his head. Then they seized him, trampled him down as if they were treading out the wine, carried him to a car that was waiting about twenty meters away, and threw him in. Then off they went. He shouted and cried out for help, but all to no avail. The people didn't want to hear.

Do you think it right that a man should get himself killed for the sake of a lot of people who can act blind and deaf when it suits them? . . .

If the *contadini* [peasants] who followed Placido had only armed themselves with one stone each weighing no more than a kilo, they could have wiped out those four *mafiosi*. But they didn't . . .

That's the saddest part of it all for me: it needn't have happened. Why didn't they all run to his help? Why did they let him be killed? (Dolci 1963: 46–47)

It is to an understanding of these and similar events that this essay is addressed.

II
The Village

The territory of Genuardo covers about 135 square kilometers and is delimited mainly by natural boundaries forming a serpentine circumference of roughly 76 kilometers. To the west and north these boundaries coincide with one of Sicily's few rivers. To the north-east, the territory is bounded by small tributaries. A large part of the southern boundary runs along a western off-shoot of the island's central mountain ridge. The area lies in the southeastern part of an extended, southwest oriented valley and consists mainly of irregular chains of hills and mountains with altitudes varying between 300 and 1,200 meters above sea level. From the southeastern upper reaches of the territory, the land slowly descends to the west and north-west and drains into the river.

The area belongs to the tertiary hill country which is one of three foremost landscapes that can be distinguished in Sicily and which are sketched by Newbigin as follows:

The triangular form of Sicily reflects the presence of its three main elements. Though exceedingly complicated in detail, it consists essentially of a prolongation of the folded Apennines to the north; of tertiary hill country which makes up much of the island, and is itself a continuation of the belt which borders the folded area throughout its extension; and of the eastern volcanic element, here external to the range . . . the tertiary hill country is made of miocene beds, for the most part but slightly folded, and pliocene ones which have been extensively uplifted without disturbance. The uplifted surface has been so eroded by the multiplicity of southward flowing streams as to present the appearance of a mountain country on a small scale, and except to the southwest, there are few lowlands (1949:198).

Though the climate of Sicily can be generally described as Mediterranean, the relatively high inland region in which Genuardo is situated lacks some of its glamorous features. To be sure, the summer is long, hot and dry—the rains fall between October and April, reaching a yearly average of about 800 millimeters. But the winter is significantly harsher than may be expected in a Mediterranean area, with frost and even snow as late as March, due to the inland and mountainous location of Genuardo. Furthermore, there is no "eternal spring," a term so often applied to Sicily. In fact spring is rather short, and winter often passes into summer without noticeable transition.

Soils are composed of clay in various combinations with sand and lime. This soil type is characteristic of southern Italy in general and of Sicily in particular, where it covers roughly three-fourths of the land (cf. Vöchting 1951: 18). On hills and mountains, soils are often thin, while in the lower parts of the village's territory soils are usually deep, and potentially fertile, as they consist of coarse alluvium washed down by streams (cf. Diem 1961 : 33). Since the original vegetation has largely vanished because of human intervention, soils are deficient in humus and exposed to landslides (*frane*). The problem of soil erosion is serious. It arises from both physical conditions and human misuse of the land, which work hand in hand. Steeply sloping land, heavy rainfall, and strong winds (*scirocco*) provide the setting while deforestation, ploughing fields unsuitable for cultivation, and overgrazing accelerate the process that produces a rapid run-off of the soils. Once forests covered a large part of the village area, and some hundred years ago there were still about 700 hectares of woodland left, about 5 per cent of the territory. These woods were located on the hills and mountains south and east of the village. By the turn of the century, a considerable part had been cut down and turned into grain fields. Afterwards, these upper reaches were used for grazing.

As elsewhere, this human interference had harmful consequences for the ecological structure. The forest provided the
peasants with important means of livelihood. Apart from
timber for agricultural equipment and construction material,
it supplied large quantities of dead wood, acorns, edible
plants, mushrooms, fruits, and game. These items were
crucial for the bulk of the peasants who lived at subsistence
level. Furthermore, the forest protected the village and part
of its territory from the *scirocco*, the hot, drying wind blow-
ing from the Sahara, which often damages crops and produces discomfort among both people and animals.

Natural catastrophes are ever present. We have seen that
the area is continually subject to landslides and soil erosion.
Hail storms, the *scirocco*, and sudden periods of drought
make conditions on the land grim and unfriendly. Malaria
was only recently wiped out in the South and is now effectively under control. The effect which malaria had on the
people can hardly be over-estimated. In this respect, Mack
Smith observes:

> ... after the second world war, the centuries-old scourge
> of malaria was being eradicated with new insecticides
> brought by the British and Americans, and it is possible
> to argue that this was the most important single fact in the
> whole of modern Italian history (1959:494).

Though the village itself was relatively free from malaria,
due to its mountainous location, large parts of its territory,
most notably the lower reaches, were virtually inaccessible
during the summer months. Moreover, the rains turn much
of the arable land into mud fields, hampering both access and
cultivation.

Sicily is also a notorious seismic zone. In 1908 Messina was
razed to the ground, and in January 1968, some months after
I had left the area, a violent earthquake hit a dozen peasant
towns in western Sicily. Five of them, just to the west of
Genuardo, are merely names on the map now, while seven
others, including Genuardo, were badly damaged.

The village of Genuardo is situated towards the center of the western interior of Sicily, some 90 kilometers by road south of Palermo. The inland area of the island contrasts sharply with the intensively cultivated coastal rim—a landscape of orchards, vineyards, and gardens. The interior is characterized by a scarcity, and in many places a complete absence, of permanent vegetation. Agriculture is and has been for centuries extensive rather than intensive. Grain fields and natural pastures extend over a bare and irregularly sloping landscape of hills and mountains. Apart from the compact settlements, the so-called "agro-towns," in which the peasant population lives permanently, the whole area gives the impression of desolation.

Genuardo is perched on the slopes of a hill. When I first saw the village on one June afternoon in 1961, I was struck by its compact appearance. At that time, I hiked through the area and was given a ride by one of the local priests. I did not come straight from Palermo, but made a detour through the southwestern part of the island in order to visit other villages and towns. So we came from the south, unable to see the village until we were rather close to it, say somewhat less than one kilometer *linea recta*. The road makes a sudden bend here, and at this point one gets a full view of Genuardo in all its grandeur. All houses are grey or white and built closely together. The physical structure of Genuardo approximates that of an amphitheater built on the slopes of a smoothly molded hill. The village faces north and overlooks the middle reaches of a large valley. From the higher points of the village, the horizon is bounded by the mountain range south of Palermo. To the south and east are higher hills and mountains which were still densely wooded until the middle of the nineteenth century. Altitudes in Genuardo vary between 520 and 570 meters above sea level.

Houses and streets generally follow the pattern of terraces. Streets are narrow and winding. Only at some points do they permit two-way motorcar traffic. They were constructed some centuries ago to serve as mere passageways for humans

and animals. The oblong village is transversed at full length
by the main street, interrupted halfway by a small *piazza*
(square). The two main churches are located at the two ends
of this street. Along the *piazza* are the public buildings, a
smaller church, a club, a bar, and some shops. In several
senses, therefore, the *piazza* is the heart of the village. All
houses and larger buildings are constructed according to an
urban pattern. They are built together and leave no room
for small fenced-in gardens or backyards, except on the outskirts of the village where gardens shade off into the countryside. For obvious reasons, shepherds and goatherds have
settled in some parts of this section of the village. Streets
alternate with rows of houses. In general, the back of the
house serves for animals and stores and is often somewhat
lower than the front, which is arranged for living. Houses are
rectangular and covered by gently sloping tiled roofs. Walls
are built up of roughly molded stones which are simply piled
up with the help of mortar. These walls are rather thick and
plastered inside and sometimes outside as well. Many houses
date from the 18th century or earlier. Houses vary in size,
though most of them are two-storied and have been equipped
with drinking water and electricity for several decades.
Recent structures and new stories are built of sandstone
blocks which are cut in quarries situated in the territory of
a neighboring town. Granite is still employed for improving
and constructing streets and terraces.

Houses vary in size according to the wealth, occupation,
and income of the occupants or owners. Roughly two types
of structures can be distinguished. First, there are several
large houses with spacious balconies, terraces, and court-
yards. These are the mansions where the well-to-do landowners and professional men live. A second type of dwelling
is much more prevalent: small, often single-storied structures
with lofts and stables. The peasants live in these. Since about
1960 this pattern has been changing as a consequence of
large-scale migrant labor, enabling poor families to construct
additional stories and apartments according to the style of
the first type.

There is no pronounced pattern of settlement in Genuardo following class lines. Mansions are dispersed rather than clustered. Some of them are situated at the outskirts while others are located towards the center of the village. Yet some pattern of residence does exist. Small herdsmen prefer to live at the edge of the village, and shopkeepers tend to settle along the main street and the *piazza*. The *piazza* is indeed the focus of public life. Here adult males meet for short leisurely walks or sit down inside or in front of the bars, clubs, or barbershops for conversation and to play cards. Women avoid being seen on the *piazza*. Their sphere is the home.

COMMUNICATIONS

Genuardo is more or less a dead end. No highways pass through its territory. In former times, the village's territory was crossed by some large public roads that served for trade and the movement of sheep and cattle. But to visit the village now one has to go there on purpose. Three roads, of which only one is fairly passable, connect the village with other towns and the outside world. Within a radius of about fifteen kilometers there are no other permanent settlements, and Genuardesi have to cover at least this distance to reach the highway to Palermo.

Most of the roads that go out from the village into the countryside are narrow mule tracks and mountain trails unsuitable for modern traffic. Only recently, in the 1950s, have some of these been transformed into roads of broken stones and asphalt. Often, however, these routes are badly constructed and are in constant need of repair. The communication problem is as acute as it was in the past. The Italian State has paid slight attention (from the point of view of welfare) to villages like Genuardo: a local report of 1914 complained that one and a half kilometers of passable roads were the only benefit the village had received from the government since Unification in 1861. In July 1967, shortly after I had left the village, the town council came together for a special meeting to deliberate about more effective ways to draw the attention of the authorities to the disastrous condition of the roads connecting the village with the outside.

In former days people travelled on horseback to neighboring villages and towns, and even as far as Palermo, where most of the local large landowners lived. At the end of the 19th century, a railway line was built to link Palermo with the foremost centers of its *latifondo* hinterland. After the World War II, the train was replaced by buses, and today two daily buses run from the village to Palermo and back. A growing number of villagers own automobiles, and with these Palermo may be reached in about two hours.

Before Unification, the people of Genuardo spent most of their lives within the boundaries of the village. Discussing Bourbon times, Brancato notes:

> Separated from other villages through the absence of reciprocal relationships, each community developed its own life. The more it was located towards the interior of the island, the less it was open to external influences. Even in language, accent, and expression each community distinguished itself from the others. . . . Neither was the sense of their isolation absent from the consciousness of the inhabitants; and for this reason the territory of the various communities was called *stato* [state]. . . . In the quasi-immobility of village life, time passed slowly and almost unnoticed. The meaning of it was only measured by the harvest season (1956:22, 30).

It must not be assumed, however, that the isolation of villages like Genuardo was ever complete. Before 1860, local markets established regular contacts beween the various towns in the interior of the island, and produce (mainly wheat) was transported to coastal towns and cities for shipment overseas. Agricultural laborers travelled southward to the coastal areas to assist in the grain harvest, returning to the hills and mountains where wheat ripened a month or so later. Furthermore, those who held supervisory posts on the large estates maintained relationships with landowners living in Palermo or elsewhere. Finally, men of learning such as, for example, priests and civil servants, had all spent years in the city for their training and, up to a certain point (to be discussed later on) kept these contacts alive.

These patterns of contact between Genuardo and the larger society gradually extended after the inception of the Italian State in 1861. Military service, large-scale emigration to overseas countries, the two world wars, and recent migrant labor to northern Europe widened the horizon of many villagers. Yet the relations between the village and the nation-State remained precarious. For the majority of the Genuardesi, most notably large sectors of the peasantry, national roles, as opposed to local roles were not readily accessible. Though the peasants paid taxes and were drafted for military service, their connection with national institutions was weak.[1] Like peasants elsewhere, they produced primarily to satisfy family and local needs and were hence only partially involved in wide-ranging market systems in which they participated to the extent of selling their labor-power. Most peasants had no direct access to land and other means of production, and were dependent upon landowners and *gabelloti* who were more directly involved in the national economy. To an extent, the local self-sufficiency of the peasantry was reflected in the use of money. Though money was employed as a standard and, occasionally, as a means of payment, it was rarely used by the peasants as a means of exchange. Various needed goods and services not produced by the peasant himself were obtained through payments in kind, that is, shares of his product. Rents and credit were paid in grain,[2] and shopkeepers and artisans were paid in similar fashion.

The general poverty of the peasants set strong limits to their participation in other national institutions, exemplified by the high rates of illiteracy in this area that persisted well into the 20th century. As a consequence, national legal systems were at best only partly understood, while formal political participation remained for a long time restricted to males with taxpaying and educational qualifications. In 1861

1. Cf. Pitkin (1959).
2. In local idiom, the word *"grana"* is still used as an equivalent of the term *danaro* (money).

the total Sicilian electorate embraced little more than 1 per cent of the population. The franchise was widened in 1882 (comprising 5 per cent of about three million Sicilians) and extended to all adult males in the reforms of 1913 and 1919. Universal suffrage was introduced in 1946.

The Italian nation-State only slowly encapsulated the village. When the State is unable to control and integrate peripheral areas, there is room for political middlemen or brokers, who are able to bridge the gaps in communication. Middlemen or the "elite of a peasant community," as Charles Tilly writes,

> ... consist of those who simultaneously carry on active roles in the community and in the national structures that intersect it. The elite are the mediators, the brokers, between those national structures and the relevant activities within the community. They gain power through their extraordinary access to information and to powerful individuals on the outside, and frequently have a good deal of influence over the contacts of other community members with "outsiders." As a rule, the fewer the elite roles and the less the specialization of those roles in one form of mediation or another, the greater the local power of the elite (Tilly 1967:80).

Though functions for middleman roles are thus generated by relative isolation or segmentation, the persistence of both these roles and the gaps they bridge is related to the degree to which middlemen succeed in dominating the paths that link the village to the larger, encompassing society.[3]

As noted above, Genuardo was never an isolated community in the strict sense of the word. But the links that tied villages like Genuardo to the outside world were limited and fragile. The prevalent organization of production and the division of labor in the inland area at large did not generate a comprehensive network of interdependent relationships between the agro-towns themselves. Each community was a replica of the next, yielding the same produce to the capital

3. Cf. Weingrod (1968:383–84); Bailey (1969:167–76).

city of Palermo and other coastal towns, from where it was exported to Europe, mainly by foreign merchants. This slight measure of social differentiation in west Sicilian society is reflected in its poor network of roads.[4] Transport of the main product (wheat) took place right after the harvest in the dry summer along trails which were permitted to wash away with the rains in autumn and winter. The scarce application of public and private capital helped maintain relative isolation and segmentation; the dominant forms of production hardly required more substantial modes of investment. To understand the particular power chances of the middlemen entrepreneurs in the countryside, we must recognize the strongly segmented character of the island society which, in a sense, neither required nor facilitated the development of more effective forms of central control. Weak development of central authority, therefore, is structurally related to relative local and regional self-sufficiency. What specifically hampered the penetration of an efficient central apparatus of coordination and control, which was imposed from above upon this segmented society, were the middlemen entrepreneurs themselves: they provided and controlled the links with the outside world, and tended to preserve local isolation by extending their control over new links that might grow with the gradual expansion of State-institutions. In this sense communications between Genuardo and the larger society have been overwhelmingly limited over the past hundred years.

EARLY HISTORY

Extensive ruins give archaeological evidence of very early settlement in the territory of Genuardo. To the north-west, a huge mountain still bears the name of the pre-Greek city once situated on its flat ridge. In the early 13th century, it was razed by Frederick II as the last Saracen stronghold. A few kilometers west of the village, the walls of a Saracen

4. For a detailed discussion of this problem, see Peter Schneider (1972). In western Europe, processes of centralization took place in close connection with growing differentiation. Cf. Elias' blueprint of State-formation processes (1969, II:222–311 *et passim*; 1970:154–59; 1972).

castle stand on the top of a steep hill, once, it seems, an almost unassailable fortress strategically overlooking a large part of Sicily's western interior. Scattered through the area are remains of former settlements, which still occasionally crop up as peasants plow the fields.

It is not before the 13th century that we hear about the existence of Genuardo in documented history. At that time Genuardo formed a *casale*, a small hamlet inhabited by villeins making part of a barony that took its name from the Saracen castle, here simply called Baronessa. Invested with the barony by the crown, the feudal lord held all judicial and administrative power. The local population was subject to his legal authority and charged with rents and services. These villeins do not seem to have been true serfs tied to the soil. Their status was halfway between that of serfs and free tenants.[5]

The institution of villeinage developed after the Normans conquered Sicily in the second part of the 11th century and set up a feudal regime (Cahen 1940:32–38, 98–99).

Ideally, feudal societies are exclusively agrarian and rest on a locally self-sufficient economy. Large estates predominate, but these are fiefs: grants of land from the sovereign to the vassal, not private properties. In exchange for allegiance (specifically, in the form of military service), these investitures entail public authority over people living on the fiefs. The political framework consists of relations between lord and vassal based on personal loyalty. Although public authority is thus fragmented, all feudal cells belong to an (at least *de jure*) recognized whole, represented by the sovereign. As fief holders, vassals constitute a distinct military class to which the peasant cultivators are subject in terms of government, taxation, and administration of justice. Economic conditions, the organization of transport, and military techniques do not permit the sovereign to maintain more efficient means of government, most notably a bureaucracy and an army, to ensure durable centralization. Feudal regimes are particularly weak in peaceful times when no new land comes up to underwrite enfeoffment. Yet the locus of

5. See Salvioli (1902). Sartorius von Waltershausen has discussed the unlikelihood of serfdom in late medieval Sicily (1913:152–53).

weakness is enfeoffment itself (the very method of feudal government), which places a military elite in a potentially strong position with respect to the central ruler.

There are thus strong elements of contradiction in feudal regimes. They contain the "seeds of their own destruction." The foremost sources of change lie in the tensions between lord and vassal. As noted above, through grants of land in return for military and administrative services, vassals increase their independence from the central ruler. When feudalization, or decentralization, whittles down royal demesnes and revenues, the authority of the king, ultimately, depends upon the likelihood that vassals will remain true to their oaths of fealty: to control a rebellious vassal or to protect a loyal one, the king has to rely on the allegiance and support of his other vassals. We know that he was often unable to do so. Supported by and living among their own vassals and retainers, feudal barons fought each other or formed coalitions against the king. In terms of effective control, the king thus became the equal of the barons.[6]

In Sicily, the tensions between the central power and the barons increased under Spanish rule from the late 13th century onwards. The crown had enfeoffed most of its domains in order to appease the baronage while no new land became available. Eventually, the barons, less dependent upon central power for protection, succeeded in changing the status of the fief into that of a quasi-allod, that is, a private domain which could be inherited, though not freely sold without consent of the crown. Therefore, instead of controlling the barons, the sovereign was increasingly controlled by them. Not centralization, but the prevalence of a strong landowning aristocracy was the most persisting feature of Norman and Swabian heritage. No independent urban power could offset the prominency of the barons, since it had been stifled by strong central control under Frederick II (Mack Smith 1968a:55–56).

According to Pontieri, the incursions of the barons into the

6. Bloch (1961); Cahen (1960); Hall (1962); and Bendix (1962: 329–84). Of particular value is Elias' essay on the sociogenesis and mechanisms of European feudalization (1969, II:14–88).

entrails of the State became increasingly visible—indeed set into high relief—with the centralizing efforts of the Neapolitan Bourbons in the 18th century: the barons wielded *de facto* power over both the parliament and the law courts; at the local level they were petty sovereigns who maintained their own government (1943:15–145). As mentioned before, their territories were called *stati*. In this way, public property and public order became virtually identified with the interests of the landowning aristocracy. By the end of the 18th century, 282 of the 367 Sicilian communities were under direct feudal control, which implied that about two-thirds of the population of Sicily (which in 1798 amounted to about 1.6 million) were subject to the authority of the barons or their agents. Genuardo was one of those communes, and this meant that it was not before the 19th century that the village became involved in a larger political system, which sought to replace baronial jurisdiction.

DEMOGRAPHY

The interior of Sicily has always been less populated than the coastal zone. Barons tried to cope with the shortage of labor by the use of violence; their henchmen captured villeins from neighboring estates, chiefly those of church domains. However, as early as the 12th century, feudal lords undertook more efficient methods to attract cultivators by granting them small shares of land in return for services. This colonization movement in Sicily's interior was initially slow, but it received a strong impetus from the reorganization of the corn trade in the course of the 15th century. The main purpose of the colonization was to reclaim large tracts of land, especially the uncultivated *feudi* (large estates) on which many hamlets had been abandoned, in order to meet the increasing demand for grain in Sicily and Europe. The extent of colonization can be measured by the growing population in this area. During the 16th and 17th centuries, some 100 new communities were founded in western Sicily, mostly in the inland region where several of them replaced vanished settlements (the *casali* or hamlets). It was also in this period that the barons became big merchants in grain (cf. Salvioli 1903; Garufi 1946, 1947; Romano 1964:196–215).

Apart from the general population growth in Europe which increased the need for food, there were other reasons for this internal colonization. As Mack Smith observes,

> a growth in population ... increased the need for food and so encouraged enterprising landlords to plow up virgin land. As prices rose, so grew both the need to make more money, and the increased demand for wheat which satisfied the need. ...
>
> The foundation of new villages simultaneously conferred on the baronage prestige and the illusion or reality of power. Socal status among the magnates was largely measured by the extent of their territory and the number of townships where they held powers of life and death. ... Founding a village with more than eighty families usually brought with it a seat in the baronial house of parliament, or an extra vote if its owner already owned this privilege. ...
>
> Another motive for internal colonization was provided by raids on the Sicilian coast, which drove people away from their farms and forced them to look for less accessible land elsewhere. Brigandage and agrarian discontent likewise made it unsafe to live in isolated farmsteads. Government policy also helped, because there was profit in selling licenses to create new villages, apart from the fact that increased food production meant more customs and excise revenue. ... At the same time there was a positive need to resettle people on the land in order to reduce the pauperism, overcrowding and disease of the cities, and to curtail the revolutionary feelings which bred in the Palermo suburbs (1968a:196–97).

The repopulation of Genuardo dates back to the early 16th century, the period of resettlement of the inland areas. In fact, Genuardo was one of these resettled communities and it distinguished itself in that many of its new settlers came from overseas. They were Albanians who took refuge in Sicily because of the Turkish expansion in the Balkans. The conditions under which these immigrants were to live and cultivate the land were arranged in a written charter issued in 1520. In this document the rights and duties of the new-comers and their lord were distinctly defined. The baron did not divide his estates among the new settlers, nor did he encourage permanent settlement on scattered farms. Apart from considerations of security, it was probably also fear that the peasants would eventually claim the land if they lived on it that led the baron to favor compact settlement. Concentrated residence of the peasants would ensure or, at least, facilitate the baron's feudal jurisdiction.[7] Therefore, the newcomers had to build houses for themselves, as well as for others still to come, on the site of the former hamlet. It was agreed that they would call for another hundred families, which indeed arrived the next year (1521) from the Greek island of Andros. The baron paid for their voyage. The new inhabitants obtained two *feudi* covering some 750 hectares close to the village. Up to the present, these estates have maintained their original names, just as the general term *"feudo"* is still widely used to indicate a large estate or *latifondo*. Initially these two *feudi* were common lands serving both for cultivation and herding. The peasants had to cede one tenth of the crops and paid a fixed amount in money for every head of cattle. They had the right to cultivate these estates with vines, olives, and other fruit trees. The tenth was gradually replaced by the emphyteusis, or copyhold contract, which encouraged investment in the land on the part of the peasant. At the same time, cultivation of grain and livestock raising were extended to the more outlying *feudi*, where the peasants constructed *masserie* and worked the land according to sharecropping contracts or as day laborers. On both these types of holdings and on the outermost waste lands, the peasants were granted common use rights of gleaning and pasturage. These *usi civici* were inherent in all feudal property and guaranteed the peasant

7. The persisting urban orientation of Sicilian peasants is much more complex than here suggested. I have dealt with some aspects of this problem elsewhere (cf. Blok 1969a).

population fundamental means of subsistence (cf. La Mantia 1904; Salvioli 1909; Genuardi 1911:60–84).

In several ways the area of intensive cultivation adjacent to the village (*corona*) meshed with the large zone of extensive cultivation and herding. The former provided continuous bonds with the land: the emphyteusis was a long-term lease of a relatively small plot which could be inherited. On the other hand, the outlying *feudi* only required a strong labor force during certain periods of the year: plowing and sowing in autumn and harvesting in summer. The emphyteusis thus appears as a necessary condition for the success of the colonization since it supplied a permanent and resident labor force for the exploitation of the large estates. In fact, the population of Genuardo increased rapidly, from some 500 people in the mid-16th century to well over 2,000 in the early 18th century. With this population growth, a second emphyteusis was granted to Genuardo in 1720. This grant involved about 450 hectares and was more or less contiguous with the first grant of 1520. The population of Genuardo continued to grow, and by 1798 it numbered slightly over 3,000 people. But there were no further grants of land. Apparently the chief purpose of the colonization—attracting labor and increasing revenues from the large estates—had been realized.

In the course of time, many barons became sufficiently wealthy to permit themselves a more attractive life in the city of Palermo. In fact, many of the numerous palaces in this city as well as several villas outside its walls were built at the end of the 17th and the beginning of the 18th century. Landlord absenteeism created increasingly more room for big leaseholders or *gabelloti*, as they will henceforth be called. Since the barons usually held many estates, the *gabella* contract had always been known in this area. Yet, in the course of the 18th century, the big lease became widespread and the most common way to run the large estates of the absentee barons. The *gabelloti* were recruited from the peasantry or, rather, from that small sector of the peasantry who owned some land and cattle, as well as from those men the baron maintained for keeping law and order and for supervising his estates: stewards, field guards, tax-collectors, and so forth. As local peasant entrepreneurs, the *gabelloti* were eager to improve their life chances by whatever means. Several circumstances promoted their social advancement: first, absenteeism of the landlords, who invested them with a formal share in local government authority; second, rising market prices of agricultural and livestock products; and finally, an increasing supply of labor.

Gabelloti managed the *masserìe*, or big farms, and established new ones which involved the occupation of more virgin land, both for herding and the cultivation of cereals. This voracity for land resulted in encroachments on the common use rights the peasant population exercised on the *feudi* which provided the lay-out of the *masserie*. Conflicts over land were settled in favor of the *gabelloti*, who were effectively in charge of local affairs. In this way, communities like Genuardo became fully dependent upon these entrepreneurs who, because of their successful enclosures, developed into landlords in their own right.[8] Although there is little information on Genuardo available for this period, some data suggest that the trend sketched out above affected the village. We know about the complaints of an 18th century local chronicler who regrets that the original and only copy of the 1520 charter had been filched and that, as a consequence, the application of it left much to be desired. A contemporary

8. Essentially the enclosure movement involved the *chiusure, strasatti,* or *difese*: large tracts of land which the baron reserved for his own herds and for hunting. The *strasatto* (from *strasattari,* which means "to arrange" or "to settle") was that part of the *feudo* which was withdrawn from the pastures on which the peasantry had common rights. With the introduction of the *gabella* contract, the *strasatto* was leased to the *gabelloto* in order that he have a fixed area to concentrate his flocks. Later on, these enclosures were followed by others as the *gabelloti* extended the area of cultivation to meet the rising demand for wheat. At the same time, a growing population facilitated the exploitation of the *masserie* by supplying cheap labor. In this way, the peasants were increasingly deprived of their common use rights, of which pasturage (especially) conflicted with the interests of the *gabelloto*. Cf. Pupillo-Barresi (1903:118–37); Salvioli (1903); Genuardi (1911:80–84); Sartorius von Waltershausen (1913:130–34); Pontieri (1943:55 ff.); Sereni (1947:175–89).

document regarding Genuardo speaks of the rise of the *gabelloti* as a dominant class, and of a growing category of poor peasants depending upon them.

Though the Sicilian population as a whole rapidly increased during the 19th and 20th centuries—from just over 1.6 million at the end of the 18th century to almost 5 million by 1961—the population figures for the inland region remained relatively stationary. The inland district of Corleone, which besides Genuardo embraces nine rural communities extending over roughly 970 square kilometers, sustained a population of about 46,000 in 1798. By 1881 it had close to 60,000, and in 1961 its number had fallen back to just over 52,000. Genuardo numbered slightly over 3,000 in 1798; it had 3,400 in 1881, and close to 2,700 in 1961 (see Table I). In the inland zone, especially in areas like the Corleone district where large estates predominated, surplus population was siphoned off through migration to coastal towns and, particularly in the decades around 1900, through emigration to overseas countries (cf. Renda 1963:13–77). In Genuardo alone between 1881 and 1911, roughly 4,000 people left for America, reducing its population from 3,430 to 2,117. Many Genuardesi returned and then left again; people from surrounding villages settled in Genuardo. In 1901, about 10 per cent of the local population had been in America. As both overseas emigration and internal migration were much restricted during the two decades of Fascism, the population of Genuardo steadily increased in this period. By the early 1950s it had grown to just over 3,000. It is likely that the peasants remained to await the results and possible benefits of the agrarian reform law promulgated after World War II. When the bill finally passed at the end of 1950, its implementation was delayed. Though many large estates were eventually divided, few peasants obtained viable plots. Credit facilities and other forms of assistance remained largely on paper. From about 1960 onwards, large numbers of peasants started to leave the area in search of industrial work in northern Europe. When I lived in the village, the population of Genuardo amounted to roughly 2,500, which included about 500 migrant laborers. The bulk of the adult male population had been abroad for work one or more times.

III
The Land

LAND TENURE

The name of Genuardo refers first of all to the village itself, that is, to the cluster of houses and the people living there—the Genuardesi. In local idiom, the village is denoted as *u paisi*; the term *paisani* is commonly used to distinguish between local people and outsiders or *strani*. Second, the name of Genuardo indicates the land belonging to the village, which amounts to just over 13,500 hectares. Together with its territory, the village constitutes the *comune*, a local administrative unit of which there are 370 in Sicily as a whole. The boundaries of this relatively large territory are precisely defined, as the Genuardo area borders all around on the *comuni* of a dozen other villages and towns. Large tracts of the village territory are owned and worked by people from adjacent communities, as these neighboring settlements are bigger but have less land. Furthermore, these villages are closer to large parts of the territory of Genuardo than the village of Genuardo itself, which lies near the southeastern boundary of the *comune*. Another reason why Genuardesi own only a relatively small section of their village territory is that until the 1950s, when agrarian reform was introduced to the area, most of the land consisted of large estates whose owners lived in Palermo and elsewhere.

The territory of the village consists of 46 estates, which range in size from 50 to 1,000 hectares. Five are smaller than 100 hectares; 31 range between 100 and 500 hectares; and 10 are larger than 500 hectares. All these *feudi* or *latifondi* have proper names, which derive from prevalent or particular vegetation, topographical features, historical events, or quali-

ties and names of former owners. It must be noted, however,
that the boundaries of these 46 estates almost never completely coincided with those of actual landed properties.
Latifondisti owned several estates which, in some cases, constituted extended clusters measuring well over 2,000 hectares.
In the course of the 19th century, when land became marketable, a new class of landowners worked their way up, and
this involved important changes of many traditional property
boundaries. The estate of Pomo, for example, which covers
roughly 400 hectares, had been part of the landed property
of the local monastery Santa Maria del Bosco since the early
15th century. When in the 1860s all church domains were
confiscated by the State and put up for sale, Pomo was
bought by five landowners who each held shares of between
30 and 180 hectares in this estate. In the beginning of this
century, large tracts of Pomo changed hands, and by 1925
the estate was owned by two landed families who lived in
Palermo. A member of one of these families, henceforth
called Mirabella (see Diagram 4), held the larger part of the
adjoining former church domains and lived most of the year
in the big house into which the monastery had been converted. In subsequent decades, Pomo was increasingly fragmented through inheritance, sale, and the impact of the
agrarian reform.

Land formed the basis for the social life of Genuardo,
which was an exclusively agrarian community. In one form
or another, the whole population of the village was dependent on the land. The majority, who did not own land or
possessed too little to live on, could only gain access to it by
coming to terms with those who either owned or controlled
large landed properties. Land, in other words, was the most
important political asset—a primary source of power. It is
thus from the changes in the distribution of land and
property titles that we might understand the dynamics of
social relationships and political activities over time.

Before the agrarian reform of the 1950s altered the traditional system of land tenure, Genuardo was a *latifondo*
village. Vast cereal-pasture holdings dominated the territory
of Genuardo, as well as in many other inland areas of Sicily,

which since Roman times had been par excellence the country of the latifundia. The origins of the modern Sicilian *latifondo* go back to the early 19th century, when feudal land was transformed by law into private property. This process took several decades. Though feudalism was formally abrogated in 1812, the land came up for sale only after the abolition of the system of entails and primogeniture in subsequent years; a third law, issued in 1824, allowed creditors to seize land in settlement of debts. Unlike the *feudo*, the modern *latifondo* was free of common use rights. The barons thus became full owners in exchange for the privileges tied to feudal property: the administration of justice, local government, and taxation, which became the right and duty of the Bourbon State—the Kingdom of the Two Sicilies (1815–59) with its center in Naples. Yet, as we shall see later on, vestiges of feudalism, especially in connection with control over land, persisted well into the 20th century. Although statistical data are lacking for this period, we may assume that these changes of titles to landed property had far-reaching consequences for the distribution of land. In the course of the 18th century, many barons had mortgaged their estates in order to carry on their life of leisure in Palermo. Large parts of these lands thus fell into the hands of new landowners, of whom the *gabelloto* as the main money-lender in the countryside was the foremost exponent. Furthermore, only few villages obtained compensation for the lost common use rights, which the Bourbon government defined as one-fifth of any territory in which these rights had been traditionally exercised, since the State lacked the force and means to implement this reform. In any event, the local peasant population lacked the resources and skills to prove illegal enclosures by the landowners who, apart from their influence on village affairs, controlled the commissions charged with the implementation of this reform. Quite unintentionally, the anti-feudal reforms of the Bourbon administration resulted in reinforcement of the enclosure movement, and thus helped ensure the predominance of the *latifondo* in the inland areas. Although the transformation of feudal property involved the fragmentation of most gigantic patrimonies composed of many *feudi*, single estates were rarely split up. It has been estimated that in 1820 the large estates covered about 80 per cent of the island, and that this figure hardly changed throughout the 19th century. Between 1812 and 1860, the total number of large landowning families increased from approximately 2,000 to 20,000 (Mack Smith 1950:203). In this way, the large estate in the interior remained the fundamental unit around which the entire life of the village was organized. It must not be assumed that the new landowners constituted a social class that was clearly separated from the relatively impoverished nobles. In several ways, the newly rich sought to emulate the life-style of the aristocracy. They had the same disregard for manual labor, as well as for productive work in general: like the members of the old landed class, they aspired to live in Palermo, thus making room for new entrepreneurs who managed their estates in the countryside. Through intermarriage and the purchase of noble titles, they gradually moved into the ranks of the nobility. This process of upward mobility, for which Pareto coined the term "circulation of elites," did not of course exclude instances of strong rivalry between "nobles" and "bourgeois": both were eager to maintain and acquire land. Invariably, however, the success of either meant increasing poverty of the peasants who, although freed from feudal bonds, lost access to the land since they were despoiled of their common use rights. Instead of a substantial class of small-holders, through whose creation the Bourbon government sought to domesticate the nobility by depriving it of direct control over land and men, hence of its power base, an utterly impoverished peasantry made its appearance in the Sicilian countryside in the course of the 19th century. The development of the market in conjunction with population increase dislocated the traditional peasant order. The position of many peasants deteriorated when the Italian State confiscated the church lands in the 1860s. Though this reform was conceived to encourage the development of peasant holdings, the majority of the shares was bought up by substantial landowners, who refused to compensate the peasants for common use rights on pasture and forest abolished by legal fiat.[1]

To what extent can this general sketch of the changes in land tenure be specified for Genuardo? We know that by the end of the 18th century three main forms of tenure prevailed in the territory of the village: land in emphyteusis (close to 10 per cent), church domains (just over 20 per cent), and feudal domains (roughly 70 per cent). As indicated above, the emphyteusis was a long lease of small holding granted by the feudal lord to the local population in 1520 and 1720. It consisted of three highly fragmented estates, situated close to the village, which covered about 1,200 hectares. The church domains measured about 3,000 hectares and included ten large estates, three of which were densely wooded. In fact, these estates made up all woodland in the Genuardo area and amounted at that time to about 1,500 hectares, that is, just over 10 per cent of the territory. The feudal domains covered the major part of the village area. They formed a barony held by a Roman nobleman descended from the feudal lord who had encouraged the re-settlement of the area in the early 16th century. On both feudal and church domains, the peasants held common use rights which included grazing, sowing, collecting wood and stones, hunting, spending the night with cattle, manufacturing lime and chalk, and collecting wild fruits, herbs, and acorns. Three distinct physical features in the territory of Genuardo symbolized three main forms of tenure: the village, the monastery, and the castle.

In 1843 the monastery still held all its estates. The barony, however, was split up into several sections owned by six noblemen (one Duke, three Marquesses, and two Princes) and half a dozen bourgeois landowners, none of whom lived permanently in Genuardo. As mentioned before, the State nationalized and auctioned all ecclesiastical property in Sicily, which amounted to about one-tenth of the island's

1. For the information on which this paragraph is based, I have relied on Salvioli (1903); Franchetti (1925:93); Sonnino (1925: 208–15); Sartorius von Waltershausen (1913:167–203); Romeo (1950: 161–85); and Mack Smith (1965).

arable land. Although the law prescribed the sale of small units to promote the establishment of an independent peasantry, substantial landowners controlled the auctions and succeeded in acquiring many such shares each (cf. Sonnino 1925:213–15; Mack Smith 1965:101–03). In Genuardo, about two-thirds of the monastery estates were bought up by Emilio Mirabella (see Diagram 4), a nouveau riche merchant from a neighboring town, who, by 1880, had most of the woods cut down and turned into cereal-pasture holdings.[2] The new landowner invested his wealth in the traditional prestige symbols which, apart from some 2,000 hectares of former church domains, included a marriage with an insolvent baroness. Both the land and the title passed to his descendants who, up to the present day, hold several hundred hectares in the village territory. Although the peasants of Genuardo tried through hopeless legal procedures to obtain indemnification for their lost use rights, the Baron, as he came to be called, wielded sufficient influence and power over civil servants to obstruct these claims. Likewise, he succeeded in covering up the illegal felling of trees on hillsides. Regalbate, another former domain of the monastery, was acquired in similar fashion by some members of the intelligentsia of an adjoining town.

According to a parliamentary enquiry carried out in the early 1880s, the sale of church land in Genuardo did not contribute to the fragmentation of landed properties (Damiani 1885). As elsewhere in Sicily, this so-called reform reinforced the predominance of the *latifondo* (cf. Sonnino 1925:212–213). In 1900, just one-tenth of the territory of the village was owned by people from Genuardo. Though the

2. According to information from the land registry, woods covered about 700 hectares in 1852. By 1900 woodland was reduced to barely 100 hectares, a figure that did not change substantially afterwards (compare Table V). Once, Sicily must have been densely afforested. Since about 1500 many forests disappeared, and today roughly four per cent of Sicily is covered by woodland. The most important factor responsible for deforestation was the burning of scrub and woodland to clear virgin land whenever high wheat prices made this profitable. See Mack Smith (1965: 109); and Mack Smith (1968a: 183–84).

fields are not specified in the report, we must assume that they largely coincided with the three estates which were given in long lease. The remainder of the area was largely held by 26 *latifondisti* (six of them nobles), who all lived elsewhere (see Table II). A second parliamentary enquiry accomplished between 1907 and 1910 registered 19 *latifondi* in the Genuardo area, all of which were larger than 200 hectares and together covered close to 7,000 hectares, just over 50 per cent of the territory (Lorenzoni 1910:358). By 1925 there were 19 estates larger than 100 and 8 larger than 200 hectares, together covering well over 7,000 hectares. Four years later, estates larger than 200 hectares still made up about 40 per cent of the territory. Accordingly, Genuardo was considered as one of the most latifundist communes of the island (cf. Molè 1929:106 and 135–139). Until 1950 this pattern of land tenure did not substantially alter. (Tables III and IV portray the changes in the distribution of land during the 19th and 20th centuries.)

In this section I have dealt with the persistence of the large estate over time. Though the State sought to modify the traditional pattern of land tenure in various periods in order to integrate a growing peasantry within its framework, the large estate maintained itself up to the mid-20th century. The main purpose of the present study is to account for *mafia*, the particular structure that accommodated these forces, most notably the impact of the State and peasant unrest. To understand this capacity of *mafia*, we must now turn to the way in which the large estates were managed and worked, and thus complete the picture of the relations between the people and the land.

AGRICULTURAL WORK

The people of Genuardo supported themselves by extensive cultivation of cereals, supplemented with animal husbandry. Additional crops of olives, grapes, and other fruits were also important but covered little area: over 90 per cent of the land was occupied by grainfields and pastures. These figures

have not changed significantly over the past hundred years
(see Table V).

In this dry-farming area there is one main harvest, that of
wheat in July. Cereals are sown between November and
April, according to the variety. As a rule the land is divided
into three fields, which are alternately cultivated as follows:
1st year fallow; 2nd year wheat; and 3rd year pasture. Although there are many variations according to terrain, size
of flocks, and market fluctuations, the essence of this three-
field rotation system is that it involves the fallow. Since one
field lies idle every year, rotations are discontinuous. The
fallow is necessary because no use is made of manure, and
there is a lack of rainfall during the long summer. Therefore,
the fallow involves various plowings to clear the field of
weeds and to conserve the moisture for the wheat crop in
fall. Traditionally, the fields were plowed and cross-plowed
with a simple wooden plow drawn by oxen or mules. After
World War I, agricultural machinery was introduced and
had found common acceptance by the 1960s. Oxen have
consequently disappeared as draft animals. Today, only very
small and steeply sloping fields are still worked in the traditional way with the use of mules.[3] The introduction of soil-
renewal and fodder crops (vetch and *sulla*) in this century
has not replaced the fallow altogether, but it doubtlessly has
contributed to a more balanced agro-pastoral economy (cf.
Vöchting 1951:294–295).

Although the *latifondi* were large in size, they were operated in small strips of land subleased to peasants on various
short-term contracts running from the 1st of September to
the 31st of August. Most commonly, the estates were managed by either leaseholders (*gabelloti*) or stewards (*amminis-
tratori*). The *gabelloto* held one or more estates in lease for
a period (usually six years) against a fixed yearly rent paid in
advance, in kind (wheat), cash, or a combination of the two.
The steward, who managed the estates on behalf of the

3. By 1966 small holdings covered close to 40 per cent of village
 territory (see Table III). The fact that the majority of the peasant
 proprietors own several extremely fragmented plots, often widely
 scattered, inhibits the use of modern agricultural machinery.

owner, was employed and paid on an annual basis. When referring to both leaseholders and stewards, I shall call them "peasant entrepreneurs," since they were persons of peasant stock who took the initiative and manipulated other persons and resources in the pursuit of profit (cf. Barth 1963:6). Though in principle their tenure was fixed for a distinct period of time, peasant entrepreneurs were often able to maintain their position for years and even decades.

The peasant entrepreneur had the fallow prepared by plow-servants. These first plowings in May (hence the name *maggese* for fallow) required teams of oxen drawing the wooden iron-tipped plow. In September, these fields were assigned to peasant share-croppers (*mezzadri*) who carried out subsequent plowings (November), sowing (December), weeding (spring), harvesting (July-August), and transport and threshing (August). As a rule, the sharecroppers had their own mules, plows, and other equipment to perform these tasks. Very often, the peasant entrepreneur provided the sharecropper with the seed and advanced loans in winter, both to be returned at high interest rates after the harvest. Pastures were utilized by the peasant entrepreneur—usually a big cattle owner himself—or subleased to others who had large flocks of cattle and sheep. Sometimes the entrepreneurs established specific partnerships with herdsmen who brought in their own flocks. The distribution of rainfall made cattle and sheep dependent on the utilization of extensive pastures, ranging from lower locations in winter to more elevated ones in summer. Shepherds traveled with the flocks and equipment while their families lived permanently in the village. Only small herds returned to the village every night. The triennial rotation system involved short-term contracts for all parties involved. From the point of view of the peasants, this cyclical pattern of land use ruled out permanent settlement on the land in scattered farms. As we have seen, the peasant population lives clustered in the village. This point receives further elaboration below.

The main domesticated animals on the *latifondo* were sheep, cattle, and mules. The latter were employed for all kinds of agricultural work, especially transportation. Before the introduction of agricultural machinery, mules were used for threshing. Since the terrain and scarcity of roads did not favor the use of carts, all transport was on muleback. Each big farm (*masserìa*) had several horses used by overseers and field-guards (*campieri*). Sheep served for the production of cheese, *ricotta* (a sort of cottage-cheese), meat, and wool; cows supplied meat and cheese; and a limited number of goats provided milk for direct consumption and cheese. The main market products of the area remain wheat and cheese. Oxen and donkeys disappeared in the course of time, and flocks of sheep and cattle diminished significantly in recent years as a consequence of the fragmentation of the large estates (see Table VI). Since both large estates and large flocks required the use of horses, the number of the latter decreased accordingly.

Two types of pastures can be distinguished: natural and cultivated grassland. The former embrace permanent pastures, that is, fields unsuited for cultivation, the fallow, and the stubble-fields. Cultivated pastures involve fields on which *sulla*[4] and vetch are sown, including hay meadows. If these fields (*maggese coperto*) were grazed for brief periods, usually a few weeks in winter and early spring, the crops could still be harvested in May. The fields were then plowed and prepared for sowing in fall. The overriding characteristic of livestock raising in this area was its strong nomadic orientation. Given the poor quality of natural pastures and the restricted availability of meadows, the flocks had no fixed residence but roamed through the country over long distances. Itineraries depended, among other things, upon the range of contacts which cattlemen and shepherds maintained with people who held or controlled land. As will be shown later on, these contacts were mainly structured along links of kinship and friendship. Since livestock could be pastured all year round, stables for shelter were unknown. There were only accommodations for horses and mules in both the village and the country. Fixed buildings where cheese could be made were also absent. Shepherds built their own temporary

4. See Glossary. Cf. Dickinson (1955:48–49).

huts of twigs and straw (*pagliai*) in the various places they tended the flocks. In these cone-shaped, thatched huts they kindled a fire both for making cheese and *ricotta*, and to keep warm during the night. At dusk, the animals were concentrated within a small area around the hut that was fenced with branches.

A nomadic tenor also characterized the life of the peasant cultivator. The vast majority of peasants, even those who held small plots of their own, depended for their livelihood on the large estates, working seasonally as sharecroppers, day laborers, herdsmen, plow-servants, pruners, or watchmen. Very often, the peasant performed several of these roles in the course of the agricultural year, and often on several different estates. With the triennial rotation system and the *latifondo*'s requirement of a strong labor force only in the summer and fall, the peasant was compelled to move continuously from place to place in search of work. Moreover, he could rarely obtain a sharecropping contract for a plot on a single *latifondo* sufficient to the needs of himself and his family, and consequently he had to lease additional plots from several other employers on different and often widely scattered estates. Even the peasant's own small plots were generally dispersed throughout the territory. Therefore, he spent considerable time traveling on foot and muleback between the village and the land, and between the several holdings on which he had to work. This itinerant character of labor, moreover, given the situation of endemic insecurity and the inability of the State to guarantee public order in the countryside, rendered the peasant vulnerable to assault and hence dependent on private power holders capable of providing "protection" in exchange for tribute—all in addition to the burdens of direct exploitation, which in certain periods left the peasant sharecropper with but a quarter of his product.

The system of land tenure as well as the nature of agricultural work did not favor permanent settlement on the land. Consequently, the agro-town in this area of large estates and surplus population functioned as the main labor market and in turn encouraged the peasants to live permanently within its walls. On the *piazza,* landowners or their agents contracted workers and sharecroppers.[5] Agro-towns like Genuardo clearly expressed the precarious employment of the bulk of the peasant population and, by their overcrowding, symbolized the alienation of the people from the land. The links between the land and the people were weak indeed, a fact which held true for all categories involved. *Latifondisti* lived off the land and were at best only marginally interested in the management of their estates, which they left to local peasant entrepreneurs. But this intermediate category of leaseholders and stewards also avoided permanent settlement on the land and lived in the agro-town where they had their families and clubs. We hear of one local *gabelloto* who managed an estate in another *comune* in the period just before World War I. When he went there to supervise work, he covered part of the way by train. This was by no means an isolated example. When I came across more recent cases in which people who owned or controlled estates and took a relatively active interest in running them, informants invariably stressed such cases were uncommon. Landless peasants have precarious links with the land from which they try to eke out a living. It might be expected that once peasants become full owners of viable units, they will settle on the land permanently, together with their family. Though this has been the case in other parts of the world, including southern Italy (Pitkin 1960; Silverman 1971), such cannot be demonstrated for the interior of Sicily. Several peasant families in Genuardo became wealthy and acquired considerable land in the course of time, but nonetheless continued to live in the village or moved to larger urban centers. The wealthier a man gets therefore, the more likely he is to sever his links with the land, that is, become an absentee.

When working in the fields or tending sheep and cattle, peasants appear morose and sullen, and are suspicious towards outsiders. They almost never sing at work, and when they occasionally do, their folksongs are melancholic and

5. Cf. Blok (1969a:129–30). It may be interesting to note that the word *piazza* in Italian has retained its original meaning of "market."

express resignation: they tell about the hardship of both man and animal. When peasants permitted me to photograph them while working, they were often embarrassed and ashamed—in sharp contrast to their eagerness to be photographed in urban or festive attires. Peasants generally avoid being seen when returning from the land, and they reach their homes by taking a longer road not exposed to the public eye. One standard answer to "How do you do?" is "*Cuntrastamu*," which means "We are resisting" or "We are struggling." I have heard this peasant salute particularly in situations involving work on the land, when peasants were actively at work or on their way to or from the fields. Francesco, a truck driver in his early forties from relatively well-to-do background, once explained: "*Caro* Antonio, you should understand one thing: work is a necessity, not a pleasure. People have to work in order not to die. Blessed is he who does not need to work. The man who lacks brains or luck has to work with his hands. He is a *disgraziato* who will never become rich or even respected. Manual work has been made by the devil." When asked what kind of work he deemed respectable, Francesco answered that supervising (*badare*) the work of other people deserved consideration in this respect, because it did not involve actual manual labor and was more remunerative.

The people in this area do not like the land, a condition I do not think common to all traditional peasant societies, as some anthropologists have argued (e.g., Foster 1965). For example, in a recently published monograph on Hungarian peasants we are told:

> "One ought to love the earth, not only to work it," said one of our informants. Especially in winter one hears much of the beauties and the joy of work in the fields and little about the fatigue involved. Be man or woman, adult or child, everyone is happier in the fields than in the home . . . (Fél and Hofer 1969:57).

This orientation of peasants having a relatively high degree of independent control over their land is completely at variance with the attitudes of the dependent peasantry discussed in this book. For them, manual work was and still is looked down upon, and those engaged in it—the *contadini* or *viddani*—are socially degraded. The peasants are said to lack *civiltà* (civility), polite forms, polish, genteel behavior. Their rustic air earns them the epithet of *viddanu*, a term with strong pejorative connotations: *viddanu* (from *villano*, villein, villain), a man from the countryside and lacking any civility (*uomo della campagna e lontano da ogni civiltà*). This basic distinction between *civili* or *signori* (gentlemen), who are addressed with the deferential *Don*, and *viddani* (countrymen) reflects a fundamental contrast between the city as a center of power, learning, and civilization and its counterpart, the uncivilized, subordinate countryside. This complementary opposition is characteristic of many Mediterranean areas.[6]

A rigid division of labor between the sexes remains one of the outstanding features of this society. Women are virtually excluded from agricultural work. Peasants take pride in exempting their wives, sisters, and daughters from labor on the land. Masculine dominance and prestige find expression in and are enhanced by the male's economic role. As the head of the family he is the main breadwinner. In this task he is usually assisted by his unmarried sons, though the responsibility is entirely his. The economic activities of his wife and unmarried daughters are confined to the home. In this connection, the family in southern Italy has been characterized as father-dominated and mother-oriented (cf. Moss and Thomson 1959). Strong restrictions exist for the sexual activities of his wife and daughters, which he is supposed to control rigidly. A man who allows his women to work outside

6. Cf. Wolf (1962); Silverman (1965, 1966). Redfield suggested that in the Mediterranean region the prestige of the *polis* carried with it the peasant's distaste for agricultural life (1960:66). This point has been elaborated by Caro Baroja (1963), Pitkin (1963), Pitt-Rivers (1963), and Blok (1969a). Honigmann's recent discussion on Austrian peasants (1970), as well as the work of Fél and Hofer on Hungarian peasants, demonstrates that Foster's proposition, that "in the traditional peasant society hard work and thrift are moral qualities of only the slightest functional value" (1965:307), requires reconsideration.

the home would jeopardize his honor in two ways: directly, by showing that he is not himself capable of supporting his family, and thus failing in his culturally defined role of the superior male *versus* the inferior females of the family; and indirectly, because he will be less able to control their sexual behavior. Hence there is a cultural emphasis on seclusion of women: most peasant women are not only socially debarred from going out into the fields, they are rarely seen in public. Very poor families cannot live up to this ideal, but most peasant families try to do so by making important sacrifices. In order to make a living at all, some peasants send their wives or daughters into the fields for light tasks such as gathering wood, or harvesting grapes and olives in personal service of the landowner. In this way labor on the land by women becomes associated with low social status. We are dealing here with an implication of the urban orientation of peasants in which labor on the land is negatively valued.

The conditions of the peasants in this area at the end of the 19th and at the beginning of the 20th century were investigated through two parliamentary enquiries. To complete this section on the relations between the people and the land, the main findings of these surveys are presented below. Most quotations are verbatim, while some passages have been paraphrased.

Genuardo is situated in the inland district of Corleone, which embraces eight towns with a total population of about 60,000 and which extends over roughly 970 square kilometers. This amounts to a density of some 60 persons per square kilometer. As for land use, cereals and natural pastures dominate with 60 and 32 per cent, respectively. There are no irrigation works, although various small rivulets (which dry up in summer) cross the area. Wheat and cheese are exported: in Genuardo a yearly amount of 900 quintals of cheese is produced. The network of roads is in very bad condition: many villages have not constructed the roads according to the law of 1869. Large estates predominate, especially so in the village of Genuardo where the land is in the hands of a few. In this

village, the sale of church lands did not have any effect
on the fragmentation of land. Public security is defective
in the entire area in so far as there is a high incidence of
cattle-rustling (*abigeato*). The large landowners lease their
estates to *gabelloti* and live elsewhere. The general form
of sublease is the so-called *mezzadrìa,* a sharecropping
arrangement which lasts one or two years and leaves the
peasant cultivator with much less than half the crops. The
peasants are frequently in debt to the landowners. Women
and children only rarely work on the land. The peasants
are sturdy-looking and feed on vegetable soup and *pasta*,
bread, and a little wine. Only very rarely does the menu
include meat. Housing conditions are unhealthy: most of
the peasants have only one room, which serves as kitchen
and living quarters, stable, store, and so forth. The peasants
are sober economically, but given their low earnings, they
are unable to save anything (Damiani 1885).

According to the second parliamentary enquiry, carried
out some 25 years later, social conditions in this area of Sicily
had hardly changed, except for large-scale emigration which
deeply affected the region. As Lorenzoni, who visited the
area in June, 1907, reports:

> The district of Corleone is one of the most characteristic
> and interesting of Sicily, because it is located at the center
> of the cereal and *latifondo* region and hence reflects its
> proper constitution. The largest part of the district consists
> of grain fields which alternate with pastures. Large estates
> predominate. Public security leaves much to be desired.
> Delinquency forms which prevail are homicide, damage
> for vengeance, and cattle-rustling. The latter is more fre-
> quent in winter than in summer, because the shortage of
> employment favors conspiracy. The town of Corleone is
> the center of *mafia*, a sentiment rather than an organiza-
> tion. *Omertà* makes both delinquency and *mafia* difficult
> to control. *Omertà* is inevitable, however, also for honest
> people, because the law is unable to offer protection. Those
> who seek redress by law can be sure to be affected by
> serious injury sooner or later. The almost complete absence

of practicable roads is a favorable condition for the lack of public security in the countryside. Genuardo is the village with the most extensive emigration in the district: between 1902 and 1907, 940 persons left the village for countries overseas. The main reason for this exodus lies in the persistence of the large estates. In the territory of Genuardo there are 19 *latifondi*, all larger than 200 hectares, which cover roughly 7,000 hectares, that is well over 50 per cent of the village area. As these estates are not sold and the small holdings adjacent to the village are extremely fragmented, there is no land that returning emigrants can buy. For this reason few returned to the village, and those who did left again. The consequent labor shortage led to higher labor costs and this compelled the landowners to abandon the cultivation of grain, at least partly, and to extend pasturage. Those most embittered by this state of affairs are the smallholders and sharecroppers who have land subleased from landowners and *gabelloti* but require additional workers to till it. As one informant put it: "This is the most terrible period we have passed through, because of the shortage of labor for working on the land and the rising costs of labor. To this should be added the seriousness of the situation." The *gabelloti* also find themselves in difficulties, because they had initiated the *gabella* contract in more favorable times and have to pay the rent while the cost of labor has been steadily rising. For this reason, they gradually yield and the *latifondisti* lease their land directly to the peasants without recourse to *gabelloti*.[7] One spokesman in Genuardo pointed out: "It is right and good that the *gabelloti* disappear. It is the hand of God that strikes them now. It is impossible to imagine the exploitation of the peasants by the *gabelloti*, especially in the recent past. Greedy to have the land in lease, they offered high rents to the landowners, and consequently tried to redeem it at the expense of the peasants. With the

7. To my knowledge, this putative crisis in *gabelloti* fortunes is much exaggerated, at least for Genuardo. See, however, Jane Schneider (1969:113), who reports serious difficulties for *gabelloti* in the neighboring town of Villamaura at that time.

disappearance of the *gabelloto*—this true vampire—both the conditions of the peasants and those of the landowners will improve. The profit of the *gabelloto* will then be divided between both." The *gabelloti* recognize these complaints as partly just, but ask for a law to change the rent according to changed conditions: "The high rents are the principal cause of the exploitation of the peasant."

[In Genuardo] there is a general request for land and the peasants ask for a law urging the *latifondisti* to lease them their estates around the village in emphyteusis [copyholding] in order to provide each peasant family with sufficient land to live on. The large estate owners, however, will be induced only with difficulty to divide their possessions spontaneously, because it would seem to them a loss in power, though they would gain in wealth. Because of widespread usury, the peasants also wish to obtain more favorable credit facilities. Existing credit institutions require loans to be guaranteed by a solvent person and therefore the peasants have to turn to others who claim a profit ranging between 15 and 20 per cent.

As elsewhere in the district, communications are very bad, and the territory of Genuardo is seriously infested by malaria (Lorenzoni 1910, II : 355–64).

As has been indicated before, these conditions did not basically change before the mid-20th century. Though some distribution of land took place in the period between the two world wars, it did not meet in any way the demands of the peasant masses. Where large estates were broken up and sold, shares were rarely less than 50 hectares, and these came into possession of peasant entrepreneurs and urban professionals. By 1930 smallholdings, most of which were unviable units, predominated only in number but covered little area, whereas the number of larger holdings was relatively low but involved the major part of the area (see Table VII).

LATIFONDISMO AND RENT CAPITALISM

The term *latifondismo* does not merely denote the presence

of large estates in a particular setting, but connotes as well the impact of the large estate upon this setting, that is, the physical and social environment. *Latifondismo,* therefore, contains the following attributes: the predominance of large estates which constitute the basis of an extensive agro-pastoral economy; the importance of agro-towns versus the absence of both permanent human settlement on the land and an adequate network of roads; the prevalence of insecurity in the countryside; a nomadic orientation of both shepherds and peasants; precarious links between the people and the land as expressed in absenteeism of the large estate owners, unstable employment of large segments of the peasantry, and the virtual exclusion of women from agricultural work.[8] The peasant entrepreneur performed a crucial role in this setting, since the most decisive features of *latifondismo* were the modes of exploitation of both land and labor. The *gabelloto* was anxious to make his fortune, and to this end any means seemed permissible (Pontieri 1943:56–57). Though his single-minded concentration on the maximization of profit brought him in conflict with the values of the peasant community (most notably his infringement of the common use rights), he was able to forestall possible levelling sanctions. As indicated above, the 18th century *gabelloto* controlled much of the social life of the peasant community in his role of *arbitro* or *arbitriante* (judge).[9] In the 19th and early 20th centuries, his power domain was increasingly based on patronage, a point that will be elaborated in subsequent chapters.

To understand the pivotal role of peasant entrepreneurs in

8. Cf. Ziino (1911:5 ff.); Navarra Crimi (1925:13–23, 71–100). Dickinson observes that when the term *latifondo* is used in its economic rather than in its etymological sense, it applies to both large and small holdings: "It is a mode of utilizing the land with a minimum of investment in improvement or equipment. It has a low input of labor per unit of area and per year, great precariousness of human settlements, extensiveness and discontinuity of cultivation—hence, the deserted and desolate aspect of such land" (1955:42).

9. See Chapter II, p. 33. The term *arbitriante* was also used to denote the *gabelloto.*

the transition from feudal to capitalist farming, we should note that they were innovators who located new resources and found adequate ways to exploit them. As we have seen, the *gabelloti* succeeded in controlling ever greater amounts of land, as it came up for sale in the course of the 19th century. The peasants consequently became increasingly dependent on them for access to land. In addition, the growing number of landless peasants and the general increase of the population in this period placed the *gabelloti* in a strong bargaining position from which to dictate the terms of employment. In several respects, these contracts were onerous and forced the peasants to accept loans advanced by their employers—the *gabelloti*. Through the institution of indebtedness, the Sicilian peasant of the *latifondo* emerged from feudal servitude only to fall into new forms of economic and political dependency. As in other parts of the world, the advent of the market and demographic growth disrupted the traditional order of lord and peasant, while at the same time, however, it provided opportunities for the rise of a new landed elite.[10]

The peasant of the inland area, and more particularly the sharecropper who brought his own mules and equipment to work on the estate, was permanently in debt to the *gabelloto* for several reasons. First, the contract left the cultivator with less than one-fourth of the crops. Second, the contract was verbal, a circumstance that left room for encroachments from the side of the *gabelloto*. Third, the *gabelloto* used two different measures: a small one when giving out seed, loans, and other *soccorsi* (aids) in grain; and a larger one when claiming these advances and dues from the crops at the threshing floor. Fourth, from his meager share, the sharecropper had to cede various "gifts" to the *gabelloto*, who distributed them among the *campieri*. These gifts were in fact tributes the peasant paid for protection. Fifth, interest rates were high; varying from 25 to well over 100 per cent. Finally, it should be clear

10. Similar conditions have been described for Eastern Europe as neo-serfdom (Mitrany 1951:43) and for the Mexican hacienda as peonage (Wolf 1959:204). Wolf has expanded this point in his discussion of peasant rebellions (1969:276–302; 1971).

that the risks of production were largely born by the share-cropper.[11]

The practices of exploiting a destitute peasantry, the disdain and lack of interest of the landowning elite for productive work and long-term investment, the social prestige attached to landownership, and the honorable way of life of parasitism are each indicative of what has been called rent capitalism. As Bobek writes:

> Rent capitalism arose through commercialization and the transformation, undertaken in a plain profit-seeking spirit, of the original lordly or feudal claims on income from the peasant and artisan under-strata. Its elaboration was definitively promoted by the keeping of accounts and other forms of rationalization of rent drawing. . . . The measures adopted [by the rent capitalist] are: appropriation of the means of production and the regular advancing of loans, i.e., the creation of indebtedness. . . . The opportunities to place the peasants in debt are favorable . . . for two reasons: one is lack of resources of most peasants that has its roots in the rent-capitalistic system. The other is the climatically conditioned frequency of crop failure. The peasant must quite often go into debt in order that he and his family can survive. It is an absolute ideal of the rent capitalist to get as many peasants as possible into debt so permanently that with all their yearly payments they can never liquidate the initial debt, which soon becomes legendary. The practices used to get around the condemnation not only of usury but of any kind of interest, so notably present in all great religions of Oriental origin, are legion. The commonest, for example, is to estimate an advance of grain at the highest price before the harvest. . . . The ideal of rent capitalism is [thus] attained when the sharecropping peasant does not touch more than a meager share of the work of his hands. But it is even possible to

11. This summary is based on interviews and written documents bearing on Genuardo and other parts of the inland area. Cf. Salvioli (1895); Lorenzoni (1910); Sonnino (1925:72, 135–36, 258–91); Ziino (1911:66 ff.); Sereni (1947:176–80); Mack Smith (1965: 107–08).

split up farm work itself (as in plowing, harvesting, sometimes care of trees, etc.) and to pay for it with appropriate shares of the product. . . . Rent capitalism was true capitalism in so far as it was characterized by a striving for unlimited gain and in so far as it adopted accounting practices. . . . It differed from the more recent "capitalism" in that it was not linked with production, but rather was satisfied with skimming off its proceeds. In regard to production it remained fundamentally sterile. For this reason it lent to ancient urbanism as a whole a definitely parasitical character, economically (1962:234–237).

To illustrate the rent capitalistic orientation of the Sicilian *latifondi*, I have reconstructed a large enterprise situated in the territory of Genuardo. Consistent with the approach followed in this book, the enterprise will be explored over time, and requires a separate chapter.

IV
The Latifondo

The enterprise with which this chapter deals consisted of nine adjoining estates covering a total area of about 2,100 hectares. I shall refer to this *latifondo*-complex as "Baronessa," not its real name but an allusion to its one-time existence as core of the barony which in feudal times made up most of the village territory. It is difficult to decide whether or not Baronessa was a typical *latifondo*, if there can be such a thing. Baronessa was much larger than most other estates in the territory; in fact it was a cluster of estates, each of which had actually been managed as an enterprise in its own right. Baronessa is particularly interesting because many of the people of Genuardo depended for their living on work they could find there. Furthermore, I was fortunate enough to obtain rather systematic information on this enterprise over time, particularly for the period after 1870. Baronessa reflected many features of other *latifondi* on which my information was less complete; its characteristics were common to many large estates in this part of Sicily, though the union of several adjoining estates into a larger complex was relatively uncommon.[1] The Baronessa *latifondi*, which varied in size from 60 to 400 hectares, covered the hills surrounding the main estate, which was located in a valley. All estates have proper names, and are generally referred to as *feudi*; the term *latifondo* belongs to technical language and did not intrude into ordinary speech.

1. In his discussion on south Italian large estates, Vöchting refers several times to Baronessa to illustrate various general points (1951:288, 299, 305). See also Buttazzoni (1939). As we will see, however, the Santa Maria del Bosco estates formed a similar complex of adjoining *latifondi*.

The central estate, for which the whole complex was named, had a large mansion from which the enterprise was directed. Apart from quarters for its personnel, stables, stores, bakehouse, chapel, olive- and wine-presses, and cellar, there were comfortable living-rooms on the first floor for the owner, who lived permanently in Palermo and occasionally visited his estates. All these buildings were joined and constituted a large square around a spacious central courtyard. The other estates also had farmhouses but these *masserie* lacked the grandeur of the central mansion; they were simple, rectangular constructions with a residential apartment, stores, haystacks, and stable for horses and mules. A system of muletracks connected the nine estates. Distances between Genuardo and the Baronessa estates range between four and fourteen kilometers.

Most of Baronessa consisted of cereal and pasture land, though some 50 hectares of olives, almonds, and vines surrounded the mansion. Such strips of intensive cultivation around farmhouses are quite common in this area, and are called *girati*. Techniques of cultivation were much the same in 1900 as they had been from about 1870 onwards in most parts of the territory. Estates were leased to *gabelloti* who divided them into three fields (cereals, pastures, and fallow) which were alternately cultivated in the course of a three-year cycle. A quite common variation on this rotation pattern was the so-called *ringrano*, the sowing of grain sown on the same field for a second year. Part of the fallow was cultivated with *sulla*, beans, or lentils, each of which is a nitrogenous crop which thus improves the soil. The tillage of beans and lentils, however, required a strong input of labor; consequently, these crops covered little area, especially during periods of emigration when the cost of labor increased. The fields marked for the cultivation of cereals were annually subleased in small plots to the sharecroppers. The other fields were tilled by wage-earners whom the *gabelloto* employed on a temporary basis varying from a few days to a season.

In 1902, seven estates of Baronessa were leased to three local *gabelloti*: the two brothers Nicola and Michele Jaconi, and their father's brother Domenico. Upon marriage Domenico had moved to a neighboring town, but all three belonged to one of the dominant patrinominal families (see Chapter VI, note 23) of Genuardo which had held large estates in lease for several generations. Domenico's brother Francesco had been mayor of Genuardo since 1873, except for one short interruption (see Diagram 1). The land, which they managed in partnership, amounted to 1,474 hectares, which were worked (with slight variations) according to the three-field system: wheat (595 hectares); barley (24 hectares); beans (10 hectares); fallow (373 hectares); and pastures (470 hectares).[2]

	hectares	*percentages*
wheat	595	40.3
barley	24	1.6
beans	10	0.7
fallow	373	25.5
pastures	470	31.9
	1,472	100.0

The partnership used most of the pastures for its own flocks, consisting of 650 sheep, 70 oxen, 20 horses, and 12 mules, as well as for 250 sheep belonging to the shepherds. Since the fallow was grazed from November till March, this together with the pastures and stubble-fields provided more pasturage than could be grazed by the animals mentioned above. Therefore, every year roughly 100 hectares of pasture land were subleased to other livestock owners.

The labor force required for the various agricultural and supervisory tasks was far from homogeneous. Three main categories can be distinguished here: permanent employees, sharecroppers, and casual laborers. There were 39 permanent employees, annually paid partly in money and partly in kind.

2. For information bearing on this period (1902), I have relied on a set of handwritten notes compiled at that time by a local young man here called Giuseppe Livornese (see Diagram 1), who was currently writing a thesis in agronomy. The notes will be referred to as MS 1902. I have supplemented his data with interviews and documents on land tenure.

Up to the early 20th century, some of them still wore special uniforms that identified them as Baronessa personnel. The most important of them was the overseer (*soprastante*). In agreement with the *gabelloti*, the overseer established the pattern of cultivation and was charged with direct and continual management of the whole enterprise. Like overseers on other estates, this man had no formal training in agriculture whatsoever.[3] As a rule, strong men were recruited for this post, from those who were able to "make themselves respected"—inspire fear—among the people on the estates as well as outsiders. In fact, the overseer was the man of confidence (*uomo di fiducia*) of the *gabelloto*. He dealt with the peasants set to work on the estates and took care of the general protection of the enterprise. In this crucial task he was assisted by five armed *campieri* on horseback who watched over the fields, crops, and animals. Like the overseer, these field guards had a reputation for toughness, which they advertised by their arrogant airs and their carrying of arms. The ways in which some of them dressed, moved around, and squinted symbolized toughness. Their reticence and the opaque ambiguity of phrases, gestures, and mimic signs they used among their peers set them apart from ordinary people. Though these strongarm men were at times strikingly polite and cordial, their general behavior and outfit expressed a capacity and willingness to coerce with physical violence. The *campieri* constituted a kind of private police force which, in the absence of an efficient formal control apparatus, claimed to maintain law and order in the countryside. Law and order should of course be understood here in terms of vested interests: conflicts were settled by and in favor of those who wielded appropriate influence and power. As will be shown in the second part of this book, positions of power were continually open to question: more violent or more shrewd contestants could oust the incumbents from

3. This was one respect in which the Sicilian overseer (*soprastante*) differed from his counterpart in central Italy, the *fattore*, who was primarily a technical expert. Cf. Silverman (1967:284–85). In Sicily the term *fattore* is only rarely used to indicate an overseer. See Prestianni (1947:146).

office. What earned these men "respect" (*rispettu*) was, first, their capacity to coerce with physical violence and thus invoke fear in others. Second, and closely related to these awe-inspiring qualities, they were able to provide access to resources, most notably land, for their followers.[4]

The other permanent employees included one book-keeper, one storekeeper, two oxen drivers, and two mule drivers. In terms of payment they were on an equal footing with the *campiere*. Their positions on the estate did not necessarily require the qualifications for toughness. The lower ranks of the permanent employees consisted of one chief herdsman (*curatolo*), six herdsmen, five shepherd boys, and 15 hired hands. The shepherds, especially their foreman, shared the orientation of the *campiere*. They were responsible for the flocks and the production of cheese. Alone with the animals on the vast pastures, they had to take care of themselves. Hence they were armed and ready to use violence in coping with rustlers and bandits.

The preparation of the fallow in spring required the employment of teams of oxen. The plowing and cross-plowing were carried out by the 15 hired hands mentioned above. Grain was sown on three types of fields: the fallow, stubble, and pasture. Its cultivation was carried out by approximately 200 sharecroppers (*metatieri*). They were left with either one-half or one-fourth of the crops according to whether or not they plowed the plots assigned them.

The recruitment of personnel was in principle controlled by the *gabelloti*. They appointed the overseer and the *campieri*, who in turn hired most of the peasants, strongly favoring kinsmen and friends from Genuardo and half a dozen neighboring towns in which some of them lived. As one informant recalled: "Each town furnished a *campiere*, who attracted his fellow townsmen." Expanding the supply of labor and, consequently, the range of patronage, the offer of

4. Compare Barth's discussion of authority and following among the Swat Pathans (1959:71–91) and Bailey's reflections (1969:39–40). The note of Elias on the concept of "*gesellschaftliche Stärke*" in his chapter on the sociogenesis of feudalism makes much sense here (1969, II:82–84).

employment was indeed a favor: the more personal the relationship between employer and job candidate, the more probable the employment and the less onerous the contract. The verbal agreements on which these contracts were based were then "respected for friendship" and involved the exchange of small services and favors.

All people employed at Baronessa were, in varying degrees, partly paid in money and partly in kind, including the usufruct of land and animals (see Table VIII). The sharecroppers were not paid in cash at all. Common to most of the contracts was the system of halves (*a metà*): peasant cultivators were paid for their work with shares of the products, either one-half or one-fourth. Eighteen permanent employees maintained a mare each on a system of halves with the *gabelloti*. The overseer had two horses on similar terms. The total of 20 mares produced 30 mules of which the *gabelloti* obtained half. Eleven employees held usufruct rights to land given out to them on a sharecropping basis: they received strips of land sown with wheat and beans, and they were assigned one-third or one-fourth of the crop. The *curatolo* grazed his 50 sheep on the pastures of the *padrone*, who took all the milk and two-thirds of the offspring for raising. In figures this reads: the *gabelloti* had 650 sheep while the shepherds had 250 of their own. All sheep were herded together on the various pastures of Baronessa. Of all 900 sheep, 522 were milked. (There were 90 rams: 152 sheep were not milked because they were too young, that is between one and two years; and 135 sheep did not produce any milk.) The *gabelloti* claimed all milk, which yielded about 80 quintals of cheese and 20 quintals of *ricotta*. The sheep that produced milk had one lamb each. Of these 522 lambs, 145 remained in possession of the shepherds; the remainder (377) were claimed by the *gabelloti*, who sold 250 of them for slaughter after one month. The production of wool was divided according to ownership of the sheep: the *gabelloti* gathered close to eight quintals of wool from their 650 sheep; the herdsmen had a production of roughly three quintals from their 250 sheep.

All contracts were arranged with the obvious aim that the

gabelloti share only minimally in the risks of production, which largely devolved upon staff and peasants.[5] To begin with, the three *gabelloti*, here called Domenico, Nicola, and Michele, had pooled part of their resources to exploit the agricultural enterprise of Baronessa. They formed a partnership (*società*). On a lower level, they established temporary partnerships with the shepherds, whom they largely paid with shares of the product. Farm work was split up to a considerable extent; plowing, harvesting, and transport were carried out by different categories while the sharecroppers performed variable amounts of each of these tasks, in addition to weeding and threshing. Virtually all employees were paid with shares of the product. Under these conditions, the structure of "enterprise" dissolved into a series of individual tasks and corresponding claims on income (cf. Bobek 1962: 235). The rent-capitalist practice of creating debtors was clearly exemplified in the cultivation of wheat and other cereals. Just under 600 hectares were sown by the sharecroppers. The fields and labor were divided as follows:

(1) Fallow land, measuring 375 hectares, was plowed up by the hired hands, who were paid partly in kind and usufruct. In September, strips were given out to sharecroppers on a system of quarters: the sharecropper received one-fourth of the crop. He performed the last plowing with the aid of his mules in November and carried out all subsequent tasks including sowing, weeding, harvesting, transport, and threshing. The seed was furnished by the *gabelloti à fonds perdu*. Production amounted to roughly 12 hectoliters per hectare.

(2) Stubble fields (*ringrano*) covered 125 hectares and were given out on a system of halves. The sharecropper provided 50 per cent of the seed and carried out all subsequent work, including three plowings in autumn. Since these fields were sown for a second year, yields were sig-

5. Hence the name *compartecipazione* that describes the system under which the risks of production fall mainly upon the cultivators and herdsmen. For the persistence of this contract throughout the South, see Franklin (1969:124–29).

nificantly lower than from the fallow mentioned above and did not exceed eight hectoliters per hectare. The crops were equally divided between sharecropper and *gabelloti*.

(3) Pasture land covered 60 hectares and was given out on a system of quarters. Plowing and sowing were carried out on behalf of the *gabelloti*. The sharecropper furnished a plowman for the last plowing in November. The seed was supplied by the *gabelloti*. Production of these fields amounted to ten hectoliters per hectare.[6]

Though Giuseppe Livornese (MS 1902), who provides most of these data, does not mention it, we know from other local and regional sources that the sharecropper often had to cede various extra amounts from his meager allotment. To understand the significance of these impositions, the reader should know that the Sicilian *salma* refers to both a cubic measure (2.75 hectoliters) and to an amount of land which is variable according to terrain but fixed for the Genuardo territory at 2.67 hectares. Though one *salma* of grain can not precisely be expressed in terms of weight, an average *salma* of wheat corresponds to 220 kilograms. Both types of *salme* (pl.) are subdivided into 16 *tumoli* (one *tumolo* equals one bushel). Among the exactions imposed on the sharecroppers, the following were the most important.

(a) A preferential share, the so-called *terraggiulo*, which varied from one to two *tumoli* of grain for every *salma* under cultivation.

(b) The repayment of more seed to the *gabelloti* than initially advanced, the so-called *addito*, which varied from two to four *tumoli* of grain for every *salma* brought under cultivation.

(c) A second increase on the repayment of the advanced seed, called *lordura*. This due consisted of two *tumoli* of

6. Salvioli mentions averages of 13 hectolitres per hectare, which he considers to be low (1895:456). It must be noted that the amount the sharecropper received depended upon the quality of the terrain, distances between the fields and the village, and the extent of competition between peasant cultivators for contracts.

grain for every *salma* of grain the *gabelloti* had provided.

(d) Claims for protection, the *guardiania* and *cuccia,* which amounted to several *tumoli* each.

These small but numerous impositions weighed heavily on the peasant, especially since most of them were fixed amounts of grain in proportion to land under cultivation, which meant that they were levied irrespective of whether yields were high or low. When claiming dues, the *campieri* used a larger measure (*tumolo di esigenza*) than the one employed in issuing seed, loans, and other advances.[7]

A local priest (Genovese 1894), who wrote a pamphlet on agrarian problems existing in this area at the end of the 19th century, calculated that from an abundant though rare yield of 12 *salme* per *salma* of land, the sharecropper obtained scarcely 20 per cent. Aided by three sons and two mules, a sharecropper was able to cultivate three *salme,* which is roughly eight hectares. His allotments, observed the priest, were barely enough to feed himself and his family throughout the year. He lacked a fund from which he could replace minimal equipment for production. In order to repair his tools, to maintain his mules, to buy clothes and shoes for his family, and to pay taxes, he could not but sell increasing shares of his grain. To make a living at all, the sharecropper had to accept loans from the *gabelloti* which, again, had to be repaid at the next harvest. To an extent, these hardships were eased by the fact that sharecropping was not an exclusive task; it left room for additional employment on small plots around the village and different kinds of seasonal labor. The hard conditions of employment, especially for casual laborers, on Baronessa at this time are still recalled in a satiric rhyme:

7. Cf. Sonnino (1925:34–39) and Ziino (1911:82–88). Favorable yields were and still are considered those called *à tumolo*: one *salma* of wheat is sown on one *salma* of land that then produces 16 *salme* of wheat. In this way the cultivator harvests from one *tumolo* sown one *salma* (i.e. 16 *tumoli*) of wheat. These figures correspond with a yield of about 13.5 quintals per hectare. Cf. Sartorius von Waltershausen (1913:94).

A Baronessa,	On Baronessa,
Pani un tozzu,	One piece of bread,
Vinu quantu ti vagni lu pizzu,	Just enough wine to wet your beak,
E li picciuli darreri lu cozzu.	No money at all.

Though all forms of share tenancy were generally referred to as *metaterìa* (from *metà*, half) or *mezzadrìa* (idem), including those cases where sharecroppers obtained much less, they fundamentally differed from the classical or proper *mezzadrìa* in other parts of Italy. In Umbria (Central Italy), for example, sharecropping involved a compact and fixed holding (*podere*) with farmstead and agricultural equipment furnished by the landowner, who took an active interest in the enterprise by appointing agricultural technicians, the counterparts of the Sicilian overseer. The tenant lived permanently with his family on the land, and though the minimum duration of the contract was one year, "it was common for a farm to be occupied by the same family for many decades and even for generations" (Silverman 1967:284). As we have seen, the Sicilian sharecropping peasant of the *latifondo* was faced with a much different situation. Since integrated farms which could be operated as family labor units were absent, he lacked any security of tenure over time. In fact, his position with regard to employment did not basically differ from that of the landless laborer. These occupational roles were often simultaneously performed by many peasants, including smallholders, a fact which, *inter alia*, weakens most official statistics on peasant occupational structures. Hence the nomadic orientation of the peasantry: sharecroppers, smallholders, and landless laborers were constantly moving from one plot to another and traveled almost daily between the village and the land.

The profile of Baronessa illustrates how limited capital investment on a short term basis inhibited the development of durable bonds between the peasants and the land. Short term leases and subleases, as well as temporary partnerships, limited the range of alternative routes and discouraged investments from the side of both cultivators and entrepreneurs. The latter, whose preeminence on the estates depended upon their capacity to generate *rispettu* rather than on anything else (least of all some scientific knowledge of farming), engaged in ruthless exploitation of land and labor rather than undertake long-term investment. As true rent capitalists they "skimmed off the proceeds." They refrained from taking any substantial share in the risks of production. The data on Baronessa suggest how, particularly, the system of shares served to pass on these risks to the peasant labor force. Among the peasant cultivators, therefore, subsistence necessarily took priority over investment. It seems that this pattern of economic organization was ultimately underwritten by demographic and political conditions. Population pressure, though at times eased by large-scale emigration, and relative scarcity of land brought those who controlled estates into a strategic position to exploit the labor force and accumulate wealth. These profits did not return to the land but instead were used to acquire more land or were spent on urban living. In this way, the peasant entrepreneur followed the course exemplified by the absentee estate owner and thus helped to maintain what has been called the paleotechnic basis of this type of agrarian society (cf. Wolf 1966b:55–56). The political conditions that help explain the rent-capitalist tenor of these agricultural enterprises will be explored in the second part of this study. But first let us complete the sketch of Baronessa and describe its development in recent decades.

ATTEMPTS AT REFORM

By 1920, the owner of Baronessa decided to cultivate his estates more intensively by substituting continuous rotations in which intercalated crops are grown for discontinuous rotations in which one field lies idle. This move was intimately connected with peasant unrest following the end of World War I. Peasant war veterans had been promised land, and several political parties advocated the expropriation of uncultivated large estates. As elsewhere in the South, peasant cooperatives occupied the land. Though the

advent of Fascism in 1922 postponed the implementation of
these agrarian reforms, the improvements introduced to
escape expropriation were nevertheless carried through.
They are described in this section.

On five estates of Baronessa, which together covered
roughly 1,100 hectares, the *gabella* was replaced by direct
management under a steward (*amministratore*). The steward,
Giuseppe Livornese, was the son of a landowning professional in Genuardo and was trained as an agronomist in
Palermo (see Diagram 1). Apart from his technical knowledge, he was well acquainted with the social conditions of
the area.[8] Giuseppe was on good terms with some estate
owners in Palermo, as well as with several *gabelloti* and
campieri in the area. He had *rispettu* not so much because he
generated fear but because he was well connected; indeed,
Giuseppe belonged to one of the families that had ruled the
village since the unification of Italy. As a man of confidence
of the estate owner and as an agricultural expert, Giuseppe
administered Baronessa, and received 8 to 10 per cent of its
net returns. Giuseppe retained his post until 1932, when
certain circumstances (to be discussed later) forced his
retirement.

The improvements introduced on Baronessa in the early
1920s affected five estates; the four remaining *latifondi*,
which made up about 1,000 hectares, were still leased for
one term to *gabelloti*. By 1932 these estates had also come
under direct management. Capital became more directly
linked with production. In a letter to the estate owner, Giuseppe mentioned "a strong employment of capital in order
to increase production in the near future." Some seven
kilometers of new roads were built to facilitate transport by
two motor trucks. Where the terrain permitted, plow teams
of oxen were replaced by a tractor to cut deeper furrows. It
has been argued that especially heavy clay soils, which predominate in this part of Sicily, require deep plowing while
shallow depths, attained by the traditional wooden plow

8. The reader will remember that this man was the author of the
MS 1902. See note 2.

(*aratro*) drawn by oxen or mules, are effective on light and friable soils (cf. Sartorius von Waltershausen 1913:85–86; Dickinson 1955:37–38; Wolf 1966b:32). A third innovation concerned the substitution of *sulla* for the uncultivated fallow. The *gàbelloti*, who were leaving at the end of August 1920, permitted that *sulla* be sown in January of that year on some 400 hectares where grain had been sown by them two months earlier. This was done to have pasture land ready during the first year from October through February and to harvest it as hay in spring. The fields were distributed as follows: cereals (500 hectares); *sulla* (400 hectares); and natural pastures (200 hectares).

Modern tractor plowing involved cutting of deep furrows instead of merely scratching the soil. The cultivation of *sulla* (a forage as well as a soil-renewal crop) increased both the production of grain and that of livestock. Some fields, particularly those planted with *sulla*, produced twice the amount of grain, well over 13 quintals per hectare. Yet averages remained relatively low. Between 1920 and 1926, the total annual production of wheat varied between 1,130 and 2,255 quintals; when all estates of Baronessa came under direct management in the early 1930s, the total annual production of wheat rose to 4,430 quintals. Fifty to 75 per cent of these yields was sold on the market; the remainder was used to pay the labor force.

On the *sulla* pastures sheep produced twice as much milk as on the natural pastures. As a consequence the former were much sought by other livestock keepers. Throughout 1920 and 1921, the flock of Baronessa consisted of just 500 sheep which grazed on less than 100 hectares. Therefore, almost three-fourths of the *sulla* fields were leased to other livestock owners: three from Genuardo and five from distant villages and towns, one of which was just over 50 kilometers from the Baronessa estates. Pastures leased to outsiders amounted to 314 hectares (see Table IX), and were grazed from November to the end of the summer. The second field of Leonardo, a *gabelloto* from Villamaura, was leased only in April after the Baronessa flock had partly grazed it. Rosario, a *gabelloto* from Prizzi, held a lease running from the beginning of January to the 15th of April. *Sulla* fields utilized by the Baronessa flock covered 77 hectares. They were used as pastures between November and the 15th of February, except for the 25 hectares which served exclusively for hay and seed. The fields that produced hay covered about 40 hectares and yielded roughly 100 quintals per hectare. The other *sulla* fields were fertilized with phosphates in February, after which they were used as pastures again for the rest of the season. The sheep that grazed on *sulla* during the winter produced twice as much milk and cheese as the sheep grazing on traditional pastures. Under previous conditions, only two flocks of about 500 sheep each could be pastured on the Baronessa estates. As may be seen from Table IX, the transformed fields provided pastures for nine flocks numbering well over 200 cattle and close to 4,500 sheep.

Most of these livestock owners were or had been *gabelloti* or *campieri*. In fact, Michele, Antonio, and Luigi held estates in lease of Baronessa before 1920. Although several of them lived in different towns, they all knew each other personally. As we have seen, ecological conditions forced the flocks to travel over long distances in search of pastures which were soon grazed off, especially if the autumn rains came too late or failed altogether. Neither natural pastures nor *sulla* fields could be grazed continually. Hence, as before, the flocks were driven from one field to the next and back again, and these movements required networks of friends and kinsmen extending over large areas of western Sicily. Such relationships were reinforced and ramified on the various cattlemarkets (*fiere*); each village and town had its own market on fixed days in spring, summer, and early autumn.

The effect of improvements carried through on the Baronessa estates was slight; average yields of wheat still remained modest and much below those attained in northern Italy.[9]

9. Cf. Prestianni (1947:164). Dickinson notes that "wheat, which provides the bulk of the peasant diet, as well as a substantial commercial surplus, yielded only 10 quintals per hectare in 1948 in the South as compared with 20.7 quintals per hectare in the North (14.5 and 30 bushels per acre respectively)" (1955:30).

Furthermore, the new techniques of cultivation were applied on a small scale: the greater part of the estates was worked according to traditional methods. As before, cultivation remained subject to the vagaries of climatic conditions; failing or abundant rains largely accounted for wide variations in yields.

Under the Fascist policy of self-sufficiency, the production of Italian wheat was strongly encouraged, and this involved subsidizing the Sicilian *latifondo* (cf. Mack Smith 1968a: 514–17). The area covered by large estates in the territory of Genuardo remained fairly stationary during this period (see Tables III and IV). Buttazzoni, who surveyed the Baronessa estates in the late 1930s, was struck by their technical and economical backwardness, which was particularly noticeable in comparison with enterprises in central Italy. In fact, Buttazzoni singled out Baronessa to illustrate some problems pertaining to the Sicilian *latifondi* in general.[10] After some introductory notes on the general features of *latifondismo*, he presents an outline of land use and division of labor (see Table X). Some of the draft animals that worked on the estates belonged to the personnel employed at Baronessa. Pastures were grazed by the flocks of the estate owner as well as by animals of outsiders (these proportions are summarized in Table XI). All the land, except for the olive grove, was divided into three main fields, each of which was cultivated in the course of a five-year cycle as follows: *sulla* / cereals / cereals / fallow and pasture / fallow and pasture. Cereals and pastures each covered roughly one-third of the land each year. The remainder consisted of *sulla*, beans, fallow, and olives. Twenty-six permanent employees and several casual laborers worked under direct management. They were charged with supervision, cultivation, maintenance, and herding. Forty-seven sharecroppers were recruited for the cultivation of grain. They supplied mules, plows, and part of

10. In his survey covering all Sicilian *latifondi* existing on January 1, 1927, Molè mentions the estates of Baronessa as being well cultivated (1929:103). Obviously, his frame of reference was different from that of Buttazzoni (1939), who compared Baronessa with northern Italy.

the seed. Each of them held about 15 hectares over two years and obtained one-third of the crops. As may be seen, deployment of capital was low. Buttazzoni calculated that the capital value of land made up 80 per cent of the enterprise, as against the 20 per cent comprised by animals, equipment, and labor. Of the gross returns, 75 per cent was made up by the cultivation of cereals; 23 per cent was drawn from the production of animals and pastures; and 2 per cent came from olives and other fruit trees. It should be noted that similar rotation patterns were found as early as 1912 in this area (cf. Sartorius von Waltershausen 1913:88–89). Clearly, methods of production hardly changed during Fascism. It was estimated that in Sicily as a whole, average yields of wheat rose just 1.6 quintals per hectare (Prestianni 1947:164). The total production of Sicilian wheat increased, but livestock keeping suffered serious drawbacks, since grain fields grew at the expense of pastures. Furthermore, clearing land for the cultivation of wheat hastened the process of soil erosion. On the whole, therefore, the Fascist agrarian policy did not promote the development of more intensive methods of cultivation and inhibited the expansion of a more balanced agriculture (cf. Mack Smith 1965:121–23; 1968a:516–17). The so-called colonization of the *latifondo* came too late (1940) to have significant results. Some 300 hectares of Baronessa were involved in this reform, which was aimed at the development of scattered settlement. Along the road that crossed the estates, 15 farmsteads were built. Each holding of about 20 hectares was assigned to a peasant family on a system of halves, while farm equipment and cattle were provided by the owner of Baronessa. After the allied occupation of Sicily in 1943, this attempt to set up the classical *mezzadria* was abruptly halted. Under the pretext of transforming the land into vineyards, the owner succeeded in reincorporating the holdings into his domain. The sharecroppers received small compensation in cash. Only two of them obtained a few hectares (one *salma*) each.

Before turning to the actual break-up of the large estates, we may well ask what conditions may account for the persistence of the *latifondo* into modern times. Several authors have been struck by its anachronistic features. Vöchting, for example, who refers to Buttazzoni's survey of Baronessa, observes that

> ... the household of the *latifondo* is divided into a multitude of individual sub-enterprises which, organizationally and socially, mesh firmly together like the wheels of a clock: as a producing community made up of a staff of estate employees along with day laborers, migrant workers, sharecroppers, small tenants, outside livestock owners, on top of whom a *gabelloto* and speculating intermediary leaseholders are often superimposed, its economic structure appears just as intricate and ingenious as do its technical processes simple and crude, like a fossilized creature out of prehistoric times (Vöchting 1951:288).

To understand the persistence of the Sicilian *latifondo* over time, we should appreciate its functions as well as its defense mechanisms. Both were strikingly similar to those of the Mexican *hacienda* as described by Eric Wolf (1956:1069; 1959: 203 ff.) First, the Sicilian large estate remained close to natural conditions. This made it vulnerable to crop failures, but the risks of bad harvests were largely transferred to the cultivators. On the other hand, this narrow ecological basis made the large estate remarkably less sensitive to market fluctuations than modern and more specialized commercial enterprises. The *latifondo* could easily shift from cereals to livestock raising and vice versa. In fact, the Sicilian large estate survived both the agrarian depression of the 1880s and the related exodus of much of its labor force in the decades around 1900 by expanding pasture land at the expense of the cultivation of wheat. Under Fascism another successful shift was made to meet the increased demand for Italian grain. Second, the cyclical patterns of land use necessitated short-term contracts and thus ruled out permanent settlement on the land. Not living on the land and even physically separated from it by fixed residence in agro-towns, the peasants could less easily lay claim to it and thereby challenge large landownership. Third, the prevailing rent systems and the pattern of convertible husbandry discouraged long-term capital investment from all categories involved: landowners, leaseholders, and peasant cultivators. As such improvements would have changed the physiognomy of the *latifondo*, their very absence reinforced its existence. Fourth, the fragmented occupational structure of the peasant class attached to the large estates stifled the emergence of class consciousness and enduring interest groups among the labor force. The way in which labor on the *latifondo* was organized inhibited sustained and concerted peasant attacks on the large estates.[11] The unstable forms of tenure and fluid organization of work were, therefore, among the most important mechanisms retarding the transformation of a laboring *Klasse an sich* into a *Klasse für sich*. Fifth, and finally, *mafia* provided the large estate with its mainstay. As will be shown in the second part of this book, physical violence dominated the social relationships through which the large estates were exploited. In this way *mafiosi* kept restive peasants in submission, while opening up avenues for upwardly mobile peasants who qualified in the use of violence. At a higher level of society, *mafiosi* lent their support and that of their vast clienteles to any government willing to abstain from too much interference in

11. Cf. Tarrow (1967:34, 51), who elsewhere states: "The fragmentation of social groups and the dominant emphasis upon landholding in the stratification system of the *Mezzogiorno* gives a peculiar character to social conflict. There is a great deal of social conflict, as any popular novel about the South suggests. However, in the absence of strong occupational classes, there is little of what could legitimately be considered as *class* conflict. Where the traditional ordering of social roles breaks down and a modern system of hierarchy has not yet been consolidated, status groups are too fragmented to coalesce into social classes" (1967:66–67). Structural fragmentation, or something much like it, has been emphasized by Wolf as one of the conditions that handicap peasants "in passing from passive recognition of wrongs to political participation as a means for setting them right.... [P]easants' interests—especially among poor peasants—often crosscut class alignments. Rich and poor peasants may be kinfolk, or a peasant may be at one and the same time owner, renter, sharecropper, laborer for his neighbors, and seasonal hand on a nearby plantation. Each different involvement aligns him differently with his fellows and with the outside world" (1971:49–50).

the affairs of the local oligarchies in west Sicilian townships. They thus kept a hold on outside influence. In turn, the large estates provided local elites with the material and human resources to build up and maintain their power domains. The Sicilian large estate had still additional functions appropriate to this wider context and which also contributed to its persistence over time. Here we should note that the rapidly developing industrial areas of northern Italy lured much government and private capital away from southern regions. As elsewhere in the world, capitalist development helped generate the underdevelopment of peripheral areas.[12]

DECLINE

Along with changes in the international wheat market and the emigration of labor, a vital circumstance may explain the nadir of the *latifondo*, in Genuardo as well as other inland areas: the peasant movement that spread across the South immediately after World War II. Several forces propelled the peasants to attack the latifundist order. The movement had a long history of agrarian unrest at its back. Since the 19th century "anti-feudal reforms," which had increasingly deprived the peasants of access to land, banditry had been endemic in Sicily, especially in its interior, and rural rebellions had shown a remarkable dispersion and frequency, exploding in 1820, 1837, 1848, 1860, 1866, 1893, and 1918. The abortive reforms of the inter-war period intensified the peasants' deeply-rooted aspiration for land. Furthermore, military service abroad and participation in partisan resistance in northern Italy and Yugoslavia helped convert resignation into militancy. What actually ignited the movement, however, was the serious political and economic crisis that followed the collapse of Fascism. A loosely organized and temporary Allied government could but partially meet the need for food and work just as it only partially filled the power vacuum. To answer the desperate demand for land, special decrees were issued by the government as early as

12. Cf. Geertz (1963); Wolf (1967); Frank (1967); Schneider, Schneider, and Hansen (1972).

1944 that authorized *de facto* occupations of estates by peasant cooperatives. For six years, one Baronessa estate was directly leased and operated by a peasant collective. Though the transformation of large estates was stipulated in the new Italian Constitution of 1947, a special agrarian reform act was passed for Sicily only in 1950. Meanwhile, the struggle for land continued.[13]

In November 1948, three estates of Baronessa were occupied by the peasants. The fields were ready for sowing when a peasant mass of about one thousand invaded them. As one of the leaders recalled:

> Women as much as men took part. Some were on mule-back, others simply walked. They carried two-hundred plows; and about 400 day laborers had the *zappa* [mattock] to work with. The *campieri* of the estates were unable to prevent the invasion. How could they shoot at us? Instead they turned to the police for intervention. Five leaders were arrested, myself included. But the same evening we were released, after a mass demonstration in front of the village prison. Afterwards we were arrested again and served a 36-day term in prison.

The occupation of these estates succeeded in obtaining the land for that year. The peasants carried out the sowing, harvesting, and threshing, after which the crops were divided on a fifty-fifty basis with the *gabelloto*, instead of one-fourth or less as was common in the past.

These invasions, as well as the support they received from the Communist Party, made many estate owners realize that agrarian reform involving expropriation was inevitable in the near future. To evade the blow of expropriation, virtually all *latifondisti* who held land in the territory of Genuardo divided considerable parts of their property among future heirs; shares of estates were sold to *gabelloti*, *campieri*, and well-to-do *burgisi*. Between 1944 and 1950, about 800 hec-

13. Cf. Marciani (1966:25) Tarrow (1967:279 ff.). Sorgi mentions that between 1944 and 1955 at least 45 peasant leaders were assassinated by *mafiosi*. Virtually all of these crimes remained unpunished (1959:626–27).

tares of the Baronessa estates were thus distributed among
the landowner's four children and just over 500 hectares were
sold. These maneuvers were widespread throughout Sicily
and the southern mainland. As Vöchting writes:

> The estate owners themselves, however, were by no
> means willing to offer their necks like lambs to the decapi-
> tation that threatened them. Since 1945, one could already
> see lawyers, notaries, assessors, and surveyors ardently at
> work in the latifundist zones dividing the land appropri-
> ately among husbands and wives as well as children and
> grandchildren, born and unborn, such that the raised arm
> of State power, instead of hitting the mark, had to expect
> to come down in a vacuum: It seemed for the present not
> inconceivable that a law for the division of *latifondi* would
> find no *latifondi* left to divide! (Vöchting 1951:309)

To appreciate the meaning of these maneuvers, the reader
should know that the agrarian reform law of 1950 stipulated
that all transfers of land after the 1st of January, 1948 (the
date when the new Italian Constitution came into force)
would lack validity. As the Italianist Barzini has aptly noted:
"In Italy any law changes meaning and purpose according
to the power of the person who applies or violates it ..."
(1965:224).[14]

The reform law stipulated that land from all extensively
cultivated properties larger than 200 hectares would be expropriated. Holdings exceeding 100 hectares were to be
transformed by intensive cultivation, while woodlands were
exempt from expropriation. Effective compensation to large
landowners amounted to an average of 40 per cent of the
market value of the expropriated land.[15] Holdings assigned

14. There are several standard phrases which illustrate the extent to
which these and other pragmatic loop-holes are generally accepted
in Italy. E.g., *Chi ha denaro ed amicizia va nel culo della giustizia*
(He who has money and friends fucks justice in her ass); *Fatta
la legge nasce l'inganno* (When the law is made fraud comes
forth).

15. See *Riforma agraria in Sicilia* (1950); Marciani (1966:31–32);
D'Aragona (1954:15).

to peasants were small and varied between three and four hectares. They were allotted under a long-term, 30-year payment arrangement. The reform had political intentions: the government provided as many peasants as possible with land to ward off the danger of Communism.[16] Small peasant property corroded the very force of the peasant movement. In this connection, it has been argued that the Italian Communist Party failed to convert the peasant movement into a truly revolutionary force that would have radically changed the structure of *latifondismo* (Tarrow 1967:291–99). Backed by a barely suppressed class war that lasted six years, the reform succeeded in breaking up the largest holdings. Since this was indeed its main achievement, it would be more appropriate to speak of *land* reform rather than *agrarian* reform: the type of agriculture that had always characterized the inland region did not substantially change under the impact of the reform, even though huge funds were allocated for improvement.[17]

Recent developments of the Baronessa estates illustrate the failure of these efforts. Between 1952 and 1963, about 780 hectares of the territory of Genuardo were expropriated and assigned to 165 landless peasants. This intervention affected 15 large estates, of which four belonged to Baronessa, which in turn lost 440 hectares to the reform. Most reform holdings are of poor quality. The better fields had been either sold or remained in the hands of the estate owners. Roughly half of the new smallholders were settled on former Baronessa estates, where they were provided with cottages near their

16. Writes Franklin: "In order to restrain growing violence in the country areas, to lessen the persuasive powers of the Communists, to demonstrate in concrete terms the power and will of the new state to provide some hope for the future—the extraordinary laws promulgated to deal with the land confiscations in Calabria and elsewhere were extended to other areas of the South. To produce a land reform whose character was determined by the political decisions that were its basis: it should at once be popular without being revolutionary or punitive" (1969:145). See also Tarrow (1967:343–67).

17. Cf. D'Aragona (1954); Rochefort (1961:105–17); Diem (1961, 1963); and Blok (1966).

land. These farm houses were grouped into two small hamlets connected with the village of Genuardo by new roads. In time the cottages were supplied with water and electricity, schools, and medical services, but most settlers lived there only part of the year, especially those who had houses of their own in Genuardo. Though some cereal-pasture holdings were converted into vineyards, the areas involved have been limited. Most new settlers each have less than half a hectare planted with vines; the remainder of the land is under wheat alternated with forage-crops and pastures. One estate owner, the son of the Baronessa landlord, cleared about 70 hectares of his land for vineyards. He acquired government funds to establish a big plant (*cantina*) for the transformation of grapes into wine, but it functioned only once. Most grapes in the area are in fact bought up by long-established plants located in Sicily's southwest. As a rule, peasants keep their grapes to make their own wine. Lacking credit and market facilities, and above all adequate technical assistance, the new settlers remain subsistence peasants rather than commercially-oriented farmers, which had been the main goal of the reform. They must supplement their annual consumption budget with casual employment on larger farms which, strongly subsidized, manage to flourish. Additional employment is also found in nonagricultural enterprises, such as the building industry. In this way, the reform has left many peasants precariously employed, especially those who did not receive any land (including the now-grown children of the new settlers). In recent years, many of them have left for the industrial North as migrant laborers. When I lived in the village, there was hardly a peasant or artisan who had not spent some time in Switzerland, Germany, or France. From the early 1960s onwards, several tens of families have permanently left Genuardo for northern Italy. The remittances of migrant laborers allow many peasant and artisan families to improve their housing conditions which, in turn, provides fellow-villagers with employment in the building industry.

A growing number of peasants purchases land (a few hectares or even less) which speeds up the process of fragmentation and dispersion of land holdings into unviable units (see Table XII).

To supplement the data on fragmentation, I shall focus on the break-up of the Baronessa estates. In 1941, the whole enterprise was still united in one hand. The first division of shares among future heirs began in that year—very likely as a response to Fascist interference with the Sicilian *latifondo*. The peasant movement generated further divisions such that, by 1947, about 1,200 hectares of Baronessa were recorded in the land registry in the names of the owner's four children. The shares ranged between 100 and 350 hectares. These divisions were indeed nominal, for no new separate farms were established. The disintegration of Baronessa took place, however, when more shares were sold in subsequent years. These sales began in 1946 and were largely completed by the end of December 1950, when the reform bill was passed. (The effects of this maneuver, as well as the impact of the reform on Baronessa, are presented in Table XIII.) Those who bought land were relatively well-to-do agriculturalists, the *burgisi*, and particularly former employees on the Baronessa estates such as overseers and *campieri*, and they acquired holdings varying from five to twenty hectares. Larger shares were bought up by *gabelloti*. One of the latter, a man called Pietro Olivieri, who had leased Ponte in partnership with his brother Aldo, purchased Rocca (see Diagram 11). When Ponte was later sold, these men acquired the lease of what remained of Zillo, some 80 hectares. In the 1960s this was the only *gabella* contract still in use in the area. Together with the shares of the Bovaro and Rello estates, Pietro owns over 130 hectares that constitute more or less adjacent fields, not far from the Zillo estate he holds in lease with his brother. The latifundist kin group has further safeguarded its property through formal internal divisions. For the 728 hectares they still control, there are 12 cadastral listings including 22 names (see Diagram 2). These listings involve shares varying from seven to 188 hectares. As may be expected, these divisions do not reflect the range and number of actually operating farms. Apart from Zillo, which is managed by Pietro and Aldo, Baronessa embraces three main farms run by stewards employed by Enrico, the son of the original owner, and his brother-in-law Diego. They are high-ranking politicians on both the regional and national level. Diego owns Sassone, a large farm located in the mountains, extending over 273 hectares, and cultivated with wheat and forage crops in alternation with pasturage. One hectare produces averages of 12 quintals requiring roughly 1.3 quintals for sowing. The steward, a former *gabelloto*, explained that the enterprise, like many others in the area, suffered from rising labor costs. Migrant labor, as this man observed, has turned the labor surplus into a serious shortage. This is why several landowners consider selling their farms or part of them, though they have reduced the cost of labor by employing modern means for plowing, harvesting, and threshing. Enrico owns two big farms. One consists of shares of Rizzo, Rello, and Piano which constitute contiguous fields measuring 195 hectares. This is the core of what was once Baronessa, containing the mansion, which has now lost its grandeur and is even falling to pieces in several places, the olive grove, and roughly 135 hectares in the valley given over to pasturage, forage crops, and wheat. Yields are remarkably high and amount to about 25 quintals per hectare. This is primarily due to more intensive and longer rotations involving several intercalated crops. But there are only two wheat crops in six years. The fields are cultivated as follows: 1st year, *sulla*; 2nd year, *sulla*; 3rd year, wheat; 4th year, vetch; 5th year, wheat; and 6th year, oats. Apart from the steward, there are only three permanent employees, a tractor-driver and two shepherds tending about 200 sheep. Casual laborers are hired for the harvest of wheat and olives. Surplus pastures are sold or leased to other livestock owners. The other farm exploited by Enrico measures 180 hectares of the estate Zotto. About 70 hectares were planted with vines in the early 1950s. To provide the area (including peasant vineyards created by the reform) with modern means to convert grapes into wine, Enrico obtained a government grant to build the *cantina* mentioned above. The plant, which has a maximum intake of 800 hectoliters and which has cost several tens of millions of

Lire, has functioned only once, in 1961, the first year after its establishment. As one informant commented: "They call the thing *cantina sociale*. Yes, '*sociale*,' in order to cheat the money from the State." It was further pointed out to me that the grants from the State not only covered part of the costs for construction, but probably exceeded them liberally. The *cantina*, however, still serves other functions, even though it does not process grapes, for the option of processing his own grapes provides the owner with the means of controlling grape prices; he sets the terms when selling grapes to the plants located in the southwest of Sicily, where the wine industry was established in the late 18th century by English entrepreneurs. The remainder of this farm consists of cereal-pasture holdings, which are being sold in small shares to peasants and others.

This rather technical chapter on the development and decline of Sicilian *latifondo* leaves us with some conclusions relevant to the subject explored in this book; they may be tested against similar experiences, both in other parts of Sicily and elsewhere. First, the large estate or *latifondo*, though in its main features "involutionary"—"the overdriving of an established form in such a way that it becomes rigid through an inward overelaboration of detail" (Geertz 1963:82) —persisted into modern times since it satisfied both local and national vested interests. Second, its decay was triggered off by the peasant movement to claim the land for those who cultivate it. In order to appease the movement, the peasants were granted a land reform which left sufficient room for evasions. Indeed, its delay, as well as the way it was implemented, suggests that the reform served political rather than economic ends. As Aubrey Diem concludes:

> The political motive behind the reform has been to assure as many agricultural laborers and needy small farmers as possible a minimum standard of living. The size of the holdings has been calculated with this in mind, rather than in the desire to achieve maximum labor efficiency. Mechanized agriculture, operating over the large farm unit, does not necessarily increase production, especially in a pre-

dominantly mountainous and hilly area like Sicily (1961: 166).

Those who benefit from government grants that accompany State intervention are persons closely affiliated with old and new vested interests; in many cases they represent these interests. Third, and finally, though integral *latifondi* are largely gone, this does not hold true for *latifondismo*. Though many substantial farms use labor-saving machinery, they are still exploited in traditional ways as far as management, cultivation, and livestock keeping are concerned. In these circumstances, the larger farms still depend on cheap labor which, however, is increasingly giving way to labor migration. These farms manage to survive therefore because of the grants, loans, and so-called integrated prices which the State provides their owners. The peasant holdings hardly deserve the name of "farms," since they are unviable strips of land. This myriad of tiny and scattered holdings exemplifies the growing marginality of the peasant sector in the south.[18]

18. "What in fact has been executed in the past fifteen years has not been the implementation of a programme of economic development—in the contemporary world no programme that in fact copes with a stationary labour force deserves the title of development—instead it has been a massive welfaristic programme of support and redistribution, engendered and maintained by the expansion of wealth in the north of Italy and in other member countries of the E.E.C., together with considerable aid from the U.S.A." (Franklin 1969:174).

PART TWO
THE MAFIA

PART TWO
THE MEDIA

...alle Begriffe, in denen sich ein ganzer Prozeß semiotisch zusammenfaßt, entziehn sich der Definition; definierbar ist nur das, was keine Geschichte hat.

FRIEDRICH NIETZSCHE,
Zur Genealogie der Moral.
Werke, Vol. II. Ed. Karl Schlechta.
München: Carl Hanser Verlag, 1966, p. 820.

V
Genesis of Mafia

As indicated earlier, the elements of *mafia* became tangible in the early 19th century when the formative apparatus of a modern central government was superimposed upon a society still largely feudal in its main features. The predominance of large landed estates, together with the considerable amount of autonomy enjoyed by local power-holders in both rural and urban areas, expressed the extent of Sicilian feudalization. During the long centuries of foreign rule, no government ever effectively penetrated this hinterland. Spanish objectives in Sicily were minimal: the production of modest revenues and the maintenance of order. For both, the outside authorities relied on the landowning barons who dominated local government. These centrifugal forces were particularly manifest in the inland region where landlords or their agents held sway in what were appropriately called "states" (*stati*). Throughout the 18th century and up to 1812, when feudalism was abolished by law, baronial jurisdiction remained in force. Noble landlords maintained private armies of field guards to keep peasants in submission. One nobleman, for example, employed a "company of twenty-four dragoons, who had their own flag and their own military band of trumpets and drums; and frequently they could be found riding through the kingdom with as much liberty and authority as a company of royal troops."[1] Neither Madrid nor Naples was much concerned with direct administration of Sicily. They abstained from interference and indulged the local aristocracy as long as their minimal demands were met. The poor development of roads, traffic, and supra-local mar-

1. Marquis di Villabianca, *Della Sicilia Nobile* (5 vols., Palermo, 1754–57), quoted in Mack Smith (1968a: 292–93).

kets preserved local isolation. Confronted with these conditions, foreign governments found the barons less costly than royal officials in local government. Spanish encapsulation was therefore largely nominal, a matter of geography: no overarching power structure assembled the various autonomous segments into a comprehensive political whole.

This situation changed after 1816 when the Bourbons were restored to Naples, capital of the new Kingdom of the Two Sicilies. Their enlightened absolutism and reformism involved a long series of attempts to curb the power of the local overlords and encourage the rise of a class of smallholders from the ranks of the landless peasants. The assumption was that smallholders would provide a more stable social base than landless laborers and would be more interested in agricultural improvements than tenants or absentee landowners. By attacking the formal institutions through which the centrifugal forces in Sicilian society found expression, the Bourbon government sought to wrest control from the hands of the landowning barons and to integrate the island into the framework of a centralized State. Government and court moved from Palermo to Naples, and Sicily was divided into seven new provinces which were administered by nominated, French-trained Intendants and by non-elected town councils.

As noted before, the formal abrogation of feudalism under the British occupation of the island (1806–15) did not seriously challenge the entrenched position of the barons. This reform instead helped reinforce the traditional monopolies of the landowning aristocracy, since the fiefs were merely converted from public holdings into private properties. Though this involved the removal of baronial jurisdiction in favor of royal courts, it also meant that the peasants lost any title to land they held under feudal conditions. In the absence of substantial compensation for the lost common use rights, the peasantry emerged from social servitude only to fall into new forms of dependency as both land and labor-power were turned into commodities. The advent of the market together with a gradual increase of population tended to reduce the Sicilian peasants to an ever-growing rural proletariat.

The Bourbons recognized this effect of the abolition of feudalism and tried to counterbalance it by introducing further, more radical reforms to break up the large estates. In the early 1820s, they abolished entails and primogeniture, and another law permitted the seizure of land in settlement of debts. Special commissions worked on the restitution of arbitrarily enclosed land to poor peasants. A law of 1841 prescribed that estate owners should compensate peasant communities by returning at least one-fifth of any ex-feudal territory where common use rights had formerly been exercised. Yet the very repetition of these laws reflected the ineffectiveness of their implementation. Quite unintentionally, Bourbon legislation aided the rise of a new and powerful landed gentry rather than promoting the emergence of a class of smallholders engaged in efficient cultivation. The bourgeois landowners partly merged with and partly replaced the landowning aristocracy but retained the noble disinterest in farming and disdain for manual labor. Their chief interest was hardly agricultural improvement. The *civili*, as these new estate owners and *gabelloti* were called, made successful bids for power and prestige: apart from landed status, several of them acquired noble titles through marriage or outright purchase, and virtually all inserted themselves firmly into local government. Those who did not move to Palermo permanently became the dominant figures in the local power structure. Agrarian reform as envisaged by the central administration was anathema to them and their main ambition was to neutralize it (Mack Smith 1968a: 351–69, 405–14).

It is only after the establishment of a monopoly of physical force, with the centralization of power, that a general law, a common legal code for large areas, can become effective (Elias 1969, II:82, 181). This may seem a commonplace, but like many commonplaces it is important and often forgotten. It is one thing to say that centralization evoked strong resistance by the privileged class that had always dominated Sicilian society and to emphasize that the State lacked sufficient force to cope with it, but quite another to explain the conditions that compelled the central ruler to come to terms with local vested interests. The government at Naples did much to challenge these interests and in the process whetted the appetite for land among the peasantry. Even after Unification of Italy, the State failed to monopolize the use of physical force in large areas of western Sicily and, therefore, could not hope to enforce legislation. It is only in this context that the origin and development of *mafia* can be understood. *Mafia* was born of the tensions between the central government and local landowners on the one hand, and between the latter and peasants on the other. At the same time, however, *mafia* helped manage these distinct but interrelated tensions and struggles since it provided a specific code through which members of the various social classes and groups arranged themselves. This chapter sketches these arrangements and rearrangements over time and, hence, the processes through which *mafia* came forth in early 19th century Sicily.

When a government makes the formal decision to encapsulate its hinterland, several conditions may impede this undertaking. One way to study this process is in terms of the determination and capacity of the central government to impose its laws and institutions upon those sectors of its territory it seeks to integrate, to consider the resistance that certain groups in these sectors are willing and able to offer, and to emphasize the differences in values between both sides (Bailey 1969:144–85). We may, however, also look at the process of centralization from a different point of view, and ask what conditions make possible and account for the growth of effective central control.

In a sense, the structure of Sicilian society militated against the establishment of central institutions (see Chapter II). The poor development of roads and markets and the rent-capitalist mode of production involved specific interdependencies between landlords and peasants in relatively small areas. These conditions underwrote a large measure of local self-sufficiency rather than generate significant links between the various communities and baronial domains. Therefore, given the segmented character of Sicilian rural society, there was, certainly in the eyes of the people who lived there, very little to coordinate. The relative self-containment of each territory hampered rather than facilitated efforts at central control and coordination. Though the Bourbon bureaucracy was imposed from without, its impact helped initiate ramifying transformations. Cutting through the cellular structure of Sicilian society, the central administration generated an increasing social differentiation. New legislation, the indebtedness of former feudal lords, and the advent of the market permitted the fragmentation of huge patrimonies. Between 1812 and 1860 the number of landowning families increased from 2,000 to 20,000 (though individual estates were rarely broken up). In proportion to the rise of bourgeois landowners, the number of landless peasants increased. A gradual growth of population intensified pressure on the land, and peasants began to roam over larger areas than ever before in search of employment. Brigandage became a way of life, and organized bands operated in almost every corner of the western and central parts of the island. The growing interdependence of city and countryside, of villages and towns themselves, and of estate owners and peasants generated new niches for violent entrepreneurs who could secure control over the tensions in this emerging configuration. *Latifondisti* and *gabelloti* retained their prominency and power as before save that scores of leaseholders acquired landed status. Commercialization of land and labor did not involve any significant technological improvement in agriculture; neither did it embody any new type of merchants or farmers. The various local segments remained therefore only loosely tied to one another, and this fact by itself restricted the possibilities of and the necessity for growing central coordination. Landed interests persisted as the chief centrifugal force in Sicilian society, dominating the paths linking the rural communities with the outside world.

The landlords and their retainers buttressed their control with the use of violence. They had done so before, in feudal times, but the important difference was that they now made successful incursions into the still fragile framework of the State, and thus forced formal authority to come to terms with them pragmatically. This collusion provided the large landowners with increasing leverage, especially on the local level. Time and again, the Bourbon government was forced to rely on privately recruited groups and squads to maintain order. The growth of unemployment, proletarianization, and brigandage made public order even more problematic in both urban and rural areas. In Palermo, the artisan guilds were still charged with maintaining order up to the early 1820s. Their formal suppression some years later did not, however, substantially reduce their control over special areas of the city. In the inland districts, the Companies at Arms were entrusted with the enforcement of law and order. More often than not, these bodies could only connive and mix with bandits and retainers of landlords to uphold the appearance of order:

> The Companies at Arms were privately recruited groups which contracted with the government for a fee and could then be held to account for thefts: sometimes they were the feudal retainers of a landowner in whose interests they continued to work; sometimes they extorted protection money much like any other gang, and acted in collusion with criminals so as to be able to find stolen property in return for payment. At worst the police companies were brigand bands in their own right (Mack Smith 1968a: 368–69).

Alongside these hybrid bodies, the government encouraged the formation of the National Guard, a volunteer class-based militia composed of well-to-do citizens, to protect property and to oppose peasant and proletarian gangs that quickly sprang up in moments of crisis.

To a large extent what was later called *mafia* coincided with these associations of armed strong men and their followers who exercised jurisdiction on the local level in conjunction with formal authority. It is precisely this concatenation that distinguished *mafiosi* from other power holders such as, for instance, the bandits and outlaws. For it is only in the context of the advent and impact of the State that we can understand and appropriately speak of *mafia*. Bandits are in open conflict with the law and the State. *Mafiosi* disregard both and act in connivance with those who represent formal law, thus validating their private control of the community's public life (cf. Hess 1970:91–92). A report from a Neapolitan magistrate in western Sicily demonstrates the extent these coalitions of *mafiosi* had developed by 1838:

> ... [In Sicily] there is not a single official who does not prostrate himself before the local men of influence and power, and who does not intend to profit from his office. ... This general corruption had induced the population to have recourse to remedies which are strange and dangerous beyond measure. In many towns and villages there are fraternities, sorts of sects that are called parties [*partiti*], without meetings and without other links than those of dependency upon a chief: a landowner or an archpriest. Common funds serve to meet certain mutual needs as, for example, to release a civil servant or to accuse an innocent person. ... The population colludes with convicts. When thefts take place, mediators emerge and offer their services to make up for the stolen goods. ... Many high-placed magistrates cover up these fraternities with an impenetrable shield ... [I]t is impossible to induce the town-guards to scout their area ... At the center of this state of dissolution is the capital [of Palermo] with her luxury and corruption ... a city in which live 40,000 proletarians whose subsistence depends on the pomp and caprices of the rich and powerful.[2]

Only three decades later these activities and relationships would be called *mafia*.

Moreover, the magistrate's report indicates quite clearly how *mafia* issued from the tensions between local and national interests, and developed within the entrails of the State.[3] In this way, *mafiosi* provided a code according to

2. Letter from Pietro Calà Ulloa (Procuratore Generale del Re presso il Tribunale di Trapani) sent on August 3, 1838 to the Minister of Justice in Naples. Cited from Pontieri (1965:235–36).
3. This point and metaphor are taken from a seminal article by Eric Wolf, who notes that "there are also resources and organizations which it would be either too costly or too difficult to bring under direct control, and in these cases the system yields its sovereignty

which the various groups in Sicilian society arranged themselves in conflict and accommodation. The new configuration, which *mafia* helped create and in which it played a
pivotal part by pragmatically mediating the tension-ridden
relations between the antagonistic but interdependent
groups, involved a *modus vivendi* between formal authorities
and large estate owners, as well as patron-client relations
between those who controlled the land and those who were
dependent upon land for their living. A vast network of
personal links thus worked to offset the tensions inherent in
the relationships between the various groups that made up
this configuration. In terms of actual control and authority,
mafia constituted a pragmatic dimension of the State.

The incursions of what I have called the centrifugal forces
of Sicilian society into the public domain did not annihilate
the State but rendered its apparatus subservient to these
vested interests. It is in this sense that we should understand
Ulloa's phrase: "Many high-placed magistrates cover up these
fraternities with an impenetrable shield." At the level of the
village and the large estate, landowners and *gabelloti* recruited their armed retainers from the peasants. They favored
with employment those who stood out as violent men or who
complied in other ways with their rule. Similar linkages tied
bandits and outlaws to the power domains of the landlords.
To survive and operate, these people had to rely on the local
mafiosi, and often became their very retainers.

to competitive groups that are allowed to function in its entrails.
. . . We must not confuse the theory of state sovereignty with the
facts of political life. Many organizations within the state generate
and distribute and control power, in competition with each other
and with the sovereign power of the state. As examples one might
cite the Teamsters' Union of the United States, the Mafia, or the
American Medical Association. Thus we could also draw a map
of political power for any complex society in which the key centers of control appeared in red—showing strong concentrations of
sovereign power—while other political regions appeared in grey
or white. We thus note that the formal framework of economic
and political power exists alongside or intermingled with various
other kinds of informal structure which are interstitial, supplementary, parallel to it" (1966a: 1–2).

These various attunements should not, however, blind us to the existence of the tensions and conflicts built into the configuration and to which, after all, these accommodations were a response. We should appreciate that these conflicts and accommodations were not separate and independent from one another. Far from it: they were complementary and operated in close connection with each other. We will briefly consider these interdependent polarities which framed the inherent dynamics of Sicilian society to place the genesis and immediate effect of *mafia* in sharper focus. Here it is worth noting the largely unplanned way in which *mafia* made itself tangible in Sicilian society. However much individual human beings helped to bring it about, "one cannot say that it was imposed on the Sicilians by anyone: in a sense, it grew out of the needs of all rural classes, and served the purpose of all in varying degrees" (Hobsbawm 1959:40–41).[4]

The growing voraciousness for land on the part of the new gentry turned the peasantry, especially its expanding landless segment, into a latent revolutionary force. Class tensions were manifest both in banditry, which was rampant, and the smoldering peasant movement which flared up and subsided in an almost cyclical way. Though there had been bandits and jacqueries in feudal times,[5] the 19th century witnessed six major risings, in 1820, 1837, 1848, 1860, 1866, and 1893, which spread over larger areas. The peasants demanded expropriation and redistribution of land, especially in the upheavals that took place after 1860. Periods of bad harvest helped ignite these insurrections, which typically dovetailed with urban risings (Palermo) for regional autonomy on behalf of the restive middle classes in coalition with

4. If sociological analysis is to make headway and enlarge our understanding of the way in which human beings depend upon one another, and to improve our knowledge about the ways in which these interdependencies are changing, the unplanned and structured course of social processes must be increasingly appreciated. Cf. Elias (1969, II:220–221); Elias and Dunning (1971:79–80). Hobsbawm's simple and precise formulation clearly summarizes the configurational dynamics of *mafia*.

5. Cf. Braudel (1966, vol. II:75–92); Mack Smith (1968a:146–51, 294–99).

segments of the nobility. The peasants of the inland area
turned on *gabelloti*, tax-collectors, and usurers only after
Bourbon authority had been openly challenged and disrupted in the streets of Palermo. Resistance to Neapolitan
centralization and a barely suppressed class war were thus
geared to each other. Bourbon rule was not wholly oppressive, but it succeeded in challenging vested interests and
whetting peasant aspirations for land. Thus pressed, Sicilian
latifondisi and *gabelloti* acted to neutralize Bourbon reforms
by "playing on local patriotism, xenophobia and the prevalent dislike of all laws and regulations; they tried to convince
people that it was not they themselves but rather the hated
Bourbons who prevented improvement and kept Sicily poor"
(Mack Smith 1968a:409). This was a powerful myth and, fed
by the ignorance of an illiterate peasantry (often deliberately
reinforced by local power-holders to ensure their control over
the means of orientation),[6] its varieties persist to the present
day. It helped unleash the forces of peasant protest into the
channels of the Sicilian *Risorgimento*, the political movement
that culminated in the successful Garibaldian revolution of
1860 that swept away Bourbon rule and from which the new
Sicilian ruling classes reaped the main benefits at the expense
of the peasantry. In their turn, the peasants became the
primary victims of the bourgeois revolution for which they
had provided the dynamite.[7]

This pattern, in which the potentially revolutionary force
of the peasantry was systematically weakened and kept
within bounds, was replicated in several realms. The tremendous increase of brigandage in the 19th century shows this
clearly.[8] The scores of uprooted peasants who took to the

6. This expression occurred in a conversation with Norbert Elias in
   reference to the interrelated aspects of elite hegemony: control
   over the means of production, over the means of coercion, and
   over the means of orientation (e.g., knowledge, religion, ideology,
   etc.).
7. See Mack Smith's essay on this revolt (1950). This particular fate
   that may await peasants after successful upheavals to which they
   lent their support is far from uncommon. See Barrington Moore
   (1966:481).
8. For a detailed description, see D'Alessandro (1959:27–84).

hills did so on account of troubles and conflicts with local power holders or formal authorities. In this initial phase of their career, outlaws and bandits embodied peasant resentment. By ransoming the rich, stealing their cattle, and sacking their *masserie*, bandits became folk heroes for doing what most of their fellows would have liked to do. This dimension of banditry, which expresses strong undercurrents of an incipient class struggle, has been described as "social banditry" for Sicily and other predominantly agrarian societies (cf. Hobsbawm 1959:1–29; 1969). Its anti-peasant counterpart is less well mapped, and this brings us to one of the main themes of the present book (see Blok 1972; Hobsbawm 1972).

As mentioned above, bandits depended upon other people. All bandits were "social" in that they were, like all human beings, linked to other people by various ties. We cannot understand the behavior of bandits without reference to other groups, classes, or networks with which bandits formed specific configurations of interdependent individuals. What seems wrong with Hobsbawm's perception of brigandage is that it pays too much attention to the peasants and the bandits themselves. We must, however, look as well at the larger society in which peasant communities are contained. Without taking into account these higher levels, which include the landed gentry and the formal authorities, brigandage cannot be fully understood, for many particular characteristics of peasant communities are dependent upon or a reflex of the impact of the larger society. Given the specific conditions of outlawry, bandits had to rely strongly on other people. As we will see in the next chapters, all outlaws and robbers required protection in order to operate and to survive at all. If they lacked protection, they remained lonely wolves to be quickly dispatched, and those who hunted them down were either the landlord's retainers, the police, or the peasants. One of our tasks, therefore, is to discover the people on whom the bandit relied.

Protectors of bandits may range from a close, narrow circle of kinsmen and affiliated friends to powerful politicians: those who held formal office as well as grass-roots politicians.

Protection thus involved the presence of a power domain (cf.
Adams 1966). Of all categories, the peasants were weakest.[9]
Hence it may be argued that unless bandits found political
protection, their reign would be short. This yields the following proposition, which can be tested against data bearing on
all kinds of brigandage: *the more successful a man is as a
bandit, the more extensive the protection granted him.* When
banditry becomes increasingly politically oriented and
evolves into what Italian scholars have called *"brigantaggio
politico,"* it assumes "anti-social" features when we take this
term in the sense understood by Hobsbawm, that is, anti-
peasant (see Blok 1972).[10] The bandits discussed in this book

9. "It is only when a cultivator is integrated into a society with a
   state—that is, when the cultivator becomes subject to the demands
   and sanctions of power-holders outside his social stratum—that we
   can appropriately speak of peasantry" (Wolf 1966b:11).
10 Sicilian brigandage of the 19th and 20th centuries provided alternately an *instrumentum regni* and a staff of the large landowners
   to suppress the peasants. Cf. Romano (1952:279 ff.). For Spain,
   see Brenan (1950:156), and Pitt-Rivers (1961:180). Van den
   Muyzenberg discusses the position of the Huks and Monkees in
   Central Luzon in the Philippines (1971). The alliances between
   delinquents and aristocrats throughout modern European history
   still await full sociological treatment. On this point Richard Cobb's
   observations on late 18th century France are perceptive: "The
   habitually violent, like the habitually criminal, do not normally
   constitute a threat to the established order, of which they form
   a semi-recognized part. Like the police, they have a stake in
   society. We do not expect to find such people in the armies of
   the revolution and in the ranks of the revolutionists. They are
   below, or at least outside, the bounds of social resentment;
   and their conservatism does not readily accept new institutions, un-
   familiar authorities, and judges with unknown faces. As far as can
   be ascertained, few such people participated actively in the
   [French] revolutionary movement at any stage, though after 1795
   quite a lot of them took to the woods in the ranks of counter-
   revolutionary bands" (1969:277). The Revolution and the Terror
   struck hard at the world of ordinary criminals (Cobb 1972: *passim*), "So the ranks of the counter-revolutionary squire could be
   expected to draw upon those who lived habitually on the border
   of crime and violence . . ." (1972:25 *et passim*). Counter-revolutionary squires, ". . . under the impact of the politics of vengeance,
   thought nothing of paying brutal, but simple, men to kill their

typically initiated their careers by redressing personal wrongs. Sooner or later, they were either killed or drawn into and constrained by the power domains of the established regional elites. Bandits, especially those whose reign was long, thus represented the other side of the class war. When assuming retainership, bandits served to prevent and suppress peasant mobilization in two ways: first, by putting down collective peasant action through terror; and, second, by carving out avenues of upward mobility which, like many other vertical bonds in this society, tended to weaken class tensions. These courses to "respectability" are institutionalized in *mafia*, on which brigandage indeed largely depended. I shall argue that actual brigandage expresses man's pursuit of honor and power. This holds true for the bandit as much

political and religious opponents, fêting them, playing on their conceit, congratulating them on their *coup de main*, calling them by their nicknames, filling them with drink, before and after, letting them go to bed with their servants, after. The poacher, the deserter, the bandit, and the corner boy must have thought that the world had turned upside-down when they found themselves invited to the local *château*, vigorously patted on the back by the squire, in the presence of his womenfolk, and told that he was a fine fellow *qui n'avait pas froid aux yeux*" (Cobb 1969:199–200). Such "anti-social" bandits were primary executors of the Royalist White Terror, operating under the protection of private lords and their official clients (Cobb 1970: 131–50). But we should be wary of focusing too exclusively on the politics of brigandage; many bandits in these troubled times had no political affiliations at all. Like the *bande d'Orgères*, which operated near Chartres in the 1790s, "There was, in their activities, no form of social protest; they were as likely to steal the only sheet of a poor widow, hanging on the line, as the whole wardrobe of a rich farmer's wife" (Cobb 1972:204–05). Together, these observations once again illuminate the difficulties inherent in the widespread vulgarization of Hobsbawm's model of social banditry that tends to see virtually all brigandage as a manifestation of peasant protest. "It is necessary to beware of romanticizing the robber as a friend of the poor, just as much as of accepting the official image. . . . Gangsterism is likely to crop up wherever the forces of law and order are weak. European feudalism was mainly gangsterism that had become society itself and acquired respectability through the notions of chivalry" (Moore 1966:214).

as his protector, who manipulates him in order to extend his power domains. This dimension should be distinguished from the myth of the bandit (Hobsbawm's social bandit), which represents a craving for a different society: a more humane world purged of injustice and suffering. These myths require our attention since they embody a latent protest element— a deep sense of injustice—which under certain conditions may "gather force and break through the culturally accepted patterns which kept it within its institutionalized bounds" (Wertheim 1964:32). But myths are imperfect mirrors of social reality and, as this study will make clear, we should treat brigandage and bandit myths as forces that weaken peasant mobilization. In the following chapters we shall see the extent to which *mafia* and banditry, complementary to one another, controlled and maintained the basic tensions of Sicilian society. By considering a series of cases from one particular village, we may attain an understanding of these interrelations between conflict and accommodation as well as their dynamics. The case material is framed chronologically to let us follow the process of change. Only at necessary points have I interrupted the narrative for occasional analyses and commentary.

VI
Expansion, 1860–1914

The popular insurrection in Palermo on April 4, 1860, which
initiated the overthrow of Bourbon government by Garibaldi
five weeks later, had immediate repercussions in the inland
towns and villages. News of the political events in Palermo
traveled fast. In Genuardo, on April 6, 35 representatives of
all classes assembled and swore to maintain order in face of
any local commotion. For the purpose, a provisional committee of internal security was elected. Most of its 16
members were landowners and professionals. That night, one
of them, a man called Luca, age 31, who is described to us
as a foreman bricklayer (*capo-mastro*), fashioned an armed
band of his own involving 22 members, most of them artisans
and peasants between 20 and 50 years of age.[1] Luca led his
companions in an attack on the police station, where they
disarmed the gendarmes. Subsequently, the band dashed
through the village continuing the disarmament, promising
to maintain order and not to molest anyone. The band then
went to the house of the two town clerks, Filippo and his
son-in-law Giovanni, and asked them for the keys to the
town hall, which were delivered at once. Afraid of being
killed, the two clerks together with their families sought
refuge with their kinsmen; taking flight, Filippo was shot at

1. For 14 members I found occupational descriptions and age. Ten
   of them were artisans (including four bricklayers, apart from Luca
   himself); three peasants; and one *milite a cavallo*. Seven of them
   were under thirty years of age; the other seven band members
   aged between thirty and fifty years (Private papers 1863). Unless
   otherwise noted, the primary source for this section and the one
   following is Private papers 1866.

twice. He cried for help and was accosted by Luca, who reassured him and asked where he was going. Filippo indicated the house of one of his cousins, and Luca brought him there. The house of the two clerks was thus abandoned, and it was sacked by members of the band. Luca and his men then headed for the house where Giovanni hid. They knocked at the door and, since it remained firmly closed, Luca got an axe and forced access to the house. The frightened Giovanni fired two shots in the air to dissuade his assailants. But when he came to the doorway, two well-aimed shots from the other side wounded him in the arm. Giovanni asked for mercy, but Luca told him that he had promised to kill him and that he could not break his word (see below). Luca pushed his victim a little to the side where he was shot to death. Right after this incident, Luca and some of his companions followed Filippo to his place of refuge. Though kinsmen and friends of Filippo urged him to flee, Filippo remained where he was as Luca himself had brought him there and had promised to save him. Luca entered the house and asked Filippo to come out in order that he might be safe. When Filippo did so, Luca took out a long knife with which he stabbed the unfortunate clerk several times. Gunshots from both Luca and his companions lying in wait around the house dispatched Filippo. Luca then asked his men to wake up the two grave-diggers of the village, and ordered them to bury the two corpses in the local cemetery. Some members of the band were sent to assist.

The next day, when the village learned of these nocturnal events (Luca made a public statement in which he proclaimed that he had been unable to restrain his companions from the killings and sacking), the provisional committee installed a company of the National Guard to "protect life, honor, and property of the villagers." One of the outstanding *civili* of Genuardo, Giuseppe Jaconi (see Diagram 1), was elected as its captain and charged with the recruitment of 30 persons. The captain was required to pay them three *tarì* per day, for which he was to be reimbursed by the committee.

Confronted with this class-based militia, the Luca band dissolved. Most of its members, including Luca himself, set off for Palermo where they tried unsuccessfully to contact the well-known band of Santo Meli. The companions of Luca who remained at Genuardo were arrested together with various close relatives of the band members. Before being sent to jail, they were lined up on the *piazza* of the village and there one of them, a man called Lopez, was slapped in the face by a landowner, a certain Foti. This incident and its repercussion bring us to the next intervention of what remained of the Luca band in early June 1860. Little information is available on the activities of the band or its individual members throughout the turbulent months of April and May. We only know that at least three members of the Luca band joined Garibaldi's irregulars after the battle of Calatafimi on May 16, and assisted in the conquest of Palermo at the end of that month. After the armistice on June 8, the three Garibaldinis, as they were called, returned to the village where they were greeted as liberators. Some days before, all persons arrested on account of the operations of the Luca band in early April were released. Luca managed to join the local apparatus charged with the maintenance of order—he commanded the *guardia urbana*. Foti, the man who had dishonored Lopez in public, found it safer to take to his farm in the country together with his wife and children. On the night of June 5 he returned to the village to visit a friend. On his way back to the farm some hours later, he was shot by Lopez who had been waiting for him in ambush. This murder, which took place at midnight in front of one of the churches, was witnessed by Luca who then followed Lopez into the house of a friend. Luca took away the discharged gun and arrested Lopez, accusing him of murder. Lopez did not offer any resistance, nor did he deny the charge. He only said: "I did it because I had to."

The same day, June 5, one of Luca's brothers was killed in the house of one of the local priests, whose sister was engaged to a shopkeeper, a man called Franco. It was generally believed that Franco did the shooting. The next day, Luca led a crowd to sack Franco's shop. He had all belongings brought into the *piazza*, where he distributed them among the village poor. Several goods which Franco kept in the house of his fiancée were similarly disposed of.

On September 1, under the pretext of maintaining order, Luca disarmed a local *campiere* whom he accused of various crimes.

On December 8, Luca incited a crowd to kill the brothers Jaconi and their friends, who held leading positions in the local company of the National Guard. The attempt was unsuccessful, and Luca took to the hills.

On April 24, 1861, Luca was arrested by three *Carabinieri* as he roamed through the country close to Genuardo. Various persons reported seeing Luca together with three members of his band near the cottage of a shepherd where they were eating *ricotta*. Though his companions sought to set him free, the *Carabinieri* succeeded in taking Luca into the village. There, a throng of women met them and urged his release. Nevertheless, Luca was jailed and the *Carabinieri* went off to a neighboring town for reinforcements. Meanwhile, a widow known as "Palermo" led an attack on the jail, and Luca was set free before police reinforcements arrived. At the head of the crowd, "Palermo" cried: "We have liberated him!"

But by the end of 1863, Luca and most of his companions were arrested and on trial in Palermo. In subsequent years, however, some of the former Luca band continued to be active as bandits. It is to one of them that we now turn.

Matteo was born in 1836, the oldest son of a yeoman (*burgisi*), Giuseppe or *Don* Piddu, as he was called, who had three younger sons and one daughter. The family owned some land in the emphyteusis area of Genuardo. The holding and cottage bordered on a large estate held in lease by one of the Jaconis. *Don* Piddu is described to us as a violent and prepotent person who indulged in stealing corn and abusive pasturing. On account of these frequent incursions, the Jaconis had a grudge against *Don* Piddu's family.

Matteo participated in the April rising staged by Luca. At that time he was 23 years old, that is, about eight years younger than his friend Luca. Matteo never married and died in 1921, by which time he was addressed and referred to as *Don* Matteo. There are several events in the last sixty years of his life that are relevant to the subject of this book, most notably his long imprisonment and the circumstances that led up to it.

After a warrant for his arrest was issued by the police chief of the Corleone district, Matteo was caught in October 1860 and incarcerated in Palermo. He was charged with participation in the Luca band and, among other things, involvement in theft and murder. Matteo was arrested again on April 26, 1861 by the police of the neighboring town of Bisacquino. He was captured together with his brother Vincenzo, barely 15 years old, following a warrant for arrest signed by the judge of that town. At the end of April, Matteo's father was also arrested. In early May, however, all were released.

Private enmity between Matteo's family and the Jaconis lay behind these repeated arrests and releases. The Jaconis belonged to the small group of local *civili* controlling a number of large estates; several members of the family played leading roles in the local company of the National Guard, and acted as informants on local affairs to the higher authorities. As one district official wrote on August 15, 1863 to the magistrate of the law court at Palermo where members of the Luca band awaited trial:

> I can neither confirm nor deny that these arrests were due to private hostility and charges from the Jaconi brothers. I can only say that [Matteo and his father] were persons inclined to disorder and enemies of the Jaconis and their friends. It is quite possible that the latter have influenced the arrests of the former since the authorities have often availed themselves of their information.

In the course of the conflicts between these two families and their followers, Matteo's father was killed at the end of June 1861. His fate was decided at a meeting of landowners and *gabelloti* from Genuardo. After receiving the news of the murder, the widow cried out in public: *"Tagghiaru l'arvulu ma ristaru li figghiulini!"* (The tree has been cut down, but the shoots are growing!) She is reported to have repeated this phrase several times afterwards. The Jaconis however, did not await the moment of vengeance implied in the widow's metaphor. On October 26, 1862, one of them, a landowner and *gabelloto* called Giovanni, sent two thugs to the country house of Matteo. Unable to find Matteo there, they massacred his three teenage brothers. Matteo took to the hills, and in 1868 he joined the famous Capraro band.

Following Unification, outlawry developed into highly organized brigandage. For example, in six months of 1871, the province of Palermo recorded 81 murders, 164 cases of highway robbery, 65 cases of cattle rustlings, 18 cases of arson, and continuous assaults on mail coaches.[2] An extortion letter sent by a local associate of the Capraro–Plaja bandit network (see below) to a relatively well-to-do peasant in Genuardo in January 1873 vividly evokes the picaresque and rather sinister bandit motif:

To the good citizen Salvatore Sacco of Genuardo

Dear Friend,
not having a reply to the *first* [letter], necessity thus obliges me to send you this *second* and *last* one, to profit *from* your goodness, hence I warmly request you to send me 80 *onze*, gold and silver, on the day of January 22 at 8 in the evening, and you *must* take it to the drinking trough. Don't fail, otherwise you will offend our usual good humor and woe to your fields, son and animals.
    Nothing else, saluting you, we remain your true friends. Moreover, I warn you not to talk, not even by the *Santo diavolo*, if not, woe for you always (quoted in Anonymous 1879:28).

The conditions that contributed to the tremendous diffusion of banditry in the inland areas included opposition to the draft and increasing concentration of land in the hands of bourgeois landowners, who often protected the bands and

2. Cf. D'Alessandro (1959:94). In the early 1860s, the annual murder rate for Sicily as a whole amounted to 1,000. In those years, scores of *Carabinieri* were killed. During the first six months of 1863, for example, 33 of them fell in battles with the bandits. Cf. Govone (1902:409–10).

used them for their own ends. Banditry flourished until 1877, shortly after the Sicilian elite was admitted to parliament. With this settlement, banditry lost much of its utility to the Sicilian upper classes. Thus deprived of protection by *latifondisti* and their vast *mafiosi* clientele, the exposed brigands fell easy prey to the army.

The Capraro band (1868–1875), the first in a series of overlapping bands known as the *banda dei Giulianesi*, evolved, typically, from another gang, that of a certain Riggio. Capraro had first served as an auxiliary of Riggio, and was employed on a farm near Sciacca. After a conflict with the owner, Capraro was dismissed. He killed his former employer and became active in the Riggio band as a lieutenant. When Riggio was killed by the police, Capraro assumed leadership in June 1868. The Capraro band was the first well-organized, disciplined, armed, and mounted band to fight the police in regular battles. It operated in the three western provinces of the island and could easily avoid and deceive the rural police, who were bound to small districts and thus unable to synchronize operations across provincial boundaries. The Capraro band's membership varied from 15 to 20, all recruited from villages and towns in the border area of the three provinces. Genuardo was one of the villages that supplied members. In the first phase, at least six Genuardesi were involved in the Capraro band. As with the other two main bands in western and central Sicily—with which Capraro cooperated—membership was loose and fluctuating. After completing an operation, the band dispersed and each member slipped back into his proper domain of kinsmen and friends. Moreover, these bands recruited new members as easily as they lost or expelled others. Each particular operation involved a unique action-set.[3]

3. As General Giuseppe Govone put it in his address to the *Camera dei Deputati* on December 5, 1863: "In Sicily bandits are not generally united in permanent bands as with Neapolitan brigandage. They constituted bands of malefactors and draft-dodgers, who committed various crimes after which each member withdrew to his own house, protected by kinsmen and friends who hid him, secure in the knowledge that no one would dare to disclose his

After Capraro was killed in a shoot-out with the police in June 1875, the *banda dei Giulianesi* split into three groups. One of them was commanded by Gaudenzio Plaja, a chief lieutenant of Capraro, who drew his primary following from Genuardo and the neighboring village of Giuliana. Plaja's band, including ten core operatives and a shifting fringe of accomplices, had its general headquarters on the wooded estates of·Santa Maria del Bosco, where they hid from the *Carabinieri* and received extortion money. From this sanctuary they scoured the Palermo-Agrigento border region, through which passed the main highway connecting Palermo with the southern coast town of Sciacca. Successful robberies, mail coach hold-ups, and acts of extortion were celebrated at occasional banquets, such as one held in late September 1876 on an estate near Bisacquino and attended by the *padrone*, two of his retainers, four bandits, and four local girls "*tutte ragazze allegre e di buon umore*" (Anonymous 1879:118 *et passim*).

In March 1871, Matteo avenged the murders of his father and three brothers. He singled out Giovanni Jaconi as the instigator (*mandante*) of the killings and forced him into a trap. Matteo drove cattle into Giovanni's planted fields and arranged to make this known in Genuardo. Though his sister, with whom the unmarried Giovanni lived, sensed trouble, Giovanni thus challenged saddled his horse and set out with a friend to inspect the damage. Their route followed a small mule track, a sort of sunken road, through a wooded area. There Matteo and his companions were waiting for them. When Giovanni passed along, Matteo jumped from above on the back of his horse and, with a knife at Giovanni's back, forced him to ride on to a prearranged spot. Giovanni's friend was sent back to the village. During the long ride, which was eventually to finish in the territory of the neighboring

---

whereabouts to the magistrate or to the *Carabinieri*. When I arrived in Girgento [now Agrigento], the bands were dissolved" (Govone 1902:414). The term action-set is used here in the sense given it by Mayer (1966:97 ff.) and ably defined by Jane Schneider as "a coalition of persons ... [assembled] for the purpose of carrying out specific and limited tasks" (1969:112).

town of Poggioreale, Matteo disfigured his victim without mercy. Eyewitnesses reported seeing Giovanni from a distance. He made the customary gesture symbolizing death (a short circular motion with his upright hand) thus expressing resignation to his fate. One informant, who as a boy heard the details of this *triste cavalcade*, recalled:

> No one interfered. Everybody knew that this was to be done one day. For the rest, there were the bandits around, and Matteo was a strong and tall man, twice as young as his victim who approached 70. When they rode along, Matteo slowly butchered Giovanni. He cut off his member and put it in the victim's mouth like a cigar. Finally, he finished him off.

Afterwards, Giovanni's sister accused the friend—an agemate of Matteo, which made him suspect—of being an accomplice. The man repeatedly denied any involvement but was nonetheless sentenced to 15 years' imprisonment. He died in jail after some years of chagrin: he maintained that he was innocent, and when he learned about the death of his only son who went to America, he pined away. Matteo remained an outlaw for several years, until he was arrested while robbing a store in Castelvetrano, one of the bigger towns in the area. He was consequently tried and condemned to life imprisonment. In 1911 he was pardoned after spending well over 35 years in prison. One of Giovanni's nephews helped arrange a pardon for Matteo.[4] When Matteo arrived at Genuardo, he made his way to the house of this man to thank him publicly. Matteo was there received by many villagers, most of whom had only heard of *Don* Matteo, as they called him, and wanted to see him first-hand. Matteo's sister, who had a family of her own, managed to disinherit him, so Matteo spent the last years of his life in the

4. No further details were disclosed to me. But compare Marc Bloch, who notes that "in the thirteenth century in the best governed cities and principalities, in Flanders for example or in Normandy, the murderer could not receive his pardon from the sovereign or the judges unless he had first reached an agreement with the kinsmen of the victim" (1961:129).

same country house where his brothers had been killed. There he lived alone and took care of himself until he died in 1921.

DISCUSSION

Although the details of this episode are fragmentary, the narrative illustrates the process of *mafia*. One aspect of the rising staged by Luca in April 1860 was open class conflict. In a letter written at the time to the magistrate in Palermo dealing with the conviction of the band members, one of the local priests of Genuardo (Stefano Jaconi)[5] observed that the unequal distribution of land in the area "accounts for the poverty of the majority of the village population, which in turn explains the latent malevolence of the numerous landless peasants and their readiness for theft and anarchy" (Private papers 1866). It is significant that the priest ascribed the concentration of land in a few hands to remote historical events and subsequent bad government, rather than to recent usurpations by the voracious bourgeoisie of which he was himself a representative.[6] The letter may be

5. See Diagram 1.
6. The abrogation of feudalism in 1812 brought, in Sicily as a whole, the collective property of two million people into the hands of no more than 177 baronial families: a serious blow for the peasants who aspired to the division of the former feudal land. Cf. De Stefano and Oddo (1963:176–77). Details on the distribution of land in Genuardo have been discussed in Chapter III. It may be of some interest to look at the situation in the Palermo hinterland at large, as Brancato briefly summarizes these conditions: "In Corleone, which had about 20,000 inhabitants in 1871, more than 13,000 belonged to the class of landless laborers (*la classa proletaria*), i.e., more than 50 per cent of the population lived from uncertain daily labor. The situation was no different in other towns. . . . Allowing for religious feasts, bad weather, and so forth, the landless day laborers (*giornatari*) remained without work for at least one hundred days each year. Thefts sometimes supplemented the shortage of work. The village of Mezzoiuso embraced only a handful of families called *galantuomini* [i.e., *civili*]; the remainder were peasants largely dedicated to robbery. . . . In some communities almost all movable property that circulated there was concentrated in one single family which, with its ramifying connections, dominated the village, monopolizing the most im-

considered an example of mystifications typically voiced by *mafiosi*.

The extent to which the priest was right for the wrong reasons is revealed by the position of Matteo's family vis-à-vis the *gabelloti* of Genuardo. What the latter described as "abusive pasturage" were no simple incursions, because the common use rights were still contested, no compensation whatsoever having been obtained. For the *gabelloti* of Genuardo, however, *Don* Piddu became a nuisance, or *insopportabile* as they put it, and they decided to get him out of the way.

The class struggle at which the priest hinted in his letter was more complex than he allowed. Not only landless peasants were inclined to "theft and anarchy." Matteo's family belonged to the category of *burgisi*—peasants who had some land and cattle of their own. This condition of tactical power[7] was shared by several members of the Luca band.

---

portant offices of the local administration, and apart from a few exceptions, the remainder continued living, but only not to die" (1956:27).

7. The term "tactical power" is understood in the following sense: "The poor peasant or the landless laborer who depends on a landlord for the largest part of his livelihood (or the totality of it) has no tactical power; he is completely within the power domain of his employer, without sufficient resources of his own to serve him as resources in the power struggle. Poor peasants and landless laborers, therefore, are unlikely to pursue the course of rebellion, *unless* they are able to rely on some external power to challenge the power that constrains them" (Wolf 1971:54–55). The peasant irregulars who joined Garibaldi in May 1860 and helped the *Mille* to dislodge Bourbon rule exemplify the importance of the intervention of a rival power for the mobilization of poor peasants. Cf. Mack Smith (1950). It would be wrong, however, to assume that these irregulars formed a homogeneous class-based body. On May 14, 1860, two days before the decisive battle of Calatafimi, one of the *Mille* reported from the nearby town of Salemi (long known as a locus of *mafia* activity): "The Sicilian insurgents come in from all sides by the hundred, some on horseback, some on foot. There is a tremendous confusion and they have bands which play terribly badly. I have seen mountaineers armed to the teeth, some with rascally faces and eyes that menace one like the muzzles of pistols. All these people are led by gentlemen whom they obey devotedly" (G. C. Abba: *The Diary of One of Garibaldi's Thou-*

In the official reports, Luca figured as a foreman. His companions included four other masons, two carpenters, two cobblers, one barber, and several smallholders. The composition of the Luca band thus bears out the proposition that "It will be the better-off sectors of the peasantry who will be more likely to organize, and certainly the most depressed sectors who will be underrepresented. Within each group, the better-off individuals, certainly not the least well-off groups, will furnish proportionally more leadership and activists."[8]

Like Matteo, Luca had his private reasons to challenge the lords of the village. Some years before the rising, Luca's sister and her husband, who held the office of town clerk, were killed by poison. Giovanni and Filippo who subsequently assumed this office were implicated as the culprits. The Palermo revolt and the constitution of the special committee of internal security at Genuardo were seized upon by Luca as an opportunity to avenge his kinsmen. Yet Luca's bid for power failed. He could not sustain the rebellion, for news of the killings triggered the constitution of the company of the National Guard by members of the local establishment. Thus intimidated, the band dissolved. After Garibaldi swept away Bourbon rule, the political atmosphere in the village changed. Luca returned and was appointed as a village guard. The three Garibaldinis were lionized. There are some reasons to assume that the local elite was too preoccupied with accommodating the new regime to bother with the former members of the Luca band. It is quite possible that they accepted Luca as a village guard to avoid the impression that they still sympathized with the Bourbons. Furthermore, Luca was more easily controlled in this capacity than as a bandit. Above all, the *civili* wanted to stabilize the existing situation, and this involved the maintenance of order in these troubled months. But when Luca tried to organize support

sand. Tr. E. R. Vincent, London, 1962, reproduced in Mack Smith [1968b:310]).

8. Landsberger (1969:39). See also Wolf (1969:289–93; 1971: 54–59).

for a second rising, he was dismissed. We should remember that Luca was extremely popular among the village poor. The new government, however, sought its mainstay among the rural middle classes, rather than among the landless peasantry.[9]

The collaboration between Italian government and the local *civili* is also revealed in the case of Matteo. The struggle with the Jaconis resulted in a terrible defeat for his family: *Don* Piddu and three of his sons were brutally killed, while Matteo had to take to the mountains to save his life. Though the Jaconis were charged with these murders, they were never convicted. Matteo's private justice, accomplished after almost ten years of outlawry, brought him to jail for most of the rest of his life.

These incidents show us three different kinds of personalities. First, the Jaconis, who indulged in illegal pragmatic action under normative cover: their membership in the National Guard and their role as informants to the authorities permitted them to use violence with impunity. Matteo lacked any normative device to cover up his extra-legal dealings. He was an outlaw, or *bandito*,[10] and represents our second type. Third, there was Luca, who has elements of both. He started as a ringleader and became an outlaw when he failed to convince the village of his peripheral role in the April killings. At an opportune moment, he returned and assumed the task of enforcing law and order. Afterwards he slid back into brigandage. He seems to have been transitional between bandit and *mafioso*.

The story of Matteo illustrates the dominant patterns of conflict and accommodation in Sicilian rural society. Through pragmatic adjustment to formal government, the *civili* sought to keep a hold on the smoldering peasant rebellion. In fact, they represented formal government at the village level or, rather, their version of it: mayors, judges, tax-collectors, priests, notaries, and *gabelloti* were recruited from a handful of interrelated families (see Diagram 1). The higher

---

9. This has been demonstrated by Mack Smith's brilliant essay (1950).
10. From *bandire* (to banish, exile).

authorities relied on them to maintain order and protect property.[11] We should be cautious about viewing these families of *civili* as a closed group, or expect that the extension of liberal institutions under the Italian government would undermine their entrenched position. These two themes will be considered below.

THE SALE OF CHURCH DOMAINS

The confiscation of ecclesiastical property did not result in a more equal distribution of land, nor did it in any way contribute to more intensive agriculture (see Chapter III). The limited effect of this reform was particularly clear in the inland latifundist areas. The experience of Genuardo demonstrates how the expropriation and sale of church domains favored the emergent gentry at the expense of the peasants.

The reform was originally intended to benefit the peasantry. Garibaldi promised land to propertyless peasants when he needed their support against the Bourbon government, but his decrees on the division of church lands were never implemented. In the laws issued by the Italian government in the 1860s, the idea of distributing small shares of former ecclesiastical domains to landless peasants was altogether abandoned. It was argued that agriculture required a reasonable amount of capital to underwrite improvement. Therefore, the law prescribed the sale of shares ranging between 10 and 100 hectares at public auction, and this measure effectively disqualified peasants from land purchase. Furthermore, the new State needed money as well as votes from the small electorate of bourgeois landowners that formed its mainstay in Sicily's interior. In this way, about 190,000 hectares (10 per cent of the island's territory) were sold in the form of 20,300 shares from 1866 through 1874. Though the reform aimed at breaking up large estates of the church, it left room for the accumulation of multiple shares in the hands of one man: it failed to explicitly proscribe such con-

11. For the involvement of *civili* in *mafia* throughout the province of Palermo at the time, see Brancato (1956:245–46, n. 8).

centrations, just as it could not prevent the auction from being controlled by private partnerships. About 75 per cent of the shares were concentrated in the hands of those who had bought several shares each.

Before 1860, about 2,000 hectares out of the 13,500 hectares of the territory of Genuardo belonged to religious corporations. The bishopric of Agrigento held one big estate of 465 hectares; six other estates ranging between 100 and 800 hectares belonged to the monastery Santa Maria del Bosco, which also owned land in neighboring communes. As the name of the monastery suggests, the area was densely wooded. By 1875, a merchant from another town, whom we met in Chapter III as Emilio Mirabella, owned both the monastery and many of its surrounding estates (see Diagram 4). The land registry describes him as a baron owning 1,200 hectares of former ecclesiastical domains, including most of the woodland. The other landowners who bought up shares were less voracious. Nevertheless, their acquisitions were significant, and none of them belonged to that *medio ceto agricolo* (peasant middle class) which the reform was supposed to create. The six persons who bought shares of the *ex-feudo* Castagneto (465 hectares) were professionals and absentee landowners. A baron called Oddo acquired 14 shares measuring between 3 and 55 hectares, a total of 188 hectares. A second baron bought up five shares making up 24 hectares. One of the Jaconis obtained 17 shares of three to six hectares, which amounted to 85 hectares of Castagneto and six shares (38 hectares) of another estate that had once belonged to the monks. The other three buyers acquired similar shares. The remainder of this big estate was obtained by Baron Mirabella who, again, held most of the adjacent estates.

Through inheritance and sale in subsequent decades some fragmentation of the estates took place. It must be noted, however, that these processes did not necessarily involve the fragmentation of landownership. Those who bought land extended their patrimony, and very often marriage between cousins brought together what had been split up through inheritance. In 1900, Baron Oddo's son inherited his father's land but sold these 188 hectares in 1904 to a man called Andrea Pizzo who had made his fortune in America. This made Pizzo's only daughter attractive as a marriage partner for the Jaconis: she married the son of the man who had helped obtain the pardon for Matteo. When I lived in the village, their two children had nominally divided the family property, but it is still managed as a big farm by an overseer (see Diagram 3).

A second example brings us back to Baron Emilio Mirabella, whose specific role in the distribution of former church domains in Genuardo will be presently discussed. When Emilio assumed landed status, he married an impoverished baroness. Both the land and the title passed on to his two daughters, who were afterwards married off with considerable dowries. The eldest, who inherited the Santa Maria del Bosco estates, had four children. The first-born, Adriano, held close to 1,000 hectares, including the shares of his brother who died shortly after marriage. His sisters Caterina and Elisa inherited 100 to 200 hectares each. Adriano adopted his brother's son Giacomo and nominated him as his only heir since he had no children of his own (see Diagram 4). Like his uncle, who died in 1943, Giacomo lives most of the year on his estates, which now cover about 750 hectares. The impact of the recent land reform has been slight on this farm, as most of the fields are classified as woodland. In fact, Santa Maria del Bosco (as the estates are still called) constitutes the only farm in the territory of Genuardo that exceeds 200 hectares. Giacomo married into a landowning family that also held former church domains. An informant pointed out that one of Giacomo's father's sister's daughters would have proved a more suitable marriage partner, since it would have brought together what had been divided after the death of his grandparents (see Diagram 4). As we will see later on, Adriano and Giacomo fulfilled important roles in village politics.

When Baron Emilio Mirabella became owner of the Santa Maria del Bosco estates in the early 1870s, he refused to recognize the *de facto* common rights which the peasants exercised on the land. As pointed out before, these civic use rights were of crucial importance to the peasants, especially the landless cultivators, who thereby obtained pastures for their work animals, wood for making implements, and charcoal for their kitchens. Additional rights involved gleaning on the stubble and the collection of fruit and acorns. These rights were immemorial customs and existed on both baronial and ecclesiastical fiefs. As elsewhere in Sicily, however, the transformation of public domains into private real estate involved the usurpation of the common use rights without any recompense to the peasantry. Baron Mirabella forbade the peasants of Genuardo to enter his woodlands and when he began to clear the trees from the land, first in agreement with the forest inspector, later on his own account, the mayor of Genuardo protested formally and the commune of Genuardo sued him. By the end of 1879, when close to 350 hectares were deforested, the issue was considered before Tribunal, which decided in favor of the village. Yet in the course of the next year, the Supreme Court of Appeal recognized the documents produced by the baron as valid, and decided that the use rights had become invalid by lapse of time. The claims of the mayor based on several historical documents (including a copy of the charter of 1520) were thus rejected, and the commune lost the case.

In this way about 600 hectares of woodland were cleared and turned into grain fields. The baron managed to obtain approval for his action from the Forestry Department, whose requirements, as its officials pointed out to the baron, were indeed minimal: major slopes had to be protected by either trees or walls.

The consequences of this instance of deforestation were both social and ecological. Deprived of an important source of subsistence, increasing numbers of peasant families emigrated. In 1880 and 1881, only one hundred persons left the village. In the next two years, well over four hundred emigrated. Apart from soil exhaustion on the Santa Maria del Bosco estates, the clearing of these upper locations produced damage to crops on lower areas, since the quiet streams changed into irregular torrents. The woods had also pro-

tected the village from much of the discomfort caused by
the *scirocco.*

The Jaconis acquired less of the former church domains
than they had hoped as substantial *gabelloti* and money-
lenders. Michele and Nicola, who had three brothers in the
National Guard in the early 1860s, succeeded in buying up
roughly 100 hectares each. But Nicola's four sons, who had
their mind on a large estate of the Santa Maria del Bosco
complex, were disappointed that they were outwitted in the
contest by Mirabella. They swore vengeance against the
local town secretary, Attilio Raimondi, who had helped
facilitate Mirabella's acquisition to restrict the growing
influence of the Jaconis in the village. As noted before, the
oldest son of Nicola, who was mayor of Genuardo between
1873 and 1882 and again from 1888 through 1902, initiated
the case against Mirabella regarding the common use rights.
At the time, mayors were appointed by the government and
wielded considerable power. They were the expression of
the strongest coalition in the village and were backed by the
parliamentary deputy of the constituency; they could favor
or ruin anybody almost at will.[12] With these resources at his
disposal, Francesco Jaconi prepared the downfall of his
rivals. Two brothers who held large estates in lease for over
40 years were removed after a visit to the estate owner by
Francesco. And the tax-collector, Livornese, was deprived
of his license through similar machinations. The conflict between the two factions escalated to such an extent that the
Prefect had to intervene in 1894, after which both parties
were forced to make peace. Francesco remained in office for
almost another decade, but the power of this branch of the
Jaconis (see Diagram 5) did not emerge from the process unscathed. The land acquired by Michele and Nicola was split
up in small shares through inheritance, and this circumstance even forced two grandsons of Nicola to emigrate.
Though another grandson held the office of mayor as late as
1914–20, there were clear signs that other families were on

12. For the power wielded by the mayor during this period, see De
   Stefano and Oddo (1963:201–09).

the rise. Before turning our attention to them, we will consider how this faction struggle affected the peasant movement of 1893.

THE PEASANT VERSUS THE GABELLOTO

The peasant movement known as the *Fasci Siciliani* (from *fascio*, league), which spread over large areas of the island in the course of 1893, differed in several important respects from previous manifestations of peasant discontent.[13] Whereas *jacqueries* and brigandage prevailed as the main vehicles of spontaneous and largely uncoordinated peasant protest, a more sustained and organized movement emerged by the end of the 19th century.

This more adequate articulation of peasant discontent can be explained in terms of a growing involvement of Sicilians in a world outside the village boundaries. One aspect was socialist influence among urban intellectuals and artisans who provided both leadership and a program to a poverty-stricken peasantry. Second, the draft brought many peasants back into their village with new experiences and an increased sense of organization. Third, the extension of suffrage to those able to read and write continued to widen as literacy advanced. And a galloping emigration rate, though in itself a safety valve to reduce the chances of revolution at home, helped overcome traditional resignation.[14]

The *Fasci* originated in Palermo and then gained ground in the inland districts. There, and especially in the latifundist hinterland of Palermo, each town had its own *Fascio*, whose actions were coordinated by the central committee in Palermo. Of the leaders on the committee, Bosco, Barbato, and Verro stood out in urging mobilization of the peasants. The goals of the *Fasci*, formulated in the two congresses of

13. For detailed accounts, see Ganci (1954) and Romano (1959). A brief survey of this movement is contained in Hobsbawm (1959: 93–107).
14. The relationship between low rates of emigration and the presence of class-based associations has been noted by McDonald (1956) and Galtung (1962).

May and July 1893, were reformist rather than revolutionary:
they sought improvement of labor contracts through legal
means including demonstrations, strikes, and electoral participation. The ultimate aim of the Socialist *Fasci* was to
generate class-consciousness among the peasants vis-à-vis the
big landowners and *gabelloti* who exploited them. Though
the movement thus remained within legal bounds and did
not, either in program or practice, aim at the overthrow of
the existing social order, successful strikes and occasional
instances of violence precipitated intervention from the
government. In January 1894, special military measures suppressed the *Fasci*, and its main leaders were arrested.

Once again in Sicilian history, vested landed interests in
alliance with formal authority muzzled peasant protest. Yet
long before the government dissolved the movement, it was
threatened from within. The course taken by the *Fasci* in
Genuardo demonstrates some of the difficulties confronting
the peasants and their leaders.

To begin with, the constitution of the Genuardo peasant
league took several months: from early May through early
August 1893. During this period, it could not avoid entangle-
ment in the bitter faction fight between powerful local
families in their contest for municipal control. As mentioned
above, the sale of church domains exacerbated this struggle.
Mayor Francesco Jaconi, unable to obtain the estates he
wanted, sought to upset his adversaries by playing upon the
rivalry between the local factions, or *partiti*. Originally, the
"Whites" and "Blacks," as these *partiti* were called, derived
from antagonism between the local parishes, and exemplified the common pattern of *campanilismo* in the South. In
practice, the division served as a tissue to structure power
conflicts between various groups in the village. But these
struggles remain incomprehensible unless we understand
their covert dimension of class conflict, as the contending
elite factions built downward coalitions with segments of the
lower classes. Tensions between landlords and peasants thus
provided the dynamic underlying the power balances of the
landed families. In this way, class tensions were converted
and maintained in a different form—were sublated or *aufge-*

hoben. Francesco's main rivals were leaders of the "Whites," the faction in control of the town council in 1893 after it had defeated the "Blacks" in the elections of 1889. With the next elections in sight, the mayor together with his brothers Pietro and Giuseppe supported the "Blacks," the core of which was formed by another pair of brothers, Lorenzo and Paolo Selvini (see Diagram 6). To broaden their electoral support, the "Blacks" invited Bernardino Verro, the peasant leader from Corleone, to address a meeting in early May. Verro, one of the main leaders of the *Fasci* and very active in his hometown, was welcomed in a splendid gathering that included the *Fascio* of Genuardo and that of the neighboring village of Bisacquino. One of the "Blacks," a certain Angelo, a physician who had recently settled in Genuardo and hoped to find employment as the second municipal doctor, was chosen president. But this was to be superseded by another *Fascio.* Though Angelo staged some meetings in May, the mayor (Francesco Jaconi) could inform the authorities as follows: "Verro and companions restricted themselves to just a visit. *Fascio* not constituted. They returned to their own village." Likewise, the incidental meetings organized by Angelo did not result in any substantial league with the presentation of statutes as happened in other villages.

In the elections of June 1893, the "Blacks" succeeded in beating the "Whites." Once they were in control of local government, the "Blacks" began to oust their opponents from office: under the pretext of cutting down expenses, they dismissed a schoolteacher and almost all civil servants, some of whom were replaced by "Blacks." On the other hand, they nominated Angelo as the second municipal doctor. The administrative muddle thus produced reached such a stage that the provincial authorities deemed it necessary to intervene. Angelo was dismissed and sent away. He had to leave anyway because he had become involved in a serious affair with a widowed member of the Jaconis, whom he sought to seduce. In the end Angelo was literally shot out of the house by her teenage son.

In the beginning of August, a different set of people successfully founded the *Fascio* of Genuardo. Membership amounted to roughly one hundred, and virtually none of them appeared to have participated in the constitution of the pseudo-*Fascio* of May. Positions of leadership were occupied by artisans, smallholders, and merchants (see note 8). The president, a waggoner, sent the following message to the mayor: "Sir, I herewith inform you that in Genuardo there has been constituted a society under the name of *Fascio dei Lavoratori* with a legal program proposing as its goal the moral and material improvement of the working classes to be reached by legal means." The statutes, which were enclosed in this letter, were similar to those of the *Fasci* in other towns, and emphasized the improvement of labor contracts through pacific means, as well as the right to strike as guaranteed by law. The new labor contracts as proposed and accepted in a big regional meeting of various *Fasci* in July approached the *mezzadrìa classica*: sharecroppers should obtain one-half of the crops rather than one-fourth or less as was common at the time. After the negotiations between the peasants and landowners (including *gabelloti*) failed, a big strike spread through the area, and lasted from August through the end of October. It was the first of its kind in inland Sicily.

During these months, the strike and occasional demonstrations alarmed the authorities as well as the landed gentry, and some of them asked for army intervention. Leaders and members of the movement who had penal records were kept under special surveillance. Some *Fasci* leaders had dubious qualifications as, for instance, the president and vice-president of the *Fascio* of the neighboring town of Bisacquino. In the police files of that town, they are described as follows:

Nunzio Giaimo, age 37, and originally from San Mauro Castelverde, has been living in Bisacquino during the last ten years. He is employed as a clerk and partner in the lease of the tax-office, and does not own any property. He is feared for his dissembling character, his imponderable indifference, and for the tendency he has—as a born delinquent—to attack life and property of others. He serves himself of alibis to commit the most audacious delicts and to ensure impunity, as happened in San Mauro in 1877 when he allegedly attempted murder and in Bisacquino in October 1892, when he unsuccessfully committed extortion, for which he was sentenced by the Court of Palermo to three years and four months imprisonment and two years of probation. He was, however, acquitted by Court on May 9, 1893, after appeal together with his inseparable friend Vito Cascio Ferro, with whose active cooperation and anarchic propaganda he leads the mass of the *Fascio* of which he is president. According to the subversive school of severe socialism, he drives the members of the *Fascio* into the resistance against everybody, and this involves attacks by surprise at the cost of the honest citizens and the public offices.[15]

Though the criminal orientation of *Fasci* leaders and the element of popular violence were greatly exaggerated by the authorities to create a pretext for dissolving the movement,[16] some local *fasci* were indeed dominated by *mafiosi*, who were fishing in troubled waters. There are strong reasons to assume that this was the case with both Nunzio Giaimo and Vito Cascio Ferro. Apart from their penal records and acquittals, indeed typical for *mafiosi*, we know that Cascio Ferro, still in his early thirties at the time, was certainly the most prominent *capo-mafia* in the area from at least 1909 until 1926.[17]

15. From a letter of the Vice Prefect to the Prefect, October 20, 1893. See Bibliography, Other Sources and Documents (183c).
16. During December 1893 and early January 1894, there were violent clashes between the public forces and the peasants in various towns as, for example, in the neighboring village of Gibellina where 20 persons were killed and many others seriously wounded. These incidents were, however, largely provoked by the authorities. Nevertheless, the central committee of the *Fasci* could not always contain the increasing agitation, and the government soon sent the army to repress the *Fasci*. Cf. Romano (1959:346, 360–72, 478–79).
17. Miniature biographies of *Don* Vito Cascio Ferro, which leave out these early years, are sketched by Barzini (1965:273–76) and Pantaleone (1966:38–42). Both authors exaggerate *Don* Vito's importance by describing him as the greatest chief "the Mafia" ever had. Though, as we will see, *Don* Vito's power was con-

By early November 1893, landowners and *gabelloti* from all over the district began to give in to the demands of the *Fasci*. The following letter addressed to the Prefect on November 9 disclosed what happened at Genuardo, illustrating the quiet and peaceful tenor of the movement.

In Genuardo on November 5, the brothers Francesco and Pietro Jaconi conceded their land in sublease to the members of the *Fasci dei Lavoratori* of this village. At 5 p.m. of the same day, about 150 members of this sodality organized a public and peaceful demonstration to express their gratitude to the brothers Jaconi for the concessions made. They walked through the village without music or banner crying: "Long live the King, the Queen, Garibaldi, the *Fascio*, the Mayor, and the brothers Jaconi!" The police sergeant in charge kindly requested the demonstrators to disperse, which they did without trouble. After some time, however, they returned, repeating the cheers for the mayor, who intervened at once, and the demonstrators, being asked to disperse, obeyed without causing any trouble.[18]

A few days later the *Fascio* of Bisacquino, with its leaders Nunzio Giaimo and Vito Cascio Ferro, marched into Genuardo. Numbering about 300, they came from the estate Moli which had been conceded to them on more favorable terms. The mayor denied them access to the village since they lacked official permission for a general meeting. When

---

siderable, including connections in the United States where he spent some years around the turn of the century, the very structure of *mafia* and the larger configuration of which it formed a part ruled out the development of pivotal chieftaincy, or any form of central control whatsoever. The same gaps in communication that inhibited State penetration and thus provided social space and leverage for *mafiosi* as power brokers, also rendered impossible the formation of a clandestine counter-State or comprehensive parallel hierarchy—of a Mafia complex embracing all of Sicily, popular mythology to the contrary. See Chapter VII. From a different perspective, Hess also refutes the folk sociological theory of a single, unified, corporate Mafia (1970:103–110, 134, 165).

18. See Bibliography, Other Sources and Documents (1893a).

I. Agro-town in the Palermo hinterland. Note
medieval castle on hilltop and zone of
intensive cultivation (*corona*) in the foreground

II. *Latifondi.* Looking north from Genuardo.
In the background, mountains
surrounding Palermo

*Photo by courtesy
of Bianca Dony*

III. Guenardo as seen from the North

IV. Boy plowing with mules

V. *Masserìa* near the Cascina estate

VI. *Masserìa* of the Moli estate

VII. Former *gabelloti* during intermezzo at threshing

VIII. Area south of Baronessa

IX. Grisafi and his companions. Top: Vincenzo Santangelo, Settimo Grisafi. Centre: the chief of the band, Paolo Grisafi. Below: Paolo Maniscalco, Giuseppe Maniscalco

Source: Mori
(1933, facing p. 130)

X. Threshing on the commons just above the village

XI. Area where Alessandro was killed

XII and XIII. *Contadini*

they refused to leave, the mayor informed the *Carabinieri*, who succeeded in making them leave after reporting both leaders. At the outskirts of the village, Giaimo made the following statement: "Companions! We have won without the use of firearms in spite of the canaille that challenges us. Keep firm! *Addio!*"

Whatever the internal weaknesses of the *Fasci* movement, that it had to be suppressed by military force clearly demonstrates not only its potential strength but also the extent to which *mafia* fell short of accommodating class conflict.[19] After the dissolution of the *Fasci* and the conviction of its leaders, radical reforms were proposed that would (among other things) split up the *latifondi*. Nothing of the sort, however, was realized. As indicated in Chapter III, the condition of the peasants in the inland districts grew even worse, and this partially explains the large-scale emigration from the latifundist zones, in particular, which sharply increased after the suppression of the movement, and continued to grow in subsequent years.[20]

THE RISE OF THE CASSINIS

During the first years of his married life, Alessandro Cassini (1829–1895) was relatively poor. He exploited a small shop in Genuardo and supplemented his income with additional retail. One of his children, Giuseppe, for example, sold wax matches for which he was called *"Lu Cirinaru,"* a nickname

19. For the relations between *Fasci* and *mafia*, see Romano (1966: 206–20).
20. See Chapters II and IV; Renda (1963:47–50). Writes McDonald: "Until 1893, emigration from the Interior of Sicily had been quite low. Then, in 1893–1894, the Italian Government suppressed the 'Fasci' trade-unions; and almost straightaway emigration rose towards the rate already prevailing in the 'typical' South. The activities of the Fasci and their cooperatives continued to a much diminished extent; and, by the years 1902–1913, total Sicilian emigration was intermediate between the low rate for Apulia and the high rate for the 'typical' South ... Did this mean that the inhabitants from the Interior of Sicily had lost faith in the efficacy of the class struggle and cultivator class solidarity?" (1956:442).

he kept long after he stopped peddling.[21] In the 1870s Alessandro became a wealthy man. Though little information on the origin of his fortune was disclosed to me, some data seem conclusive. A grandson, a man called Nene, who was one of the three drunkards in Genuardo when I lived there, dropped hints that his grandfather became rich when the government crushed organized brigandage in 1877. Published documents on the operations of bands in the area at that time provide no evidence that Alessandro was ever active as an outlaw.[22] It may be assumed, however, that his retail business procured him considerable profits from bandits, who had to rely on people like Alessandro in order to dispose quickly of their booty (cf. Hobsbawm 1969:73–76). That many bandits were either killed or arrested and convicted in the course of a few months may have facilitated or even increased Alessandro's gains. It was precisely to this position—a strategic location in a network of "friends"—that the reticent grandson offered some clues.

Alessandro did not invest his wealth in land. Neither his name nor those of his three sons Vincenzo, Giuseppe, and Giacomo figure among those listed in the land registry of this period. The Cassinis capital was invested in leases (*gabelle*). By 1890, Alessandro's sons held several large estates in lease. In the beginning they formed partnerships (*società*), but later on, when they married, each son managed estates on his own account, and with various measures of success until the early 1920s. Their control over land gained them authority over people who depended on the land for their living, particularly sharecroppers, shepherds, and landless laborers. Their numerous employees, both actual and potential, used to call them *"Don,"* addressed them with *"Vossìa"* (*Vossignoria*, Your lordship), and saluted them with *"Bacio la mano"* (I kiss your hand). This marked their social ascent as well as their growing political influence. The Cassinis became members of

21. From *cera*, wax; hence *cerini*, wax matches, and the Sicilian *cirinaru*, seller of wax matches. As customary in the area, the nickname passed on to the children.
22. Cf. Anonymous (1879); D'Alessandro (1959:94–100); Marino (1964:205–21).

one of the two social clubs (*circoli*) where the local elite assembled, relaxed, and discussed village politics. This drew them, as early as 1894, into the main conflict evoked by the Jaconi mayor who, as we have seen, played upon the long-standing strains dividing the "Whites" and "Blacks," each with its own *circolo*. Before Vincenzo Cassini became mayor (1907–1914), the Cassinis had participated in the local administration as councillors since the early 1890s.

Alessandro, who died in 1895, married his two daughters off into neighboring towns. Vincenzo's wife also came from another place but lived in Genuardo. Giacomo married into the local elite and one of his sons, Ignazio, reinforced these ties by marrying a cousin (see Diagram 7). Another son, Antonino, married a daughter of a local landowner. One daughter of Giacomo married a *gabelloto*, a nephew of Pizzo, who bought up the land from Baron Oddo in 1904 (see Chapter VI). Another daughter married into the Jaconi family. Giuseppe's wife was of peasant background. The violent reputation of Giuseppe's family will be discussed in the next chapter.

The wealth of the Cassinis must have been considerable, at least by village standards. Their revenues from cattle and estates, which they also leased in neighboring communes, enabled them to live as *signori* in attractive and spacious houses with servants to do the manual work. One particular incident may illustrate Vincenzo's power and the range of his network. In 1911, his nephew Gioacchino, son of Giuseppe, challenged the fiancé of an artisan's daughter whom he claimed for himself. Though the girl felt no sympathy for Gioacchino, the latter, only nineteen years old, told her fiancé to stop his visits to the girl and threatened him. When the young man continued his visits to her family's house, Gioacchino waited for him outside in the night and shot him dead as he came out the door. In the early morning, Gioacchino reached the *masserìa* his father held in lease and told the employees boldly: "*Cadìu u porcu!*" (The pig has been killed.) Gioacchino succeeded in hiding from the law and eventually escaped to New Orleans, where many village emigrants had gone. The girl and her family, inconsolable, also went to America to find a better home and settled in New Orleans. There they were threatened by Negro thugs who told them to refrain from any action against Gioacchino.

I have carefully scrutinized the two main Palermo newspapers of the time to find additional details on this homicide, but no mention of it was made whatsoever. Yet some clues are offered in the Genuardo council deliberations of 1914, which were published that year in the form of a pamphlet dealing mainly with the classification of fields in the territory of the village. The preliminaries contain the following passage: "No less unfortunate than the conditions of transportation were and still are the conditions of public security. Four *Carabinieri* protect well over 13,000 hectares of territory. Cattle rustlings, the killing of persons and animals are such a normal thing that the newspapers do not even record them . . ." This was discussed and written down just after Vincenzo resigned from office. Though the text does not of course suggest, let alone specify, Vincenzo's part in the manipulation that enabled Gioacchino to escape safely, it seems more than likely that uncle and nephew *si intendevano* (agreed). In fact, some informants suggested that Vincenzo might have facilitated the emigration of his brother's son, but they added that evidence for this and similar cases is hard to find: "*Sono cose che si capiscono.*" (You can make out what happened.)

This instance incidentally illustrates the important difference between *mafiosi* and bandits or outlaws. Bandits must hide from the law, since they do not have their *carte in regola* (papers in good order); *mafiosi*, in their role of accomplices (*manutengoli*), do: no evidence can or will be produced against them.

Vincenzo retired as mayor some time after he gambled away his fortune one night in his *circolo*. At the end of the sitting he ventured to make up for his mounting losses and put at stake his whole *mandria*—his entire herd including appurtenances—in a contest with Pizzo, who did the same. At the time both herds were pastured on Pizzo's estate, and hence formed appropriate stakes. Vincenzo's defeat made his wife pine away; she died in 1918, only 45 years old. The children were reduced to beggary. Save one who died in an asylum, all emigrated to America, and none contracted a favorable marriage. As two informants recalled: "Nobody was concerned with their fate anymore. Yet, before his ruin Vincenzo as well as his children did not try very hard and indulged too much in luxury. As we say: *Una generazione fa i soldi, l'altra li fa perdere. In somma, la vita è come una ruota: c'è chi scende c'è chi sale.*" (One generation makes money, the next one loses it. After all, life is like a wheel: there are those who go down and there are others who go up.)

A STRUGGLE FOR GABELLE

Between 1902 and 1914, the brothers Nicola and Michele Jaconi managed a large estate in partnership with their father's brother, Domenico, who exploited three adjacent *latifondi*. The organization of this agricultural enterprise, which embraced close to 1,500 hectares of the Baronessa complex, has been discussed in Chapter IV. The reader will remember that the Jaconis held large estates in lease for several generations and that some of them were big landowners in their own right. Since 1861, mayors and councillors had been recruited from their ranks. In 1914, Nicola succeeded Vincenzo Cassini as mayor of Genuardo.

In early September 1914, bandits unsuccessfully tried to kill Nicola and one of his plowmen. Their attempt to steal cattle from Domenico likewise failed. Yet they succeeded in killing fifteen of Domenico's oxen and injuring several others that were plowing the fields that day. Some years before, Domenico had been blackmailed. Subsequent investigations revealed that all these operations had been undertaken by the Grisafi band and were part of a strategy plotted by a rival clique of entrepreneurs from the village of Adernò, situated some ten miles south of Genuardo. Through this maneuver, Domenico's own *campieri* sought to usurp his position as *gabelloto*. The stratagem succeeded and Domenico was forced to retire. His former henchmen acquired the lease for the next six years. Before discussing in detail the genesis, composition, and role of this rival clique, known as the *mafia* of Adernò, we must first understand the position of the Grisafi band.

The Grisafi band owed its name to its leader, a former herdsman in his early thirties from Caltabellotta, another small town in this mountainous border region of the provinces of Palermo, Agrigento, and Trapani. Paolo Grisafi, or "Marcuzzo" as he was called, had been active as a bandit for well over 12 years before he was arrested together with four of his companions in January 1917. Mori, the police officer who accomplished the roundup, provides the following description of Grisafi and his band:

The *latitante* [outlaw] Grisafi, a mountain-dweller of thirty-six years of age, originally a shepherd, who commanded the armed band . . . , was a consummate bandit. Fierce and cautious, most redoubtable, up to all the tricks and stratagems of guerrilla warfare, and protected by a thick net of local favour strengthened by terror, he had been a *latitante* for quite twelve years; and he had set up in the western part of the province [of Agrigento] a kind of special domain over which he ruled absolutely, interfering in every kind of affair, even the most intimate, making his will felt in every field, including the electoral field, and levying tolls and taxes, blackmailing and committing crimes of bloodshed without stint. Some thirty murders were put down to him, besides an unending series of crimes. Perhaps he had not committed so many: possibly he had committed more: certainly he was ready to go on committing them. They called him *Marcuzzo* (little Mark), but he was a man of thews and muscles, inclined to stoutness.

Aided not only by his boldness but by constant good luck, and being a good shot, he had always succeeded in escaping from the toils of the police; he had escaped unhurt from several conflicts and had sometimes inflicted loss on his pursuers. Not long after I came to the province of Agrigento, during a raid on the southern part of the province of Palermo, he had run into a group of five police agents with his whole band. Instead of opening fire, as was his wont, he had beaten a hasty retreat over the gentle slope of a small hill, disappearing from view over its shoulder. The police agents had immediately rushed in pursuit, but in their zeal they had not thought of the trap laid for them. Instead of coming on in open order, they had kept close together. Grisafi and his companions were waiting for them on the other side of the slope: and a well-aimed volley caught the pursuers full at their first appearance on the skyline, killing two brave men.[23] For some time, too, Grisafi had had such a reputation for being uncapturable that the country folk began seriously to believe that he was *maato* (bewitched). . . .

. . . [M]y arrival in the province of Agrigento had aroused some anxiety. I was told that, a few days after my arrival, the Grisafi band, which apparently numbered nine men at that time, had been reduced to six. Three of the bandits had preferred to go off on their own affairs. After a little time had elapsed, another bandit had gone away, owing to some dispute with the leader, and the band had been reduced to five—Grisafi, his brother, the two brothers Maniscalco and a certain Santangelo. At that rate there was the risk that the famous band would disappear into thin air, and I wanted to capture it, not to break it up . . . (Mori 1933:130–132).

The composition of the Grisafi band was continually subject to modification. Given the relatively long period during which the band maintained itself (1904–1917), the fact that some members were still teenagers as, for example, Santangelo, suggests that older members were regularly replaced by youngsters. This organizational feature is not uncommon among bandits and may even be inherent in brigandage. In this respect, it has been argued that:

. . . [S]ocial banditry is universally found, wherever societies are based on agriculture (including pastoral economies),

23. This incident took place in October 1916 in the territory of Genuardo south of Baronessa.

and consist largely of peasants and landless labourers ruled, oppressed and exploited by someone else—lords, towns, governments, lawyers, or even banks. . . .

. . . [N]ot everyone in such regions is equally likely to become an outlaw. However, there are always groups whose social position gives them the necessary freedom of action. The most important of them is the age-group of male youth between puberty and marriage, i.e. before the weight of full family responsibilities has begun to bend men's backs. . . .

The second most important source of free men are those who, for one reason or another, are not integrated into rural society and are therefore also forced into marginality or outlawry. . . .

. . . The characteristic bandit unit in a highland area is likely to consist of young herdsmen, landless labourers and ex-soldiers and unlikely to contain married men with children or artisans (Hobsbawm 1969:15–28).

On this point, we may remember Matteo's career in the 1860s and 1870s and understand how his unmarried status facilitated his activities as an outlaw.

Apart from the core of the Grisafi band, which consisted of two sets of brothers who were all from Caltabellotta, people from various neighboring places formed a catchment for the band, though they were not recruited on every occasion. Up to a certain point, membership was intermittent. This was even more evident for the network of support on which the band relied to carry out its activities and, indeed, to survive. After Grisafi and his companions killed the police sergeant and a policeman from Genuardo in the incident described above, the band dispersed. Characteristically, the bandits did not take to the mountains, but moved to different towns where "friends" hid them from the authorities. In this connection, Prefect Mori refers to a "thick net of local favour" and observes that the Grisafi band "had eyes everywhere." Mori's keen insight into Sicilian social life in terms of networks—over 30 years ahead of network analysis in anthropology—had immediate implications for the roundup:

... I began to send out my men ... into the various places that had been the scenes of the bandits' crimes in order to collect—without raising the alarm and so without any official formality—all possible current news on the past activities of the band and especially the necessary indications for identifying their habitual and occasional helpers, whether voluntary accomplices or compelled by fear ...

... [T]he network of assistance that had been drawn round the Grisafi band had grown wide, thick and strong in the course of time. The whole system was welded together by complicity in crimes, fear of reprisals, terror, espionage on behalf of the bandits, conflicting interests and equivocal alliances for the most of varied ends, to an extent that made it almost impenetrable. ...

One night, therefore, by sudden simultaneous action in different places, I made an attempt to arrest all the helpers we had identified and against whom—at my request, which had been kept secret—the judicial authorities had issued warrants of arrest: 357 persons in all, of whom ninety were in Caltabellotta alone (Mori 1933:133–34).

This brings us back to the location and composition of the rival clique that made use of Grisafi to intimidate and disrupt the Genuardo partnership, and thereby forced Domenico Jaconi's retreat. Its location was clear: all members of the clique lived in the village of Adernò and were employed as *campieri* on various estates of the Baronessa complex, including the four estates leased by Domenico and his nephews. Its composition was mainly structured along links of cognatic and affinal kinship and contained sections of three patrinominal families,[24] the Cosimas, the Ginnettos, and the Co-

---

24. Specimens of patrinominal families have been discussed before when dealing with the Jaconis and the Cassinis. They are distinctly noncorporate units which are open to alliances with affinal kin and friends. See Firth, who notes that "In the ordinary European system of patrinominal families the use of the patronymic in successive generations as surnames does allow of the recognition of a kin group (not necessarily *descent* group) of members of two or more generations. A European patrinominal kin group is not exclusive, that is, kin bearing other patronyms combine as working

fanos. (See Diagram 8. The solid triangles designate the *campieri* who supervised the estates leased by the Genuardo partnership. The striped symbols represent members who exercised similar functions of surveillance on three other estates of Baronessa leased by an impoverished nobleman, a certain Baron Francesco, who had moved from Genuardo to Adernò. His mistress's brother was set up as an additional *campiere* on one of these farms.)

As appeared from legal documents and interviews with older people, the central focus of the Adernò clique was Edoardo Cofano. He is described as *capo-mafia* of Adernò, that is, the primus inter pares of the clique. Grisafi acted by order of Edoardo, who kept him under cover. As one inform-ant put it: "Edoardo *garantiva* [protected] Grisafi." We are here concerned with institutionalized proceedings in which people distinguish between the *mandante* (principal) and the *mandatario* (agent). These specific interdependencies be-tween bandits and *mafiosi* are somewhat obscured in the otherwise highly interesting account of Mori, who tends to overemphasize the role of Grisafi in the area. Though it is true that Grisafi intervened in many affairs (taxation, elec-tions), it is wrong to ascribe to him qualities like "absolute control." Grisafi's power was largely derived from the power domains of local *mafiosi*, people like Edoardo, who were Grisafi's patrons. As mentioned above, Grisafi was in fact captured as a result of Mori's technique of rolling up part of his network of support. After the arrest *en masse* of his friends, "the Grisafi band, now on foot and without support, moved very little, owing to the fewness of the houses where it could take refuge, had necessarily to go round the caves . . ." (Mori 1933:138).[25]

---

members within the same social entity. But the continuity of common name gives a fairly ready means of identification" (1963: 24–25). See also Wolf (1966a:3–10); and Peter Schneider (1972).

25. In any context the term "absolute control" is inappropriate. Our understanding of power and power dynamics will be considerably enlarged if we see them as a process of interdependencies, as a structural aspect of all human relationships, rather than as a substance or an attribute of a single human being or social group.

Cliques like the one formed around Edoardo, which sought
to gain access to and control over resources for their individual members by means of violence and intimidation, were
called *cosche*.[26] As a noncorporate group, the *cosca* should
be understood in terms of a set of dyadic ties linking each
member to every other member. In turn, these dyadic ties
were part of larger, overlapping networks involving other
mafiosi, kinsmen, friends, and many others. The *cosca* was
thus an integral part of these networks, and cannot be understood in isolation from them. Each member, most notably the
leader, was connected in a ramifying order with people outside the *cosca*, either directly, or indirectly through intermediaries. The position of the leader depended upon his
range of contacts with persons who were important to him
and vice versa: the smaller the number of steps that the leader
had to take to reach these persons, the stronger his position.
Yet this reachability accounts for only part of the leader's
strength. The number of lateral linkages between these contacts, especially links between persons adjacent to the leader,
should be controlled and kept to a minimum to ensure his
monopoly as broker: when people learn to make their own
contacts, the leader will be out of a job.[27]

The importance of dyadic bonds in Sicilian social organization was expressed in several social fields. The dyad was a
salient feature in *gabelloto* partnerships, the *cosca*, and the
brigand band—a clique in its own right. Dyadic kinship
relations, especially sets of brothers, as in the Genuardo
partnership, the Grisafi band, and the Adernò *cosca*, pro-

Where people depend upon one another, we are ipso facto concerned with power-balances. This is equally true of extreme cases
such as master-slave or jailer-prisoner relations. Cf. Elias (1970:
76–77); Adams (1966:5).

26. Singular: *cosca*, which etymologically refers to artichoke (Italian:
carciofo; Sicilian: *cacocciula*), especially the hardest parts of the
leaves. The term *cacocciula* is also used to indicate a local clique
of *mafiosi*: "*è della cacocciula*" (he belongs to the local *mafia*).
The closely folded and spiny leaves very clearly symbolize the
tightly knit and fearsome features of the *cosca*.

27. Cf. Mayer (1966:111–12); Barnes (1968:110 ff.); Clyde Mitchell
(1969:15–19); Boissevain (1973:Ch. 2, 6).

vided crucial building blocks for the relatively durable units
I have called cliques. Dyadic links were also significant in
less permanent groupings—action sets—that emerged in
specific situations for specific goals and dissolved when these
had been accomplished. The Grisafi–Edoardo axis demonstrates the extent to which dyadic relationships were
prominent in less durable but crucial groupings. The term
"coalition" seems appropriate to describe these different
forms of noncorporate units: dyads, action-sets, and cliques.
"Coalition" retains the meaning it has in ordinary language,
where it is understood to be a temporary combination for
special ends between parties that retain distinctive prin-
ciples.[28]

Returning to the coalition that emerged to oust the Jaconis
from the Baronessa estates, we may assume that Edoardo
had long coveted the estates controlled by Domenico, and
seriously considered a leaseholding partnership with some
of his kinsmen. Domenico was faced with the choice of either
renewing the lease for another six-year term (September 1914
through August 1920) or leaving. Though he had opted for
the first alternative (he was in office when Grisafi challenged
him in early September 1914), he changed his mind after this
violent confrontation. That Edoardo and some of his kinsmen
had already established themselves as *campieri* on the very
estates they intended to lease facilitated their attack. Their
key positions as "men of confidence" provided them with the
intelligence to subvert the Genuardo partnership from
within, and brought them into regular contact with the
casual laborers set to work on the estates. We know that
some of the latter were used by Edoardo to carry out thefts
and rustlings suffered by Nicola. Again, these laborers acted
under the guise of their role as employees. Likewise, Grisafi
must have been informed about the appropriate time and
place for his attacks on Domenico and Nicola. Such double-
dealing stratagems were by no means rare: *Di dintra veni*

28. See *The Concise Oxford Dictionary of Current English.* I am
    much indebted to Boissevain (1968; 1973 and personal communi-
    cation) for insights into this problem.

cu lu voscu tagghia (He who cuts down the forest comes
from inside), runs an oft-quoted Sicilian proverb.

The Jaconis had to accept their defeat, though Nicola and
Michele were allowed to maintain their lease of one estate.
They lacked the human resources to resist Edoardo, who was
becoming very prominent at the time.[29] Whereas Edoardo
could rely on several adult male kinsmen, the Jaconis lacked
these crucial assets. Domenico, already aging (he died in
1916), had only one son, also called Nicola, who had married
a sister of Michele's wife (see Diagram 9). These two sisters
belonged to a once powerful family, the Selvinis, whose
male members died out by 1914. Though Nicola and Michele
had three other brothers, two of them had left for Argentina
while the third had a nonagricultural profession, running the
local chemist shop. Nicola's son was, moreover, too young to
provide support. Nor could Domenico mobilize other
nephews.

The position of the Jaconis was also threatened by some
disappointed Cassinis. Giuseppe and his eldest son, Alessandro, were among Edoardo's allies. We may assume, indeed,

29. We hear that Edoardo carried a reputation for his strength and
skill. An informant from his home town recalled the following
anecdote, which illustrates that physical appearance and daring
were crucial determinants of the prestige, respect, and social standing of males in rural Sicily: One day, at the beginning of his career
as a *campiere* on Baronessa (about 1910), Edoardo went to Palermo
to see the estate owner, Ippolita Vassallo, on business. He wore
a peasant outfit and traveled by train from Corleone to Palermo,
taking a carriage from the railway station to the palatial town
house of the latifondista. As the carriage stopped before the house,
the owner and some of his relatives chanced to be standing on the
balcony. They witnessed a scene in which the cabdriver over-
charged Edoardo, whom he took for another country-bumpkin
ignorant of city life and prices. When the driver demanded his
inflated fee, Edoardo (aware of his audience) dragged the man
down from his seat, and shoved his head under the carriage wheel.
Pinning the driver there with his feet, Edoardo threatened to spur
on the horses . . . Our informant spoke with great admiration and
respect for Edoardo, who by this show of prowess displayed the
very attributes necessary for survival and advancement in the
Sicilian countryside.

that they were eager to curtail the power of the man who seized the office of mayor from their brother and uncle. It is to the Cassinis and the larger network of *mafiosi* of which they were part that we turn in the following chapter.

VII
Heyday and Decline, 1914–1943

The period of World War I and the years immediately following showed a recrudescence of *mafia* activity all over western Sicily, the proliferation of the use of private violence for political and economic ends. The experience of the war, the growth of democratic institutions (most notably the extension of the suffrage to all adult males through the reforms of 1913 and 1919), the persistence of large estates in conjunction with the lord–peasant complex, and the restrictions on overseas emigration aided, each in its own way, to exacerbate class tensions. Supported at the national level by the new mass parties of the Catholics and Socialists, which were particularly strong in the North, the peasants were growing into a significant social force. In Sicily and the South, peasant leagues and cooperatives occupied large estates, and radical land reform to break up the *latifondo* was proposed in a parliament on which the Liberal Sicilian landowners were losing their grip.[1]

This development of Sicily and Italian society made the estate owners increasingly dependent upon a growing number of *mafiosi* retainers to offset the restive peasant labor force as well as to control the elections to which the poor peasants had recently gained access. Yet, what thus appeared as the zenith of *mafia*—a situation in which the retainers came close to dominating their lords—rapidly plunged to its nadir. On the one hand, tensions and conflicts arose between the *mafiosi* retainers themselves, especially when new and younger members asserted themselves in competition for

1. Cf. Raffiotta (1959:181–98, 208–21); Romano (1966:237–62); and Tarrow (1967:164–70).

control over resources. On the other hand, the *latifondisti* became increasingly receptive to a regime that would, on both the national and the local level, safeguard their interests less expensively and more adequately than their *mafiosi* retainers, who had become a liability. The advent of Fascism in 1922 excluded any prospect of radical agrarian reform that would benefit the peasantry. In 1925, elections were abolished, and a more comprehensive party system and the Fascist militia destroyed the gaps in communication on which the *mafiosi* had thrived. Under the new political structure, with the emphasis on a strong State, private police bodies became both anomalous and superfluous. Thus isolated and deprived of protection, the retainers were rounded up as common criminals shortly after the establishment of the Fascist dictatorship in 1925. Before this was accomplished, however, *mafiosi* were powerful, perhaps more powerful than ever.

THE NETWORK OF COSCHE

In a report of October 1925[2], the local section of the *Carabinieri* in Genuardo described in detail an impressive recrudescence of delicts committed by members of a "vast association for criminal purposes" (*associazione a delinquere*) operating in the area for several years. It was argued that the audacity of these crimes and their impunity required urgent measures of control.

The "association" involved well over 150 *mafiosi* from seven different villages and towns situated in the Genuardo area along the western border of the provinces of Palermo and Agrigento. The offenses attributed to it included homicides, cattle and sheep rustling, and various forms of extortion. The association is described as firmly organized with a hierarchy of leaders and sponsors, and characterized by a distinct specialization of functions, with a division of its territory into smaller sectors, thus resembling public agencies in many respects, including the imposition of taxes. There were frequent and secret meetings in a variety of locations where

2. See Private papers (1928).

mafiosi discussed their operations, which were facilitated by a dense network of accomplices that had grown up around them in the course of time. The report emphasized the quick and unwarranted enrichment of several members, most notably the leaders. The alleged kingpin of the association was *Don* Vito Cascio Ferro, a man we have met before in connection with the *Fasci*. The report provides the following vignette.

Chief (*capo*) of the association was Vito Cascio Ferro from Palermo, residing for many years in Bisacquino. In 1900 he went to America and soon became one of the major exponents of the *Mano Nera* (Black Hand). He was expelled from the United States as the author of a serious crime. Back in Sicily, he resumed his ordinary criminal activities with old and new affiliates. In 1909 he was involved in the killing in Palermo of the well-known American policeman, Joseph Petrosino, who had come to Italy to investigate Cascio Ferro's criminal career.[3] From the statements of various persons the absolute preeminence of Vito Cascio Ferro in the "association" emerged clearly. According to some people, he was one of the most distinguished chiefs if not the supreme chief of "the Sicilian *Mafia*." At his house in Bisacquino there was a continual coming and going of people, and it was a place of nocturnal meetings. In his hometown alone, Cascio Ferro disposed of a dozen henchmen (*bravi*). Pantaleone presents the following, somewhat dubitable portrait:

> Many people, especially in the province of Palermo, still remember Don Vito Cascio Ferro. He was a tall, distinguished-looking man, and his gentlemanly appearance was made more venerable by a long flowing beard; certainly no one would have suspected him of being an old, semi-literate criminal. His prestige reached unimaginable heights; high-ranking authorities were obsequious to him,

3. For details of Petrosino's mission in Sicily and his violent death in Palermo on March 12, 1909, see the original documents reproduced in Reid (1952: 160–76). Cascio Ferro's involvement in the assassination is discussed in Pantaleone (1966: 40–41) and Petacco (1972: 111 ff., *et passim*), which only came to my attention while correcting page proofs.

and he was a welcome and gratuitous guest in the best hotels. He was generous, too, in the way typical of people who do not have to count their money or even know where it comes from, and it is said that when he went to visit "his area" the mayors of the towns through which he passed met him at the town gates and kissed his hand in homage (1966:40).

It is worth noting that the term *"associazione a delinquere"* was invented by the judicial authorities to facilitate the mass arrests of *mafiosi* during 1926 and 1927 carried out by Mori, Prefect of Palermo at the time. Regarding its meaning, Mori writes in his memoirs:

> ... [I]t sometimes happened that after long, careful and close inquiry we had succeeded in collecting strong evidence against numerous individuals who had been guilty of crimes committed some time before. However, the state of flagrancy having elapsed, it was not legally possible for the instruments of the judicial police to act on their own initiative. Under the ordinary criminal procedure the collected evidence should have been transmitted to the judicial authorities, who would then take action as they were competent to do after having followed the prescribed procedure (interrogations, confrontations, etc.), which meant that they could only act after having raised the alarm sufficiently to render all the criminals in that particular district immediately undiscoverable, and in consequence to induce all those who had given denunciations, indications, testimony, etc., to retract all they had given. In order to avoid this it was necessary to create a state of flagrancy which would allow the instruments of judicial police to act directly. This was obtained by formulating the offence of "association for criminal purposes," particularly on the ground that the same individuals committed the same crime. This was a permanent state of crime and, therefore, flagrant; and on this basis we proceeded to make a sudden and simultaneous round-up with all the necessary subsidiary action and denunciation to the judicial authorities (1933:182).

Thus, to be a member of such a "group," a legal fiction created from above, was defined as a criminal offence. No specific indigenous term exists to denote an assemblage of *mafiosi* in areas larger than the local commune. Each village or town had its own *cosca*.[4] Its members exploited a distinct and limited territory. This territory generally coincided with the commune itself, but sometimes the *cosca*'s domain extended beyond as well; the *cosca* of Adernò, for example, entrenched itself in the estates of the Baronessa complex. The local *cosca* was a small, relatively autonomous unit—a clique as I have called it. Though most of its members maintained more or less regular relationships with *mafiosi* from neighboring towns, these interdependencies did not grow up into a comprehensive, hierarchically ordered association embracing various *cosche*. As we have seen above, and will see again, there was no evidence for the operation of a supra-local chieftainship. Though certain local chiefs succeeded in extending their power domains far beyond the boundaries of their hometowns and gradually developed into dominant *capi-mafia* in larger districts, as happened with Cascio Ferro, such developments did not turn them into supreme chiefs of corporate associations. To an extent, the same segmented or cellular structure that characterized Sicilian society at large was reflected in the way *mafiosi* themselves were organized. The various local *cosche* maintained loose relationships with each other without, however, yielding their relative autonomy to any overarching or sovereign power. These local clusters of *mafiosi* were thus structurally complementary to the segmented framework of the larger society in which they bridged, exploited, and maintained the gaps in communication. What the so-called association for criminal purposes actually stood for can therefore best be understood in terms of social networks.

The interrelations of Sicilian *mafiosi* may thus be analyzed in terms of interlocking and ramifying dyadic ties building

4. Some of the larger towns in Sicily's western interior had two (rival) *cosche* as, for example, Corleone during the 1950s (Pantaleone 1966:113–28). Cf. Mosca (1900, 1933); Candida (1960: 125–83); Boissevain (1966b:224–25).

up into an open-ended field. The chains of relations emanating from a particular *mafioso* did not necessarily lead back to him (that is, all the "friends" of a particular *mafioso* did not always know one another), though they did of course in the *cosca* in which each *mafioso* was adjacent to (knew) all the others. The organizational principle involved is very neatly phrased in the term "*amici degli amici*" (friends of friends), an expression used in everyday language to refer to *mafiosi* and their patrons.

When discussing the early 1920s with a former *gabelloto*, who at the time together with his father and two brothers managed a large estate in the area of Genuardo, it was pointed out to me that they had to pay for "protection" from pillage. Of particular interest was his use of the network metaphor to unveil a crucial dimension of *mafia*:

> We kept enormous bloodhounds to prevent incursions and thefts. Cattle rustling was rampant at the time. But our own measures were all to no avail. We were robbed all the same. When we employed a *campiere-mafioso*, who was, you might say, imposed upon us by the *mafia* of Bisacquino [Cascio Ferro's hometown] which was very powerful then, the robberies stopped. We paid the man a regular yearly salary, but he only rarely inspected our farm. Now and again he turned up. You may well ask what his surveillance actually meant. Yet he did not need to bother about much more than just these occasional visits, since he let it be known that he kept watch over that particular estate. Our man was an "*amico degli amici*" as we say, and this made the robbers stay away. We were "respected."[5] In some way, *mafiosi* from different places

5. The specific meaning of "respect" in this context was summed up by Mori as follows: "[The Mafia] ... demanded complete subordination, absolute obedience and *rispetto* (respect). This last was even required in exterior forms and was understood particularly as a concrete recognition of the prerogative of *immunity* belonging to the *mafioso*, not only in his person but also in everything that he had to do with or that he was pleased to take under his protection. In fine, evildoers had to leave the *mafioso* severely alone, and all the persons or things to which, explicitly or im-

[he named half a dozen neighboring towns] are in contact with one another. The *mafia* is a sort of network [N.B.] spread out all over the area.

The purpose of the present and following section is to describe a series of events in which *mafiosi* were involved. By analysing them we can gain some insight into the organizational features of the *mafia* network and the way it operated to satisfy specific ambitions of its members. The account will be focused on the Cassinis, since this family formed the center of *mafia* activity in Genuardo during the decade preceding Fascism.

As suggested in the previous chapter, where I have dealt with the capture of the Baronessa estates by the *cosca* of Adernò, *mafiosi* chiefly aimed at and engaged in the control over land by violent means. Once they obtained a foothold on the large estate, either as leaseholder, *campiere*, or supervisor of the herds, they sought to accumulate wealth in various ways. Apart from the ordinary revenues from crops and animals and the various levies they imposed upon the peasant sharecroppers, the rustling of cattle and sheep was one of the most important stratagems for accumulating

plicitly, he had given a guarantee of security. That is the meaning of the word *rispetto* in this connection.

"For instance, among field-watchmen or *campieri* who had to be taken on and paid by the big landed interests, at the behest of the Mafia, to look after the estates, there was the *campiere di rispetto*, so-called not, as some think, because his employment was an act of respect towards the Mafia, but because he guaranteed the security of the estate of which he was guardian, through the *rispetto* for his person that was due, in a subordinate sense, from the malefactors and, out of solidarity or reciprocity, from the Mafia itself. In fact, the *campiere di rispetto* did not usually carry out the functions of his office continuously or in person, and often he did not even reside on the estate entrusted to his care—or rather which he had seized—but he simply allowed his name to be used. That was usually enough. It is to be noted that the Mafia laid great store by this *rispetto*, not out of concern for personal safety, but for reasons of prestige, since it saw in every injury inflicted upon it by criminals or others an insubordination, an insult or an act of contempt rather than an act of material damage" (1933:69–70).

wealth. Ecological conditions strongly favored the theft of animals (see Schneider 1971). Natural pastures and their relative scarcity entailed a migratory orientation of animal husbandry, and this ruled out fixed boundaries and fenced places where the herds could be kept under adequate surveillance. The same ecological constraints that brought cattle and sheep on long migratory routes and kept the herds roaming over desolate and distant *feudi* demanded, on the part of the successful owner, a maximum number of relationships with persons on whom he could rely for pastures, accommodation for his herdsmen, transport and marketing of the products, and several other facilities according to the circumstances. These network relations of support and intelligence were not only crucial for the successful pastoralist, but also for the successful rustler. They provided the organizational grid of rustling operations as well as the secure disposal of the booty. Not all thefts of animals were organized, but those that were, especially large-scale rustlings (*abigeati*), required careful preparation. It is to the organization of one particular set of thefts that we now turn.

During the summer of 1915, animals were stolen at three different places adjoining the Baronessa estates leased by members of the Adernò *cosca*. A fourth raid, involving 14 head of cattle, two mares, and one mule, took place near the estate controlled by the Cassinis (Giuseppe and sons) at the end of October of the same year. Subsequent investigations revealed that the four thefts (all suffered by owners from Genuardo) were organized by one and the same coalition, consisting of 17 *mafiosi* from Genuardo, Adernò, Bisacquino, and several other neighboring towns, all situated along the borders of the three western provinces of the island. Apart from the *mafiosi*, six of whom acted as accomplices, seven landless laborers from Genuardo and three outlaws from distant towns took an active part. Each of the four occasions involved unique coalitions or action-sets which, however, had overlapping membership. Regarding the participation of the seven casual laborers, we know that they appeared on the estates under the pretext of seeking employment and left one or two days later; each time a theft took place shortly thereafter. The first theft (June) involved A and B; the second (August) involved C, D, and E; the third (September) involved B and F; and the fourth (October) involved again A and B. The role of the seventh laborer (G) was not specified in the records. The fourth rustling, which took place on October 24, was prepared during two banquet meetings: one on September 29 in the house of Cascio Ferro at Bisacquino; the other on October 21, at the *feudo* Misilbesi located in the commune of the neighboring town of Villamaura, and also presided over by Cascio Ferro. About 16 persons participated in the latter assembly. The six accomplices mentioned above were *gabelloti, campieri,* and livestock supervisors engaged in the management of the Misilbesi estate. It was at this place that, a few days after the fourth rustling, a third meeting took place during which the money from the sale of the stolen animals was divided. These fragmentary details on the rustlings became known when the police sergeant of Genuardo[6] tracked down one of the outlaws involved in the thefts, and stole in upon him at the Misilbesi estate on October 30. Betrayed by one of the stolen mares, the man was identified as a certain Zarzana, 28 years of age and from a town called Partanna located some 50 kilometers west of Genuardo. Several warrants for his arrest for murder and extortion had been issued by the judicial authorities in the area in the course of the past few years. A cash reward of 500 *Lire* was offered for his capture. On Zarzana the police found a booklet that contained a note regarding the division of the spoils. From the total amount of 2,460 *Lire* obtained from the disposal of the stolen animals, Zarzana had received 150 *Lire*. The rustlers were brought to trial and consequently acquitted under a general amnesty. When their case was reconsidered in 1928, they were acquitted again since no conclusive evidence could be produced.

As far as the organizers were concerned, we note, apart from the presence of Cascio Ferro, who has already been mentioned, the following names: Edoardo and Aldo Cofano;

6. It was on one of these enquiries on horseback that this man met his death at the hands of the bandit Grisafi in October of the next year. See Chapter VI.

Giuseppe, Antonino, and Ermenio Ginnetto (all belonging
to the *cosca* of Adernò and in charge of several Baronessa
estates; see Diagram 8); Giuseppe Cassini and his son Alessandro (the axis of the *mafia* of Genuardo; see Diagram 7),
and Aloisio Olivieri, also from Genuardo, whom we shall
meet later on. The names of the other participants do not
concern us here, since they play no further part in this book.
We should note, moreover, the striking flexibility of organization reflected in the considerable range and diversity of
the relationships contained in the successive coalitions, some
of which we have encountered before in the Edoardo-Grisafi
action-set which drove the Jaconis from Baronessa in the
autumn of the previous year (see Chapter VI).

In the absence of corporate kin groups, relations with cognates, affines, friends, patrons, and clients were emphasized
according to the circumstances of strategy. In this respect,
it has been argued that the freedom to form strategic groups
requires a flexible social matrix offering multiple channels of
association.[7] To a certain extent, this flexibility is provided
by the bilateral kinship structure, in which the operation of
ascriptive kin groups of a corporate type is de-emphasized,
and in which ties with nonrelatives are promoted. As in other
societies with bilateral kinship, relations between friends
were a salient feature of Sicilian social organization. As Freeman writes :"The development of the institution of friendship
is marked in bilateral societies, for the formation of personal
friendship is not impeded by loyalties to this or that segmen-
tary descent group" (1961:212). However, one may well ask
what is actually meant by friendship in this part of Sicily.
It has been observed that friendship in Sicily, as in other
Mediterranean societies, is instrumental rather than emotional: each member of the dyad is a sponsor for the other
and acts as a potential connecting link to other persons outside the dyad.[8] When people exchange favors voluntarily,
they call each other "friend." They rely on the idiom and

7. See Paine (1970:64–66). Jane Schneider (1971) provides several
   insights into the importance of contractual affiliations in pastoral
   societies.
8. Cf. Boissevain (1966a:22–23); Wolf (1966a:10–18).

connotations of intimacy, trust, and affection to cover the practical utility and sometimes the exploitative nature of their dealings. As Wolf has clarified his distinction between emotional and instrumental friendship: "Despite the instrumental character of such relations, however, a minimal element of affect remains an important ingredient in the relation. If it is not present, it must be feigned. When the instrumental purposes of the relation clearly take the upper hand, the bond is in danger of disruption" (1966a:13). In his discussion of patron–client relations in Sicily, Boissevain maintains that, given the great inequality in the distribution of resources, friendship may become asymmetrical and shade off into patronage (1966a:23). We should not, however, emphasize too much a conceptual division between friendship and patronage: in Sicilian peasant society, patrons and clients were and still are conceptualized as friends (*amici*). Where the West European middle-class notion of friendship is largely bounded to personal relations between social equals, the Sicilian folk classification of friendship involves personal relations crossing class lines. In this respect, Pitt-Rivers' original term "lopsided friendship" seems appropriate to describe the relation between patron and client in Mediterranean societies where patronage seems to be largely coterminous with "friendship."[9]

As indicated above, livestock and crops could be "protected" against thefts through payment. Persons who refused to pay or were unwilling to come to terms with the *mafiosi* who controlled the area suffered damage to crops and animals, and even risked their lives. Punishments involved theft, arson, and destruction: crops were set on fire or stolen; trees and vines were cut down; and animals either disappeared, or were wounded or killed on the spot. Sometimes cattle owners succeeded in recovering part of their stolen flocks for a ransom. Such protection was always a racket: it was forced upon people by intimidation and violence.

9. Pitt-Rivers (1961:140). In western Sicily no specific terms exist to denote patrons and clients; both are referred to as "friends" (*amici*). It is from the context that one learns about this differentiation.

The most characteristic manifestation of the protection racket was the imposition of a tribute system. According to legal documents of the time, *mafiosi* had attained such prominence and were organized so well that they felt strong enough to place themselves above the authority of the State and imposed an actual tribute on the landowners and peasant sharecroppers in the area they controlled. The tribute was called *pizzu* or *cuccia* and consisted of two *tumoli* of wheat for every *salma* of wheat under cultivation.[10] The territories of the various communes in the area were divided into districts, each of which consisted of several large estates controlled by a single *cosca*. The *campiere* was the guardian of the estate, and it was under the cloak of this role that he imposed and collected the tribute, half of which he kept for himself while the other half went to the *capo-mafia* of the district. Regarding the supervision of one estate, one used the term *campierato*. When surveillance by *mafiosi* was extended to various contiguous estates, it was called *guardianerìa*. *Campieri* not only extracted tributes from the peasant sharecroppers but, as noted above, also imposed themselves upon the manager of the estate. When *mafiosi* did not actually run the estates themselves (as they did at Baronessa between 1914 and 1920), they sought through more or less veiled threats to induce the manager or owner to employ one of their company. Though these "men of confidence," as *campieri* were called, made themselves "respected" by keeping rustlers and petty thieves away from the farm, their presence often proved a burden to the manager or owner. Some of these men of confidence became rich in the process and attained landed status. The common phrase "*Un uomo fa un altro uomo*" (A man makes another man) suggests that this evolvement was by no means rare. One case clearly demonstrates the dilemma. A landowner had replaced his

10. See Chapter IV. *Pizzu* (Sicilian) means beak. The expression is: "to pay for wetting the beak [of a *mafioso*]." Originally, quite small quantities might have been involved. In fact, the equivalent of *pizzu*, *cuccia*, also refers to a very small portion of grain: boiled and seasoned grain, which as a small meal is offered to guests on the day of Santa Lucia (December).

thieving *campiere* by another man of whom he expected less exacting behavior. After some time the landowner met his former employee. They exchanged a salute, whereupon the landowner asked how the *campiere* had fared since his dismissal. The man rearranged his jacket to cover only one shoulder, and answered: "You clothed me only partly, Sir. What about the man who has taken my place?"—a typically oblique *mafioso* expression reminding the *padrone* that he would needs begin anew to make the replacement *campiere* a reliable client, during which time the new man would surely pilfer enough goods to "clothe" himself fully at the *padrone*'s expense, whereas the fired *campiere* was already "half dressed" and, hence, a less costly liability.

At this point we are a long way from the 18th century feudal landlords who mobilized and equipped a personal following of armed retainers to maintain law and order in the countryside. To appreciate the differences and similarities between 20th century *mafiosi* and their feudal counterparts, we should distinguish between cultural form and function. Both types of retainers used a similar code of communication in which highly personal relationships and the element of toughness were emphasized. Yet the social context in which *mafiosi* operate differs fundamentally from the institutional setting of the feudal henchmen. Whereas the mediating functions of the latter were minimal and strictly locally phrased, those of the former attained major strength and significance in connection with the impact of the State and the advent of the market. We should remember that similar cultural forms and codes can be used in different social contexts in which they may have quite different functions. The persistence of the overriding elements of loyalty and physical violence should not blur the gradual change of the power balance between landlords and their retainers in favor of the latter. A configurational approach to society brings out the fact that the dependence of Sicilian landlords upon *mafiosi* increased as the peasantry posed an ever growing threat to vested landed interests.

Mafiosi were ruthless when they required the payment of tributes and ransoms. At times, they paid heed to the request of the poor peasant and allowed for a slight reduction, especially when harvests failed. When they collected extortion money, *mafiosi* quite often referred to others in the interests of whom they said they acted. These persons were the *amici* and *picciotti* (lads), who made up a part of the *cosca* or who formed its penumbra. The following examples and conversations, taken from Fascist court proceedings,[11] illustrate the reserved manner and veiled threats that differentiate *mafioso* behavior from the less restrained conduct of those in open conflict with the law. All cases took place in the Genuardo territory *circa* 1920.

A landowner called Teodoro said that he was compelled to take as *campiere* a certain Salvatore, known to be affiliated with the *mafia* of Bisacquino. Landowners were left undisturbed only when *mafiosi* knew them to be protected by some *pezzo grosso* (big shot). Teodoro had to pay without stint, and part of the money went into a common fund. When he ventured to ask for a reduction, Salvatore answered: *"Che le pare che me le mangio io solo?"* (What do you think, that I take it all for myself?)

A peasant called Nicolo, from whom two mares and a mule were stolen (see below), tried to recover them and addressed himself to a go-between, who told him that the *picciotti* wanted 4,000 *Lire*, about 40 per cent of the market price of the animals.

A peasant named Filippo worked a small strip of land, part of the *feudo* Coda di Volpe and located in the border area of the communes Bisacquino and Fioravante. He put himself under the protection of a *campiere*, Giuseppe Damati, one of Cascio Ferro's right-hand men who lived in Bisacquino. Filippo had promised to pay the required tribute at the end of the harvest. After some time, the *capo-mafia* of Fioravante, a man called Francesco, addressed himself to Filippo and demanded the *cuccia* with the following words: *"Voi sapete che io non ho bisogno, ma ci sono i picciotti e la cuccia ce la dovete dare."* (You know that I do not need it, but there are the lads and the tribute has to be given them.)

11. See Private papers (1928).

Filippo argued that he had already promised to give the tribute to Giuseppe, whereupon Francesco insisted that Coda di Volpe fell under his jurisdiction. It was decided that things should be straightened out in a conversation with Giuseppe. When the three men met, Francesco said: "*Don Pippineddu, Lei sape che nella riunione che abbiamo tenuto nella casa che Lei sape, abbiamo stabilito che la cuccia di Regalbate deve essere Sua e quella di Balatazza deve essere nostra: che diritto ha perciò di pretendere la cuccia di lui?*" (*Don* Pippineddu, you know that during the meeting we hèld in the house you know about, we have established that the tribute of Regalbate[12] should be yours and that of Balatazza[13] should be ours: what reason therefore do you have to pretend to claim the tribute from him?) Giuseppe answered that he thought Coda di Volpe part of Regalbate, since it was separated from Balatazza by a country road. And he added: "*Dopo sei mesi che servo questi signori debbo rubare senza niente, ma i patti si debbono rispettare.*" (After six months serving these gentlemen I have to leave without any reward, yet one has to respect the agreements.) Giuseppe then addressed himself to Filippo, and said: "*La cuccia la dà a Don Ciccio.*" (The tribute has to be given to *Don* Ciccio [Francesco].)[14] In fact, at harvest time two members of the Fioravante *cosca* presented themselves to Filippo and requested the tribute in the name of Francesco. The following year (1924) they did likewise. In the summer of 1925, however, no one appeared to collect the tribute from Filippo: Francesco had been killed by *picciotti* of the Bisacquino *cosca* who, under the aegis of Cascio Ferro, asserted themselves in the area through a series of staged incidents—rustling that

12. An estate in the territory of Genuardo along the border of the commune of Fioravante. Giuseppe acquired supervision over this estate after killing Bernardo, the incumbent *gabelloto* (see below). He succeeded in extending his control over various adjoining estates during 1922–23, but shortly thereafter had to take refuge in America. When he left he was 27 years old.
13. Situated in the commune of Fioravante.
14. Pippineddu and Ciccio are diminutives of Giuseppe and Francesco, respectively.

infringed the jurisdiction of established *mafiosi*—which provoked the anger of these older *mafiosi,* whom they then
subsequently murdered and then replaced. Francesco was
approaching 50 while his three killers were under 30. (This
pattern of inter-*cosche* conflicts will be discussed below.)

The sharecroppers employed on the Baronessa estates also
submitted to this collective extortion. They paid tributes to
the members of the Adernò *cosca* who, after the change of
management in 1920 (see Chapter IV), had nevertheless
remained on the staff of Baronessa as *campieri.* According to
some informants, the *mafiosi* from Bisacquino and Adernò
held the territory of Genuardo tightly in their grip. It was
indeed from Cascio Ferro and Edoardo Cofano that this network of control radiated, especially over the eastern and
northern parts of the commune of Genuardo. This network
was reinforced by links of cognatic and affinal kinship, which
in turn were strengthened by bonds of ritual kinship when
mafiosi acted as baptismal sponsors for each other's children.[15] *Campieri* and *picciotti* of the *cosche* from these two
towns situated on the fringes of the territory of Genuardo
thus closed in on the large border estate of Moli managed
by the Cassinis, Giuseppe and his sons (see Diagram 10 and
Map of Commune). Before exploring the kind of relationships that emerged, we will first consider the position of the
Cassinis in Genuardo. Two central incidents in which they
were involved illustrate how they fared in their hometown.

On the night of October 25, 1919, two mares and one mule
were stolen from a peasant named Pasquale. The value of
the animals amounted to roughly 10,000 *Lire.* Seven local
suspects were tried and subsequently released, since no evidence could be produced against them. Two weeks later, on
the night of November 9, Andrea Raimondi, a medical
student and son of Attilio, the town secretary (see page 120),
was killed on the outskirts of the village; his head was
crushed with a big stone. Legal action was brought against
two brothers named Fazelli, after Andrea's parents, especially

---

15. Whether they were co-parents (*cumpari*) or not, *mafiosi* quite
 often addressed each other as such.

his father, had leveled strong charges against them. However, the accused were acquitted. On account of new investigations, the police reported that both delicts were interrelated: the murder had been committed as a consequence of the theft of Pasquale's animals. The main offenders were members of the Cassini family. The Fazellis, poor to the extent of approaching the status of village outcasts, had nothing to do with either crime.

It turned out that Pasquale paid 2,500 *Lire* for ransom to a go-between named Malacarne, who delivered the money to Giuseppe Cassini, who in turn distributed it among the members of the *cosca*. Both Malacarne and Andrea Raimondi were among the seven suspects arrested on account of the theft. Through his eldest son, Alessandro, Giuseppe told Malacarne to keep quiet, and it was thus that the main authors of the theft were not arrested. Though Pasquale had paid in order to recover his animals, he did not get them back. At this point, Andrea, who was a relative of Pasquale, interfered and urged the Cassinis to return the animals to his kinsman. We do not know the precise extent of Andrea's involvement in the Genuardo *cosca*, only that he was well informed about this particular operation. One informant mentioned that Andrea kept the accounts of the local *mafiosi* —something which could not be checked since other informants side-stepped the issue or simply said they did not know. Yet the very fact that some informants were touchy about the subject, and the circumstance that many of the local *mafiosi* were illiterate or semi-literate, besides being Andrea's age-mates, imply that Andrea was deeply involved. At any rate, these circumstances help explain his father's behavior. His father had been at odds with the Cassinis for some time, and so had reason to fear disclosures from them about his son's involvement should they be arrested for the killing. Hence the persistent charges of Andrea's father against the innocent Fazellis. In any event, it was on account of Andrea's incessant attempts to get the animals released and the arrests of two rustlers that the Cassinis, afraid of being detected, decided to eliminate Andrea. After a series of discussions with Alessandro and Ferdinando Cassini and two other local *mafiosi*, the group finally reached the edge of the village, where Andrea was murdered. Giuseppe Cassini severely reproached his sons for killing Andrea. Not so his wife, who is described to us as a "terrible woman." She not only approved of the action of her sons, but broadcast the news in vulgar terms before anyone in the village knew about it.

On the night of May 5, 1919, three men presented themselves at the *masserìa* of the Cascina estate, held in lease by the Tortochettis from Genuardo and attended that night by two brothers of that family named Saverio and Benedetto. The three men asked for bread. When, however, Saverio made a movement to reach for his gun that was hanging on the wall, one of the visitors shot him in his arm, wounding him seriously. (It took four months to recover from the fracture.) The intruders went off and took Saverio's gun with them. The police arrested a certain Vito from Bisacquino, but the court released this man for lack of evidence. In the course of the judicial enquiries, Saverio's father mentioned that he had a serious dispute with Giuseppe Cassini in 1913 on account of the shot-gun marriage of Giuseppe's eldest daughter Anna that followed after her abduction by a poor villager, a mason called Bruno. Giuseppe believed (correctly) that the Tortochettis, who lived opposite his house, had facilitated the elopement. About 6,000 *Lire* and clothes for the girl were brought from her house to that of the Tortochettis, from whence the couple set out.[16] This constituted a serious insult to the Cassinis and gave rise to a long-standing rancor between both families. The grudge the Cassinis held against the Tortochettis was also fed by the latter's prosperity which in no way depended upon the good favor of the Cassinis.

On May 18, 1920, when two other brothers of Saverio pastured the family herd in an area fairly close to the village, they saw two individuals approaching the herd in a suspicious way. One of the brothers ran to the village to inform his

---

16. Two forms of elopement can be distinguished: with and without the consent of the girl. Both proceedings were institutionalized.

family and the police. After a brief chase, in which Saverio took part, the intruders were arrested. One of them confessed that they had come from the estate of Moli, where they had decided—together with the Cassinis and a *campiere* from Bisacquino—to rustle the cattle of the Tortochettis; hence it was with this goal that he and his companion (also from Bisacquino) had approached the herd, while others, armed, were waiting at some distance. All persons involved were arrested. After some time they were released when the man withdrew his testimony. Moreover, the court later found no evidence for an attempted rustling.

On September 30, 1921, Saverio was shot to death on the road along the Cascina estate. The murderers also took his gun. Saverio's father ascribed the killing to Giovanni Cassini, adding that one of his sons had also recognized Giovanni among the three men who had attacked Saverio at the *masserìa* two years before. Fearing reprisal, however, his son had kept silent. It turned out that Giovanni's mother—the "terrible woman" who had encouraged and openly approved of the killing of Andrea, the son of the town secretary—had uttered constant threats against Saverio, because he had told the father of the murdered youth Cesare (see below), that public opinion in Genuardo held Alessandro Cassini responsible for the killing. Four days before Saverio was killed, Giovanni's mother appeared at her window and said to Saverio: *"Poco ne hai di gridare."* (You have but a short time to live.) The next day, Giovanni Cassini passed along the house of Saverio and said to one of his companions: *"Questo è l'amico. Guardatelo bene!"* (This is our man. Have a good look at him.) Some weeks before the killing took place, one of Giovanni's uncles, who happened to be Saverio's godfather, had advised his co-parent to prepare for his son's emigration to save him from some ill fate. Some time after the murder, Giovanni confided to a local girl he had seduced that he had killed Saverio at the instigation of his family. These facts only became known during the Fascist trials. By then Giovanni had long since left for America. But shortly after the assassination of Saverio, Giovanni had been arrested by the local police who, after a careful investigation of the ambush site where Saverio was shot dead, found the hoof-marks of two horses and two mules belonging to Giovanni and three *mafiosi* from the Bisacquino area. The tracks of Giovanni's mare led to the *masserìa* of the Moli estate held in lease by the Cassinis. The marks of the other animals went in another direction where they were soon lost. The court, however, acquitted Giovanni and his companions for lack of evidence.

One objective of the present essay is to gain some under-standing of the conditions that promoted and actively en-couraged the use of physical violence in Western Sicily. From 1916 to 1966 no less than 39 homicides were reported in the territory of Genuardo. Two-thirds of these killings took place in the decades following both World Wars: 13 from 1916 through 1924 and another 13 in the period 1944–52. These figures are by no means exceptional for Sicily. Between 1918 and 1956, the nearby village of Godrano (population 1,400) witnessed 49 assassinations in a factional struggle that embroiled two patrinominal families; in the larger town of Corleone (population *circa* 14,000), 62 persons were killed in the 15 years following World War II.[17]

The recourse to violence and homicide in this area of large estates worked by a poverty-stricken peasantry is matched by the Tarascan community of Naranja in Michoa-cán, Mexico described by Paul Friedrich.[18] This pueblo of peasant cultivators—impoverished since the usurpation of most of its fertile land by Spanish entrepreneurs in the de-cades around 1900—registered a total of 77 political homi-cides between 1920 and 1956. Though there are important differences between Genuardo and Naranja, both communi-

17. In the province of Palermo as a whole, the yearly average rate of homicides, which amounted to 250 in the early 1920s, dropped to 50 in the mid-1950s. See Mori (1933:223); Pantaleone (1966: 221–22, 233); and Dolci (1963:311–15). See, however, Chapter VIII, note 19.

18. Friedrich's studies of *caciquismo* and his recent monograph on agrarian revolt provide valuable insights into the problem of homicide and the various mechanisms that channel physical vio-lence in Mexico which, "until at least the early 1950s, had the highest homicide rate in the Western Hemisphere" (1965:208).

ties show striking parallels. The similarities bear on a violent struggle for land geared to a flexible social framework in which links of bilateral kinship are supplemented by ties of ritual kinship and friendship. The most comprehensive social units in both areas are patrinominal families, called "political families" by Friedrich, involving several persons allied by marriage. The periphery of these loosely defined bilateral kin groups is made up by ritual kinsmen and friends. The most outstanding parallel, however, is the violent competition for control over land, which manifests a specific orientation towards death and an acceptance of the inevitability of homicide as a means of attaining particular goals. Violent death is a familiar and necessary part of both cultures. People often dicuss it. In particular cases, homicide is encouraged and justified. In both villages, indeed, people kill because as they say: "I had to do it. What else could I do?" In the previous chapter we have encountered this attitude among people like Luca and Matteo, who killed to avenge their kinsmen. Lopez shot dead the man who affronted him in public. However strongly we may feel about the killings described in this book, we should refrain from condemning or praising them out of hand. Likewise, we must resist the temptation to describe homicide in terms of social disorder, as has so often been done. These heteronomous evaluations are extraneous to social analysis and do not help us to understand the issue. The anthropologist or social historian who seeks an understanding of the regularities underlying homicide should avoid sharp moral dichotomies. Why did Giovanni Cassini kill Saverio Tortochetti? Was it only because of envy, or because his family ordered him to do it for vengeance? Let us first look at the larger network of *mafiosi* and at the patterns of conflict it generated to place these questions in their proper perspective.

COSCHE IN CONFLICT

In 1920, the *mafia* of Genuardo became involved in a serious conflict with the allied segments of the *cosche* of several neighboring towns. These feuds and the conditions that precipitated them illuminate the central theme of the present study: the connection between the extent of socially permitted, unlicensed physical violence in a society and its specific stage of State-formation.

At the time, members of the Cassini family constituted the inner core of the Genuardo *cosca* (see Diagram 10). Its outer shell comprised a dozen persons linked to the Cassinis through ties of marriage and friendship. Some of these rank and file were related by cognatic ties among themselves. The *cosca* embraced a total of 20 persons, three of whom lived in Bisacquino. Giuseppe Cassini had seven sons. The eldest, Alessandro, assumed leadership until his violent death made room for his younger brother, Giovanni, who in turn was succeeded by Ferdinando when he was forced to emigrate to America (as indeed, his brother Gioacchino had done in 1911 for similar reasons; see Chapter VI). Vincenzo was killed in World War I. By the end of the 1920s, all members of the Genuardo *cosca* were in jail, except for four of them who had been assassinated and another four who had managed to emigrate.

One afternoon in early May 1920, a *campiere* from Corleone named Cesare was shot; his body was found in a green wheatfield at the fringe of the Regalbate estate. It became clear that Cesare had been killed at the bordering Moli estate, and his corpse removed to Regalbate. The Cassinis and three *mafiosi* from Bisacquino were charged with this homicide, but they were acquitted for lack of evidence. Some days before he was killed, Cesare attended a dance feast at the house of the Cassinis. As one informant, then in her early twenties, recalled: "Cesare was a *bel giovane* [handsome, strapping lad]. He danced with little bells attached to his legs below the knee. He was a great success. Perhaps the Cassinis killed him out of jealousy. Who knows?" Another informant pointed out that Cesare was indeed a coming man. He was charged with the supervision of an estate located in the commune of Corleone adjoining the Moli estate held in lease by the Cassinis:

They knew each other well. They were all *picciotti schetti* [unmarried youngsters]. Hence the invitation for the party at Genuardo. Perhaps Cesare's behavior was a bit too presumptuous and might have offended the Cassinis. *Quando uno si sente troppo mafioso* . . . [When a man is overbearing . . . (he is heading for trouble).] In any case, a few days later the Cassinis invited Cesare for dinner at Moli. There, at their *masserìa*, they held a banquet. They had invited others as well so as not to raise any suspicion. They were particularly kind to Cesare. *Mafiosi* always are, especially when they are going to kill somebody. Perhaps Cesare lacked experience to see the trap they laid for him. Whether or not he sensed that he was in danger of losing his life, one can never know. At any rate, when he left they secretly followed him and shot him. People said that it was Alessandro who killed him, just to show that he was the boss in that area. They took him on a mule to the *feudo* Regalbate to cover up. But it was found out that Cesare had been killed elsewhere, for on his clothes were traces of sandy soil of the Moli *feudo*.

This homicide triggered off enmity, which subsequently developed into a feud between the Genuardo *cosca* and *mafiosi* from Adernò, Bisacquino, and Corleone who felt challenged by this display of dominance. We should remember that several of these *mafiosi* were supervisors on the Baronessa estate. Hence they resented any change in the local power balance that might threaten access to the estates in their custody.

One year later, on the night of May 14, 1921, four armed men intruded into the *masserìa* of Moli. After they tied the hands of Simone Cassini and three shepherds, they stole the entire herd of two mares, three mules, 190 sheep, 87 goats, and some cash all together amounting to about 52,000 *Lire*. One mare, two mules, six goats, and 53 sheep belonged to the shepherds; the other animals were the property of the *gabelloto* Cassini. The rustlers were not identified. In the late afternoon of June 22, 1921, Vittorio, a *campiere* from Corleone, was killed in the neighborhood of the Moli estate.

Nothing could be ascertained about the authors of this murder.

At about three o'clock in the afternoon on July 1, Alessandro Cassini was killed along the mule track that led from the Moli estate to the village of Genuardo. Witnesses claimed to see four armed and mounted men who came from the direction of the Baronessa estates. Alessandro, who had set out from Moli shortly after two, approached from the opposite direction. At some distance, the four men stopped their horses, and one of them is reported to have said: *"Così si fa. Non di dietro!"* (This is the way it's done, not from behind!) —referring to the way Alessandro had ambushed Cesare. Then two shots were heard whereupon the four men quickly made their way back in the direction of Bisacquino. Subsequent investigations revealed that three of them were *campieri* at the Baronessa estates and members of the Adernò *cosca*. The fourth man was never identified. A squadron of four *Carabinieri* scouting the area did not find these *campieri* at their estates.

Later on, Alessandro's father Giuseppe mentioned that the rustling and the murder of his son were connected. The theft had been carried out for political reasons. The Cassinis supported the candidacy of the parliamentary deputies of the Liberal Party (*Partito Liberale*) Lo Monte and Finocchiaro. When the rustlers tied up Simone and the three shepherds they remarked sardonically: *"Domani sono le elezioni, eh?"* (Tomorrow [May 15] are the elections, eh?) Giuseppe added that he had addressed himself to the *campiere* Vittorio to recover his animals. A few days later, this man told him that the theft had been organized by Edoardo Cofano and other *mafiosi* from Adernò. Vittorio suggested that Alessandro should discuss the matter with the rustlers themselves. Alessandro then talked with Vittorio and afterwards with the others in Adernò. He learned that it would be very difficult to get the animals released. The *mafiosi* from Adernò made Alessandro understand that the animals had been rustled to discourage the Cassinis from taking part in the election campaign. As for the assassination of Vittorio, Alessandro explained to his father that this killing had been decided and carried out by members of the Adernò *cosca* because of his (Vittorio's) insistent attempts to recover the stolen herd. On June 30, one day before he met his death, Alessandro told his father that he had an appointment *cogli amici* (with his "friends") at the market of Bisacquino, and asked him for money to buy some gifts for the man who was supposed to return the animals to him. On his way to the market, however, Alessandro was killed by the very "friends" with whom he had made the appointment. During the trial, Alessandro's father explained that Edoardo Cofano and his companions sustained the candidacy of the deputy Ippolita Vassallo (see Diagram 2), the owner of Baronessa, and that the theft was organized to draw him away from the campaign. The court acquitted Edoardo and his friends for lack of evidence.

The next year, on the night of November 5, 1922, two pistol-shots put an end to the life of Bernardo—Giuseppe Cassini's sister's husband. Bernardo was killed near his house at Bisacquino. For some time, Bernardo had feared for his life. He did not leave his house after sunset and occasionally even slept elsewhere. During the parliamentary elections, Bernardo had supported the Liberal deputy Lo Monte, while Edoardo and the Adernò *cosca* had relentlessly sustained Vassallo, of the *Partito Popolare*.[19] Just before the elections, Edoardo appeared at Bisacquino together with his henchmen and enjoined the electorate to vote for Vassallo. Some people including Bernardo, however, answered that they were committed to Lo Monte. The enraged Edoardo snapped in a loud voice: "*Chi non è per me è contro di me!*" (He who is not for me is against me.) In Genuardo, Edoardo made a

---

19. As a young boy in 1919, one of Giuseppe Livornese's sons listened to a conversation in the mansion of Baronessa between his father, then steward, the estate owner Vassallo, and the *campiere* Edoardo Cofano. The three men discussed the canvassing of votes in the area, and Vassallo asked Livornese and Edoardo to have "their" people vote for the *Partito Popolare*, the Catholic mass party founded after World War I. Staunch atheists, Edoardo and Giuseppe vented their anti-clerical feelings, deriding "the party of the priests" that could not bring or lead to any good. They consented, however, to campaign on behalf of their patron.

similar appearance on Vassallo's behalf. Giuseppe Cassini vigorously refused to give his vote to Vassallo, whereupon Edoardo said: "*Se ne parlerà!*" (We will see.)

In Bernardo's house, the police found and sequestered a letter in which Bernardo, in anticipation of his death, identified his executioners. Bernardo named the leaders of four *cosche* along with several followers. The *Sezione di Accusa* (Grand Jury), however, in a verdict of March 9, 1925, declared itself unable to proceed since the authors of the murder of Bernardo remained unknown.

Because of renewed investigations undertaken by the Fascists in 1927, a new indictment was brought against the same set of *mafiosi* for their alleged involvement in the rustling and the killings. Of particular interest in this respect is Bernardo's letter[20] in which he specified those who threatened him:

> If I shall have trouble, my persecutors those who let [other people] take the mares, while now they have commissioned to kill me are: Giuseppe Battaglia from Corleone. I have done much for him and he owes me money since 1891 and 1892 and he has never given it to me. I have even a bill on the Balatelle affair. I have paid many sums of money and to get me out of his eyes, he made me do all those things and let me get murdered in cooperation with his *compare* Vito Cascio Ferro, Pietro Scialabbra, the *campiere* of the famous Margiotta from Burgio, and also from Burgio Baiamonte, the brothers of the archpriest, and other friends of him, and the Adernesi Edoardo Cofano, Ginnetto and all the malefactors of Adernò together with all these towns in the neighborhood, these terrible *signori*, all these things they have told me and a friend of mine said to me that they conspired against me. They had a meeting at Palermo and then at Corleone in March and again at Corleone in April to eliminate me. What have I done against them? Am I a traitor? You jury-

20. In translation I have tried to convey the rough, semi-literate, passionate tenor of the letter. Pseudonyms have been inserted where necessary.

men if you release all these malefactors, one day God and the Blessed Virgin Mary have to curse you as also all the lawyers and who protects them, especially the deputy Ippolita Vassallo, who practices the Catholic and protects all the malefactors. His followers kill anyone, steal all days and he, the villain, in order to be deputy, protects them. Vile rogue! Do not give him your vote, for he is a terrible assassin who protects in order to be a miserable deputy. Villain and infamous together and all his men—that in the beginning I have always worked with sweat on my brows.

God and his Holy Mother have to send you, jurymen and judges, many lightening in your heart if you release these malefactors. Permit to be told to you by the gentleman Vito Cascio Ferro why his friend Grisafi wanted to kill him, and how there came other persons to stop him from it. Other friends who had committed a murder came here in Bisacquino to hide themselves and they were sent away not rudely but gently and with honeyed words telling them that it was not fair to kill and many other things. But you rotter are alive in order to conspire against me and let a father of a family be killed. Villain! You and all the others, especially your *compare* Battaglia. That is the good done to all by you. If you release them, God will harm you and your family as far as the seventh generation. Cursed by God will be all of you. I hope that God will have mercy on me and that he will forgive me.

I have many things to write, but I cannot write them all down because I am not well, thinking about my family and my children and all this without doing anything.

And you, who represent the law, if you don't administer justice God will administer justice upon you, and if you protect them, you will be more assassins and dishonored than they are. I am speaking with frankness about these things, and about my spontaneous wish my family does not know anything. I have done so because I have always been a good man and I have been a friend of all that canaille for fear. I have been good to all of them, and now they are going to reward me by eliminating me from their midst. Do not release this canaille, because tomorrow they will commit things which are worse than those they usually do.

Bernardo's son testified that his father knew who had been singled out to kill him and who would assist. The accuracy of Bernardo's misgivings were verified after the assassination when his son learned the details. Bernardo was killed by Giuseppe (*Don* Pippineddu) Damati, a man we have met in connection with the tribute *mafiosi* levied on the peasants who tilled the fields of Coda di Volpe (see pp. 154–56). In this way Giuseppe obtained the *campierato* of Regalbate. Giuseppe, who was forced to emigrate the following year on account of this killing, was assisted in this murder by his brother, also *campiere*, another kinsman, and two additional *mafiosi* from Bisacquino, one of whom was married to a daughter of Edoardo Cofano from Adernò. Bernardo had been eliminated because of a longstanding dispute that originated as follows.

In 1914, Bernardo entered into a partnership with Battaglia, *capo-mafia* of Corleone, as well as with another man named Vincenzo, to pool resources to buy and subsequently sell in small shares at a profit the estate of Balatelle, located in the commune of Corleone, and belonging to the Passatempo heirs living in Palermo. Bernardo anticipated some of the expenses, but afterwards the affair failed because of the outbreak of the war. In 1920, Bernardo entered into a new partnership with two *gabelloti* and succeeded in selling the share of one of the heirs, Elvira Passatempo, deducting a profit of about 40,000 *Lire*. Before drawing up the contract, Bernardo wrote to Battaglia and invited him to pay his share of 14,000 *Lire*. Battaglia, however, did not answer the letter. The following year, Bernardo sought to acquire another share of the same estate also belonging to Elvira Passatempo. He was preferred above the others who had presented themselves, among whom were the two *gabelloti* mentioned, Cascio Ferro, and some *mafiosi* from Burgio—the arch-priest Baiamonte and his brothers. In order to sell this share in small holdings, Bernardo entered into a partnership with his lawyer and the owner. Cascio Ferro sought to wreck the deal by frightening off prospective buyers. This was made clear in a letter Bernardo received from his lawyer.

Sometime before the elections in May 1921, Bernardo's brother-in-law, Giuseppe Cassini, was arrested together with all his adult sons. Bernardo made a great effort to get them released. He first made his way to the house of the deputy Vassallo at Palermo. He was not received. Then Bernardo called on the deputy to Lo Monte, who succeeded in getting Giuseppe and one of his younger sons out of jail just before the elections. This was why the Cassinis and Bernardo campaigned for Lo Monte. In the club of the *civili* at Bisacquino, Cascio Ferro was known to have received 25,000 *Lire* from the deputy Zito. Bernardo subsequently repeated this allegation, and he added that Cascio Ferro *aveva mangiato* (spent it). There ensued an incident between both men. The evening preceding the elections, Edoardo Cofano, together with a number of his supporters and Baronessa employees of the deputy Vassallo, went to Bisacquino. Edoardo entered the club of the *burgisi* and urged those present to vote for Vassallo. Edoardo also invited Bernardo's son to vote for this candidate. He answered that he was always *Popolare*. Edoardo then remarked scornfully: *"Ma papà suo no, ma papà suo no!"* (But not so your father.) Apparently, Edoardo had already addressed himself to Bernardo and Giuseppe Cassini, and had learned that they were committed to the Liberal Party candidate, Lo Monte. Meanwhile on the *piazza*, Emanuele Ginnetto tried to enjoin Bernardo to vote for the *Popolari* by uttering threats. The frightened Bernardo then refrained from participation in the electoral struggle.

When the Cassinis' animals were rustled that very night, and Alessandro was assassinated a month later, Bernardo became still more worried. He asked for a gun license. Edoardo absconded because of the accusations of Giuseppe Cassini. Indirectly, he tried to induce Bernardo to make Giuseppe refrain from mentioning the Adernesi as being involved in the killing of Alessandro, but Bernardo bluntly refused. Then the warrant for arrest against Edoardo was revoked, whereupon Bernardo grew even more frightened and let it be known that he was willing to intervene among his kinsmen in favor of the arrested Adernesi. Edoardo, however, answered with contempt: "*Sono fuori!*" (They have been released.) One night in early February 1922, three mares belonging to Bernardo were stolen from the pastures he held in lease. Shortly thereafter, one of Bernardo's daughters encountered two unknown armed men lying in wait near the family country house. They asked for her father. When the girl told them she did not know his whereabouts, they went off. Bernardo then asked for a pistol license, specifying the reasons. He further addressed himself to *gli amici* from the various towns in the area and asked them to use their influence. Yet nothing was decided. Bernardo then applied to the deputy Lo Monte, who merely answered that the matter was very serious but had nothing to do with elections.

Finally, Bernardo addressed himself to the godson of a local judge who had been district judge at Corleone. A meeting was arranged in his house in Monreale near Palermo in which Battaglia and Bernardo participated. The Corleone chief complained about Bernardo's behavior in the Balatelle affair. Bernardo had offended Cascio Ferro and Baiamonte from Burgio by buying up the second share of this estate, even though he knew they had also made bids. As for the first share, acquired by Bernardo and the two *gabelloti*, Cascio Ferro and the others were disappointed at not having received any profit. Bernardo answered: "*E per cosi poco pensavate di ammazzare un padre di famiglia!*" (And for such small things you think it's necessary to kill a father of a family!) Retorted Battaglia: "*Tanti picca fanno assai!*" (Many small things make up much.) It was agreed that Bernardo would provide 5,000 *Lire* for the sale of the share of Balatelle, and Battaglia promised that he would settle things with Cascio Ferro and Edoardo Cofano. Later, Bernardo brought some of the money to Battaglia, in whose house in Corleone he met the sons of Cascio Ferro and Edoardo, who stayed with their godfather while they studied for their school examinations. Bernardo then paid the balance to Battaglia's son, guest at Cascio Ferro's house in Bisacquino. Cascio Ferro himself and the other *mafiosi* involved reassured Bernardo, and told him that he could leave the house without incurring any danger. Thus appeased, Bernardo did not suspect that the "friends" were preparing his elimination.[21]

Bernardo was shot twice by *Don* Pippineddu (Giuseppe), one of Cascio Ferro's right-hand men. His retreat was covered by other of Cascio Ferro and Edoardo Cofano's henchmen, themselves related by ties of kinship. *Don* Pippineddu's brother kept at bay Bernardo's son, who nonetheless succeeded in following the killer right after the two shots had been fired. He lost the trail when the fugitive reached the house of Edoardo's son-in-law, who lived at Bisacquino. Shortly after the killing, Bernardo's wife received an anonymous letter warning her to refrain from any action.

It was subsequently revealed that the three mares had been stolen from Bernardo to affront him, because he had spoken ill (*amatula*) of "certain Adernesi" whom he accused of murdering his nephew, Alessandro. This sequence of confrontations between the *cosca* of Genuardo and those of four neighboring towns that culminated in the death of Bernardo resulted in an enforced agreement through which the Cassinis accepted defeat. It was agreed that the Cassinis should pay a yearly tribute of 3,000 *Lire* to Edoardo, chief of the Adernò *cosca*. On this occasion, Giuseppe Cassini is reported to have said: *"Sono loro che tengono il coltello per il manico."* (They hold the knife by its handle.)

THE STRUCTURE OF VIOLENCE

Mafiosi go in for violent political–economic games. Whatever the specific goals of *mafiosi*, their operations should be understood in terms of the particular means used to attain any

21. As suggested before, *mafiosi* used to stress relations of friendship in order to accomplish a killing effectively without raising the suspicion of either the victim, public opinion, or the law. Cesare, Alessandro, and Bernardo were killed through this stratagem. Similar modes of intrigue prevailed in quite different societies. Writes R. F. Fortune in his book on the Dobuan Islanders of the Western Pacific: "False friendship is suspected. I heard from three different sources: If we wish to kill a man we approach him, we eat, drink, sleep, work, and rest with him, it may be for several moons, and we wait our time; we *kawagosiana*, call him friend" (1963:155).

goal: these means involved the use of physical force. To ask to what extent the use of violence by *mafiosi* was legitimate is beside the point. The term "legitimacy" is fraught with so many implications and value judgments that it may best be avoided. From the viewpoint of the State, *mafia* was a form of unlicensed violence. *Mafiosi* therefore differed fundamentally from policemen, soldiers, or any other agents publicly charged with the maintenance of law and order. However, and this is crucial for the whole argument sustained in the present study, formal authorities pragmatically accepted the "rule," that is, the power domains, of *mafiosi*. Though judicial proceedings were staged to appease certain sectors of public opinion when the law had been violated, most Sicilians realized that State sovereignty existed mainly on paper. For security and protection they had to rely on private power holders. In this regard, Franchetti, a Tuscan nobleman who wrote on the subject as early as 1876 after having studied it from close quarters, hit the mark when he stressed the patron–client relationships involving government officials, members of the landowning elite, and the "malefactors" as salient features of *mafia*.[22]

The use of violence and intimidation was part of the regional culture; the capacity to coerce with physical violence was valued in itself. Those who qualified for it commanded respect and were singled out as leaders. As mentioned before, *mafiosi* were referred to as *uomini rispettati* (respected men); their younger peers were designated as *bravi*.[23]

22. Cf. Franchetti (1925:128–40). The Italian term *manutengolismo* denotes a state of affairs in which "delinquents" are protected by local power holders or formal officials. The latter are designated as *manutengoli* (from *mano*, hand; and *tenire*, to hold). Franchetti's book and its companion volume written by Sonnino, which were first published in 1877, received strong criticism in certain Palermitan circles where these studies were considered as mere fiction (cf. Alongi 1887:9). Barrington Moore's remark, which serves as the motto of the present book, comes to mind: "Any simple straightforward truth about political institutions or events is bound to have polemical consequences."

23. In Italian the term *bravo* is used in two different but related

The way in which young *mafiosi* asserted themselves clearly illustrates the extent to which violence was linked with respect, and how it was indeed required to exact deference. Giuseppe Damati (*Don* Pippineddu), whom we met as one of Cascio Ferro's henchmen, was only 26 years old when he killed and replaced the much older and established Bernardo in November 1922. As we have seen in the Coda di Volpe affair (pp. 154–56), this assassination not only gained him control over land (a part of Regalbate) but also yielded

---

senses. As a noun its meaning ranges from a brave and valiant man to a (hired) assassin. Used as an adjective *bravo* means valorous, brave, bold, clever, and fearless. The terms *manutengolo* and *bravo* therefore refer to complementary roles: *Manutengolo*, he who favors thefts and frauds committed by others, and gives assistance or means of refuge to convicts. (*Chi tiene mano a furti e frodi altrui, e porge aiuto o modo di salvarsi ai rei.*) *Bravo*, bandit, criminal who took refuge with a powerful man to assure himself, by serving him, impunity and maintenance. (*Bandito, malvivente che si rifugiava presso un potente assicurandosi, col servirlo, impunità e sostentamento.*) Cf. Zingarelli, *Vocabolario della Lingua Italiana* (1965).

The term *rispetto* has similar connotations. As in the expression "a man who makes himself respected," the notion of respect implies deference based on the capacity and willingness to coerce with physical violence. Though the etymology of the term *mafia* is uncertain, we know that from the early 1860s onwards the term *mafioso* has been used to describe a man "able to make himself respected." Cf. Novacco (1959; 1964:192).

The anthropologist's concern with semantics is not otiose, since the specific meaning of words and the way they are used yield insights into social structure. The perception of violence is much to the point here. Most social scientists come from societies in which the use of physical force is monopolized by the State, and in which the claims of the State in these matters are widely accepted. This condition has often tended to bias our appreciation of violence in other societies. In his study *Revolutionary Change*, Chalmers Johnson exemplifies this when he argues that violence is a form of "anti-social action": ". . . we may define violence as action that deliberately or unintentionally disorients behavior of others. Violence is either behavior which is impossible for others to orient themselves to or behavior which is deliberately intended to prevent orientation and the development of stable expectations with regard to it" (1968:8).

him the honorific title of *Don* by which authoritative persons in Sicily were addressed and referred to. Likewise, the assassination of Andrea in Genuardo in 1919 and that of Cesare the following year were carried out by Alessandro Cassini to get his territorial claims recognized. In the village of Genuardo, these claims were not disputed: Andrea's father accepted defeat, and even complied with the action of the Cassinis by charging innocent persons. Cesare's violent death at Moli, however, antagonized other *mafiosi* in the area and precipitated a series of violent confrontations in the course of which Alessandro was killed. Animosities born of Bernardo's past dealings and the electoral conflict escalated the struggle. After accounts were settled with Alessandro, his brother Giovanni succeeded him as leader of the *cosca*. He took just three months to prove himself: in the early autumn of 1921, Saverio Tortochetti was liquidated, and this enhanced the position of the Cassinis in the village arena. As noted before, this was not a random assassination for there were longstanding hostilities between the Cassinis and the Tortochettis. Yet the fact that Giovanni had assumed leadership of the *cosca* and the circumstance that he was still very young (barely 21 years) and largely without a reputation for toughness did much to precipitate the killing. The domination of the Cassinis and that of the Genuardo *cosca* at large remained, however, strictly locally phrased. Its members had to yield control over large sections of the village territory to *mafiosi* from other towns.

The recourse to violence prevalent in this part of Sicily and expressed in theft, extortion, ransom, arson, shooting, and homicide was taken for granted and accepted rather than questioned. The use of violence was encouraged and justified, though people were never aimlessly harmed or killed: violence was prescribed in those situations where people sought to get their claims to honor and power ultimately recognized. Similar attitudes prevailed and still prevail in other societies. When dealing with the problem of violence and physical destruction among the Sarakatsan shepherds who live in a mountainous redoubt north of Corinth, Greece,

Campbell observes that "there is no more conclusive way of showing that you are stronger than by taking away the other man's life" (1964:318). Campbell shows how the concern with violence among these shepherds is related to three basic features of the social structure of Sarakatsan society: (1) the complementary opposition of the sexes; (2) the solidarity of the family; and (3) the rivalry between unrelated families. Friedrich, to whose work I have already referred, tries to account for Tarascan homicide by relating it to attitudes toward death and the competition for control over land:

> Neither police laxity, nor communal autonomy, nor the ethics of kinship can fully account for the perennial recourse to homicide. Homicide has continued and will continue to erupt mainly because of the competition for the control over land. . . . Political violence, in any case, is causally linked to the peasants' ultimate life symbol: *la tierra* (1965:206).
>
> Violent agrarianism in the Zacapu valley is related to Tarascan and Mexican peasant attitudes toward death. The child is exposed to mortality early, and a consciousness of death is pieced together from personal, concrete experiences. The adolescent listens with interest to the cases of village homicide, a customary way of settling adultery, land disputes, and other kinds of conflict. Death is a familiar and necessary part in the cycle of things. . . . Patterns of local violence were reticulated with Tarascan and Mexican attitudes toward the inevitability and irony of death . . . (1970:76, 139).

Both Campbell and Friedrich attempt to explain the prevalence of violence in terms of the local culture. Though this is an important and even necessary step toward an understanding of the phenomenon of overt violence, the analysis can and should be pushed further. It is one thing to single out the aspects and the context of the use of violence, but quite another to account for their interrelations. Specific attitudes toward death do not explain high rates of homicide. Nor do conflict over land, *machismo*, rivalry between unrelated families, and family solidarity account for the recourse to violence. Both Campbell and Friedrich evade asking why in the particular local settings they investigated these cultural features (high rate of homicide, resigned attitude towards death, struggle for land, etc.) show coherence.[24] To explain these patterns, we should look beyond the level of local culture, and ask how these communities were related to the larger society. "Police laxity" and "communal autonomy" tell us something about the extent to which the use of physical force was organized and monopolized by the State. In western Sicily, as well as among the Sarakatsani and in the Tarascan communities, the State failed to monopolize the use of physical violence and had to yield its sovereignty to local power holders. Without taking into account this obvious yet crucial dimension, we can never understand why Bernardo accepted his fate as inevitable, and even found time to express his resignation in a letter. This letter, moreover, illustrates his strong ambivalence toward State institutions and officials: though Bernardo addressed himself to those who administered justice, he expected punishment of those involved (including the judges themselves) only from supernatural forces. Such attitudes toward death, the use of private violence, conflict over land, and family rivalries can be understood as interrelated aspects of one and the same configuration, characterized by a weak development of stable, central, impersonal control over the means of violence. This development influences human interdependencies, most notably the overt level of socially permitted physical force between individuals as well as their prevalent attitudes and sentiments regarding violence and death.[25]

24. For a recent and rather unsuccessful attempt to understand the use of violence in terms of a distinct subculture, see Wolfgang and Ferracuti (1967:esp. 158–63). All such arguments in terms of values and subcultures alone are innately circular, and thus beg the very question they propose to answer.

25. See Elias' theoretical model of civilizing processes (1969, 1972), according to which, one may expect "that state formation and conscience formation, the level of socially permitted physical violence and the threshold of repugnance against using it or witnessing it, will differ in specific ways at different stages in the

A second important element emerging from the description of conflicts between these local *cosche*—related to the theme of violence and striking close to the heart of the present study—concerns the role of *mafiosi* as brokers or middlemen. With the penetration of the State and the market into the Sicilian hinterland in the course of the 19th and 20th centuries, *mafiosi* succeeded in dominating the paths linking the local community to the outside world. By assuming positions of supervision and management, they controlled the large estates of absentee landlords, and this granted them control over the local peasants who depended upon the land for their living. The struggles between *mafiosi* disclose how virtually all of them controlled large estates as *gabelloti* and *campieri*. When an estate came up for sale, as in the Balatelle affair, *mafiosi* inserted themselves as brokers and formed partnerships in order to acquire the land and then sell it to the peasants at a considerable profit. In return for access to the land, the peasants provided *mafiosi* with periodic electoral support for national deputies, most of whom were owners of the estates managed and supervised by the *mafiosi* power brokers. *Mafiosi* thus acted as links between the candidate and the electorate. This patron–broker–client network extended with the growth of peasant voters and reached its full strength after the World War I when the entire male peasantry was enfranchised. The critical leverage of the *mafioso* over peasant votes was appreciated by his urban patron, who protected him against the demands of the law, covering up his illegal dealings with a cloak of immunity. We have seen how such patrons intervened on behalf of the

---

development of societies" (1971:95). Lawrence Stone's magisterial study of the crisis of the English Aristocracy demonstrates these interconnections very clearly, most specifically in his discussion of the Tudors' concerted efforts to strip the nobles of their independent means of violence (retainers, client gentry, fortifications, etc.) which, after a long and sanguinary struggle, succeeded in forcibly promoting the development of elite civility. Deprived of the capacity to wage intramural violence, nobles resorted to bouts of litigation, safely confined within the juridical institutions of the State (1965: esp. Ch. V).

Cassinis and members of the Adernò *cosca,* whom they succeeded in getting released from jail.

Relations between patrons and clients cannot be built up
in a moment, but must grow over time and be tested in a
number of contexts. They include multiple aspects of the
persons involved.[26] Before Edoardo became prominent at
Baronessa, his father had been employed for several years
as a domestic in the Vassallo family in Palermo, and it was
during this period that "confidence" was built up. Apparently, only segmented single-interests (*viz.,* electoral) were
involved in the relationship between Bernardo and the
deputy Lo Monte. This circumstance and the fact that Bernardo was rapidly losing power in his home area may
explain why Lo Monte let him down at a critical moment. As
we will see in the next section, there are specific circumstances pertaining to the development of the larger society
that may even lead to the severance of intimate and long-
standing bonds between patrons and clients.

A basic pattern of patron–client relationships was thus replicated on different levels of organization and in various
institutional contexts. Looking outward from the village,
mafiosi had exclusive and direct access to the larger society
since they successfully controlled the economic and political
positions linking the village to the outside. In fact, the network of *mafiosi* provided the main effective organizational
framework that covered the middle ground between the local
and national levels. They controlled the land whose owners
lived elsewhere; they dominated the markets and auctions;
they alone were able to grant effective protection in the
countryside; and they "fixed" elections. Characteristically,
however, *mafiosi* often exercised these functions of brokerage
without seeking formal office themselves. In this connection
it has been argued that the power and flexibility of brokers or
middlemen can often be maximized by acting informally:
"... it is often obviously disadvantageous to accept formal,
overt, and institutionalized statuses when one's essential job

26. In his discussion on peasant coalitions, Wolf defines the patron–
    client bond as a manystranded, dyadic, and vertical coalition
    (1966b:86–87). See also Wolf (1966a:16–17).

or game is to interrelate neighborhoods, factions, communities, clans, and party segments that are characterized by serious and logically irreconcilable discontinuities and hostilities" (Friedrich 1968a:203). With the notable exception of the arch-priest Baiamonte (nicknamed *il Santone*), who together with his three brothers formed the core of the Burgio *cosca*, the *mafiosi* discussed above did not assume formal offices such as those of parliamentary deputy, mayor, judge, lawyer, notary, teacher, priest, tax-collector, or policeman. Rather than occupying these offices themselves, *mafiosi* controlled access to or wielded influence over these junctures that tied the village to the encompassing society. *Mafiosi* helped to shape these relations and in some cases even determined the operation of these offices. As brokers of a violent type, *mafiosi* were poised between the peasants (from whose ranks they sprang) and the State, and succeeded in maintaining a grip on the tensions between what have been called the "Little Tradition" and the "Great Tradition."

A third salient feature of the *mafia* network in this area has been kinship. Bonds between cognatic kin, especially those between siblings, proved very powerful devices in the operations discussed above. In fact, the cores of the various *cosche* were chiefly structured by these relationships. Again, it is important to note that these relationships were to a marked degree optative. Many of the idioms, codes, and functions of these relations were extended to the spheres of affinal and ritual kinship, friendship, and patronage which supplemented the highly particularistic precincts of distinct segments of cognates.

Though much of anthropology has been primarily concerned with kinship studies, the relative importance of kinship *per se* is often taken for granted. Only rarely are we told why, in particular societies, kinship rather than some other principle of organization structures human relationships in pervasive ways. Nor have anthropologists dwelt at length on the conditions that may explain how and why solidary kinship bonds have gradually lost their overriding importance in certain societies. The historian Marc Bloch has demonstrated for Medieval Europe how ties of kinship were tightened when public authority became weak, while the development of the institutions of the sovereign State contributed to a gradual weakening of the kinship bond (1961: 123–42). When neither the State nor kinsmen could provide adequate protection, men were obliged to seek or to accept other ties:

> ... the weak man felt the need to be sheltered by someone more powerful. The powerful man, in his turn, could not maintain his prestige or his fortune or even ensure his own safety except by securing for himself, by persuasion or coercion, the support of subordinates bound to his service. On the one hand, there was the urgent quest for a protector; on the other, there were usurpations of authority, often by violent means. And as notions of weakness and strength are always relative, in many cases the same man occupied a dual rôle—as a dependant of a more powerful man and as a protector of humbler ones. Thus there began to be built up a vast system of personal relationships whose intersecting threads ran from one level of the social structure to another (1961:148).

Bloch shows how these patron–client relationships (bonds between lords and vassals) were patterned on kinship relations, both in terms of mutual obligations and sentiments. "In relation to the lord," writes Bloch, "the vassal long remained a sort of supplementary relative, his duties as well as his rights being the same as those of relatives by blood" (1961:224). These structural features were reflected in a terminology that did not distinguish sharply between ties of kinship, friendship, and vassalage. In some areas, the term "friend" (*ami, Freund*) was used to denote a kinsman as well as a vassal.[27]

To appreciate, therefore, the predominance of bonds of kinship, (as well as their substitutes, and complements of ritual kinship, friendship, and patronage) among *mafiosi* and in west Sicilian peasant society, we must look at the stage of

27. Bloch (1961:123–24, 231). See also Boissevain (1966a:30–32); Wolf (1966a:9–10); and Blok (1969b).

development of the larger society—especially at the protective capacity of the State. Bernardo's case clearly demonstrates what happens to a man when public law cannot guarantee protection and when there are neither kinsmen nor friends to whom he can look for help.

The conflicts between the Genuardo *cosca* and those of the surrounding villages and towns were only partly structured along generational lines. Here it was not just younger *mafiosi* who fought older ones. The *bravi* or *picciotti*, who did the killings, were between 20 and 30 years old. Though they operated against older, more established *mafiosi* whom they sought to replace, they killed under the aegis of their leaders, who were often twice their age. Cascio Ferro was in his sixties at the time; his *compare*, Battaglia, was approaching 80.

The killing of rivals was the main way of asserting oneself, not only because of the office which thus became vacant, but also to prove that one was able to make oneself respected. The capacity to generate fear was a necessary qualification of young *mafiosi*. They had to build up a reputation for violence to assume the intermediate position of broker between landlord and peasant. As mentioned before, tensions between landowners and peasants had grown in the immediate postwar years when agrarian reform was discussed but not implemented. To cope with peasant restiveness, to safeguard their estates, and to control elections at the village level, estate owners increasingly had to rely on local strongmen. The leverage thus granted to *mafiosi* soon became an embarrassment to the estate owners. As we saw in the Balatelle affair, *mafiosi* controlled the sale of this estate by intimidating and thus preventing prospective buyers from taking part in the auction. As for management and supervision of large estates, the tough rather than the high bidder was favored. Young and aspiring *mafiosi* were eager to see rivals cut a poor figure (*mala figura*) in front of the estate owner. They committed *sfregi* (affronts) by stealing animals, which thus questioned the reputation for violence of the man in charge. The owner would then dismiss the man and

employ a tougher *campiere*.[28] We have seen this happen
in 1914 when Edoardo succeeded in replacing the Jaconis
at Baronessa (see Chapter VI). Competition between *mafiosi*
exacerbated after the war, and their "protection" became
ever more burdensome for the estate owners, who could not
but give in to the demands of *mafiosi*, who, according to one
observer, "extended their high-handed and oppressive treatment even to landowners. . . . They started by systematically
withholding payment of their rent either in money or kind,
and they often finished by forcing landowners to sell off land
at ridiculously low prices" (Pantaleone 1966:43).

Looking back on this troubled period, one informant remarked: "*Chiddi ricchi cadero, e li rugnusi acchianaru.*" (The
rich fell, and the scrofulous ascended.) The changed power
balance in the countryside, and the fact that estate owners
were losing control of parliament where socialist and reformist Catholics proposed radical change of the *latifondo* structure, induced the large estate owners to support the Fascists
in the elections of 1924 (Mack Smith 1968a:506, 508). With
the consolidation of the Fascist regime, involving the abolition of the electoral system and the nationalization of the
Fascist militia, *mafiosi* as local strongmen were deprived of
their *raison d'être*. Those who did not change sides found
themselves increasingly isolated from both landlords and
peasants, whose interrelations were redefined in terms of
enforced centralization. Where the Fascist State guaranteed
vested landed interests and established effective security in
the countryside, *mafiosi* were rendered obsolete. This state
of affairs helped the Fascists to deliver a severe blow to *mafia*.
Successful operations against *mafia* were thus rendered
possible and, furthermore, would enhance the prestige of
the new regime.

THE ROUNDUP

In early 1926, Prefect Mori was given extraordinary powers

28. The standard phrase *Levati di ddocu chi mi ci mettu iu!* (Move
aside, I am replacing you). suggests the extent to which this
procedure was institutionalized.

in Sicily to repress *mafia* and banditry. He created an inter-provincial police force, an autonomous and highly mobile instrument directly under his personal control and not re-strained by considerations of provincial jurisdiction. "My specific function," wrote Mori in his memoirs, "was to co-ordinate and direct the activities intended to protect public safety in Sicily towards a single end. My powers were those of the common law, with the additional authorization to make applicable all over the island the ordinances I had issued as Prefect of Palermo" (1933:161). One of these ordinances regarded the lease and supervision of large estates, the control over *campieri*, waggoners, and herds-men, and the branding of animals. The local authori-ties issued identification cards and restricted the licensing of firearms. Transfer of animals was registered on title-deeds (*bollete*). These regulations aimed at providing the police with more effective means of operation.[29]

In conjunction with the local police forces, the interpro-vincial police service directed personally by Mori collected evidence regarding people to whom injured persons and witnesses had attributed responsibility for crimes over the past ten years or so—crimes that had remained unpunished. To avoid sending suspects into hiding, "action had to be taken suddenly, aggressively and simultaneously at different and distant points over well-defined districts and set in motion from without.... [T]he district, however large it might be, was invested in a single night by a force that had been cautiously concentrated on the spot at the opportune moment" (Mori 1933:184). All persons under suspicion were arrested *en masse*. We have seen before how the formulation of the offense of "association for criminal purposes" facili-tated these operations. After the interrogations, which nearly always involved brutal means,[30] convicts were handed over to the judicial authorities. Mori conducted these operations all over western Sicily, and it took him two years to complete

29. For details of these ordinances, see Mori (1933:234–40).
30. Confessions were often extracted after long sessions of torture. See Pantaleone (1966:49–50); Maxwell (1959:217–18).

them. In this way hundreds and hundreds of *mafiosi* were rounded up, tried, and imprisoned for many years.

What kind of persons did the Fascist regime settle accounts with, and who remained beyond its clutches? It has been argued that mainly minor and middle range *mafiosi* fell into Mori's web: people who were actually involved in the use of violence, the *campiere* and *gabelloti*, as well as their immediate satellites. Their patrons—the large estate owners and deputies—either actively or passively facilitated their demise by accepting Fascism as a more appropriate and much less burdensome means of defending their large estates. What happened in the area of Genuardo in this period confirms this point of view, not to mention Mori's public statement in which he explicitly referred to the large estate owners in whose interests the State was operating. In his address on May 16, 1926 to 1,300 *campieri* who had sided with the regime, and who had gathered for the occasion near Roccapalumba, located in the western interior, Mori said that

> it was easy to understand why in the past, seeing the insufficiency of State power, the owners of landed property had had to look for *campieri* in the Mafia and to submit to receiving orders from the Mafia as to whom they should employ, but that now that the State was vigilant, present and operating, it must never happen again. . . . [T]he *campiere* would keep his traditional figure and function . . . (1933:193–94).

Earlier that month, on May 1, Mori arrived with some of his men in Genuardo for the preliminaries of the arrests. He was received by the local Fascist authorities, among whom were the estate owner Mirabella and exponents of the Jaconis. They organized a public meeting in which Mori addressed himself to the people in his usual magniloquent style. People still recall his words: *"Io mi chiamo Mori e farò morire! La delinquenza deve scomparire come scomparisce questa polvere che porta via il vento."* (My name is Mori and I shall have people killed. Delinquency must disappear just as this dust disappears which is carried off by the wind [the *scirocco* which blew at that moment across the *piazza*].) Then Mori lionized two local peasants who had recently hunted down cattle thieves. They were awarded medals to underscore the type of behavior that was now expected and encouraged. After this public meeting, Mori was invited to dinner at the barracks of the local *Carabinieri*, According to one informant, some *mafiosi* served the guests at table "with their tails between their legs." They had indeed good reasons to be scared: after a week, on May 9, Mori returned to Genuardo at night, accompanied by a strong police force. They broke into the houses of those against whom evidence had been collected. On Mori's list were 35 local names, including 11 of the Cassinis; ten peasant smallholders (*burgisi*); four shepherds; two *campieri*; two artisans; one waggoner; two day laborers; and one butcher. Apart from these 33 men, the list included the names of two women: that of Giuseppe Cassini's wife (the "terrible woman") and a friend of hers, the mother of a local *mafioso*. Those actually arrested numbered 27, since three men had died while five others had managed to escape overseas. After some time, three of those arrested were released for lack of evidence; the others were imprisoned to await trial. The operation in Genuardo took place in conjunction with roundups in the neighboring towns and villages of Bisacquino, Adernò, Corleone, Fioravante, and Burgio in which well over 150 persons were arrested who, together with those of Genuardo, were held to constitute one single "association for criminal purposes," charged with no less than 22 homicides and scores of cattle rustlings.[31]

31. For a brief survey of the roundups, see D'Alessandro (1959: 109–17). Mori justified these drastic measures as follows: "Much has been said about these police operations, and in particular there has been a good deal of exaggeration as to the number of arrests. Of course, three hundred, four hundred or five hundred arrests must make a certain impression: but two things must be borne in mind. In the first place, that each operation covered four, five or sometimes more villages at the same time; and in the second place, that they were the result of a long period of criminal activity. Three hundred arrests carried out in all in five villages each of five thousand persons, for crimes committed in the course of ten years, does not really represent anything abnormal. The

Cascio Ferro was also arrested. One of his godchildren tried to get him released, and addressed himself to the estate owner Adriano Mirabella, who told him that he could not do anything for him since the times were different now: *"l'época è cambiata."* Edoardo, the chief of the Adernò *cosca*, had escaped abroad before the roundups. From the various testimonies of non-*mafiosi* estate employees during the trials it seems clear that *latifondisti* helped provide evidence against their former henchmen. They made it appear that they could not but accept the impositions of *mafiosi*, and obscured the fact that the *mafiosi* who now faced trial had been their main tools in safeguarding the large estates vis-à-vis the peasants. Thus the patrons or *manutengoli* emerged unscathed. It could not be otherwise, for the large estate owners were the main partners of a deal with the Fascist government in which *mafia* was replaced by new and less expensive forms of defense of the *latifondo*. Apparently, Mori did not quite understand the significance of his actions in this larger context. When he began to extend his investigations and denunciations to members of the Palermitan aristocracy, the regime dismissed him. Fascism thus settled accounts with *mafia* by providing a substitute: it monopolized the use of violence without fundamentally changing the social milieu in which *mafia* had flourished. When the Sicilian *latifondisti* sided with the Fascist regime and became one of its main exponents on the island, they no longer needed the compromise of *mafia* to cope with the landless and restive peasant mass.[32] The tensions between landlords and peasants, between what we have called national and

---

abnormality was simply to be found in the impunity which had lasted ten years" (1933:185).

32. With the rural retainers gone, the crucial task of controlling class tensions fell upon the regime. Rural discontent was largely soaked up through the recruitment of landless peasants into the police and the army (particularly for overseas adventures). It is obvious, moreover, that much of the present-day nostalgia of the landowning peasants for Fascism can be traced to the connection between a strong State organization and the security of private property in capitalist societies. Both points deserve further study.

community-oriented groups, were effectively controlled under the Fascist dictatorship. The relationships the Fascist State established with the local populations were exclusive: they ruled out any rival power structures, either of peasants or *mafiosi*. Thus the late 1920s marked the decline of *mafia*. We must expect the re-emergence of violent brokers with the collapse of Fascism. This development was foreseen as early as 1926 by Grieco, a Party colleague of Gramsci, who noted that

> The immediate postwar years have widened the bases of the rural *mafia* of peasant origin, especially in connection with the restrictions on emigration. This mass has opposed Fascism which—through its program of the conquest of Sicily—presented itself as the substitution of the old by new leaders on the local, regional, and national level. Since the Sicilian agrarian system remains unimpaired, Fascism represents the substitution of the *mafia* through a new organizational form of defense of the large landed estates. The struggle which Fascism conducted against the *mafia* in Sicily, with police measures, strikes the lower ranks of the *mafia*, but not its chiefs who are closely related to feudal forms and who cannot be overcome if not together with these forms, except through the revolution of the Sicilian peasants (1964:601).

During the period from 1927 to 1943, relative security prevailed in the countryside. Some of the older *mafiosi* died in prison, including Giuseppe Cassini and Vito Cascio Ferro. Those who returned in the course of the 1930s had to accept humble roles in village affairs. Together with his brother Melchiore, who had been arrested but was released shortly afterwards for lack of evidence, Simone Cassini worked on road construction. An incident that took place in Genuardo at the end of 1934 may illustrate the atmosphere in the village under Fascism. At that time Simone, who was back from prison, started to haunt his cousin Ignazio (see Diagram 10) who, though involved in a serious crime together with Simone and others, had not been arrested. Simone told Ignazio of his sufferings and humiliations in prison, about the interrogations and the terrible things they had done to people to extract confessions. Simone dragged up Ignazio's part in a killing a decade before, for which only *mafiosi* from Burgio had been tried.

In May 1924, a young man called Silvio from Burgio was killed in one of the outlying *feudi* along the northwestern border of the Genuardo commune. At the time he was employed by a partnership of three *mafiosi* from Burgio who managed the estate. After some discord over a certain amount of money his employers refused to pay him, Silvio left and found employment on a neighboring estate. Silvio told his mother about these things, and explained the involvement of his former employers in homicides and large-scale cattle rustlings through which they had enriched themselves. They made part of a "terrible" association, together with persons from adjoining towns and villages, dedicated to the sale of stolen animals. Since Silvio had left nursing a grievance, the *mafiosi* were afraid he might reveal these things to the authorities. Silvio's mother understood this and tried to convince her son to leave the area. When she met one of her son's former employers in her hometown, she told him that if some accident might happen to her son, she would not refrain from action against him. Subsequently, Silvio was reproached by this man, who told him: "*Tu uomo sei che vai a riferire a tua madre le cose che succedono fra di noi?*" (Are you a true man telling your mother about the things that happen between us?) When cattle were stolen from Ignazio's sister's husband (see Diagram 7), Silvio presented himself to the Cassinis as a go-between and promised to get the animals back. When he failed, however, he was murdered. The *mafiosi* from Burgio were indicted and tried for this murder. Yet public opinion regarded the Cassinis as the authors, particularly Ignazio, who was said to have participated in the killing. Later, when his cousins were imprisoned under Fascism, Ignazio rented a small estate near the village and fared relatively well. Simone, reduced to poverty and humiliated, could not endure this and started to harass him. Time and again he hinted at the fate that might befall Ignazio should his involvement in Silvio's death

become known to the authorities. These continual sugges-
tions, during which Simone did not spare his cousin horrible
details of the treatment he and others had endured in prison,
frightened Ignazio and drove him to despair. One day in
January 1935, he took his pistol and killed himself.

The conclusion of this section must be that the Fascist
roundups dealt a severe blow to the local *cosche*. *Mafiosi* like
the Cassinis suffered a strong setback. Some of them succeeded in re-establishing themselves after the demise of the
regime. As we will see in the next chapter, moreover, scores
of new *mafiosi* sprang up to bridge and exploit the gaps in
communication between the local and the national level that
re-emerged in 1943. This rapid revival demonstrates that
Fascism had avoided coming to grips with Sicilian problems
by considering *mafia* merely in terms of "rural delinquency"
while leaving intact the organization of the large estates.
The resurgence of *mafiosi* quite naturally followed the collapse of the dictatorship.

VIII
Re-emergence, 1943 and After

In early July 1943, the Allies landed on Sicily's southern coast, and in the course of a few weeks the Fascist forces retreated to the mainland, leaving behind a power vacuum which the Allied Government (AMGOT)[1] was unable to fill from its own ranks. To maintain order, the Allies relied on the local men of influence—the exponents of landed interests which were largely left unimpaired under the reign of Mussolini. In their turn, the large estate owners had to look for local support to safeguard their land and property from attacks of a starving peasantry, who were the main victims of the black market of grain and foodstuffs that flourished on the terrible scarcity of those years. In various parts of Sicily as well as elsewhere in the South, peasants invaded and occupied large estates or simply took to the hills to form or join armed bands of outlaws. By the end of 1943, already thirty of these armed companies of discontented peasants and ex-soldiers were operating in the inland districts of the island. Several large landowners came to terms with these bands and employed them as private guards on their estates. Homicides and robberies rapidly increased. In the province of Palermo alone, the annual rate of homicide increased from 84 in 1943 to 245 in 1944; the number of robberies grew from 148 in 1943 to 646 in 1944. In most of the cases, those responsible remained unknown (see Gaja 1962:140–42; Di Matteo 1967:262). In October 1944, the new Italian government, which had succeeded AMGOT some months before, issued a decree authorizing the occupation of poorly cultivated estates by peasant cooperatives and regulating a more equit-

1. AMGOT, Allied Military Government of Occupied Territories.

able partition of farm produce. This ordinance, the so-called Gullo Land Act, named after the Communist Minister of Agriculture, was followed by the Segni Land Act in September 1946 which dealt with the same issues (cf. Marciani 1966: 25; Di Matteo 1967:305–07, 483–84). In the struggle for the land that enveloped the South from 1944 through 1952, the peasants of the *latifondi* were encouraged by the left-wing and center-left parties of the North which advocated radical agrarian reform. "The actions of these reconstituted political parties," writes Marciani, "contributed to the rapid affirmation of a new class consciousness and a progressive modification of the attitudes of the peasants: the poor awoke from traditional resignation and assumed an ever more conscious attitude of vindication and protest against their condition of *miseria*" (1966:25).

There were thus several conditions in western Sicily that favored the restoration of *mafiosi* as power brokers linking people at different levels of integration. There was, first of all, a weak government unable to organize control over the means of violence, especially in the inland districts where the *latifondi* had been left intact under Fascism. Second, the organization of production on the large estates favored the establishment of relatively autonomous power domains which constrained the peasantry and provided local strongmen with specific power chances. The struggle for the land challenged the organizational set-up of the *latifondi* and the associated power domains. The outcome of this confrontation depended upon the extent to which the peasants could rely on the new sources of power that opened up at the national level. Moreover, the occupation of Sicily by the Allies was, as far as we can tell, facilitated by the intelligence and actual services rendered by certain American *mafiosi* and their Sicilian counterparts who survived Fascism.[2] Though this

2. For the role of overseas gangsters, see Gaja (1962:75–91); and Pantaleone (1966:54–72). Regarding the part played by Sicilian estate owners, Gaja observes: "For fifty years already the English nobility and bourgeoisie had landed property, villas, friendships, and also ties of kinship in Sicily. The Sicilian nobles, on the other hand, were impregnated by English culture and tastes, and sent

condition alone cannot entirely explain the rebirth of *mafia* in western Sicily, the leverage granted to large estate owners under the Pax Americana surely promoted the entrenchment of old and new *mafiosi* who professed an anti-Fascist and anti-Communist bent. This leverage was manifest above all in the color of local administration. In close to 90 per cent of the 352 Sicilian communes, the Allies appointed authorities who represented landed interests. As two decades before, large estates were again placed under the protection of bandits and *mafiosi* and managed by the latter.

In the beginning of 1944, right after Sicily came under Italian administration, the decentralizing forces embodied in estate owners, *mafiosi*, and assorted components of bandit-gangs assembled in the upper echelons and right wing of a vigorous though short-lived separatist movement for an independent Sicily to safeguard traditional class privileges which were threatened from the mainland. Public statements of Separatist spokesmen emphasized liberation for Sicily from Italian rule and clearly revealed the foremost issues: the persistence of large estates was to be guaranteed, and allusions were made to the historical role of bandits and the "necessity" of *mafia* in moments like this. Andrea Finocchiaro Aprile, a former deputy of the pre-Fascist Liberal Party in the constituency of Corleone (see p. 164) and one of the main leaders of the Separatists, is reported to have eulogized in public meetings the large estate and *mafia*.[3] But even before Sicily was granted regional autonomy in May 1946, Separatism had lost much of its significance. Apart from internal conflicts, the failure to field an adequate bandit-army, and the strong action the Italian authorities took against it, the

---

their children (as they still do) to English schools. These relationships were very useful to the Intelligence Service" (1962:88).

3. "*Il latifondo resterà cosi come è.*" (The *latifondo* will remain as it is.) "*Se la mafia non ci fosse bisognerebbe inventarla. Io sono amico dei mafiosi, pur dichiarandomi personalmente contrario al delitto e alla violenza.*" (If there were no *mafia* it would have to be invented. I am a friend of *mafiosi*, although personally I am opposed to crime and violence.) See Rochefort (1961:106); Romano (1966:302–03).

collapse of the movement must be chiefly ascribed to the willingness of the "reformist" Christian Democrat Party to open its ranks to the Sicilian estate owners and their satellites, thus offering prospects of accommodation to vested landed interests in Sicily. This made many landowners and *mafiosi* change sides, for they understood too well that they had to make some sacrifices in order to offset the tide of Communism that could sweep away all existing privileges. To make the best of a bad bargain, the landed classes realized that they had to come to terms with the political party that was in power in Rome. The Christian Democrats, entrenched in the network of the Church and equipped with a strong conservative wing, rather than the Separatists, or the Monarchists for that matter, were indeed most appropriate for a new *modus vivendi* on both the regional and national level through which the Sicilian agrarian elites hoped to check the peasants' struggle for the land. The next section describes this contest in the area of Genuardo.

THE STRUGGLE FOR LAND

As noted in Chapter III, Genuardo, up to the mid-1940s, was one of the most latifundist communes in Sicily. At the time, less than a dozen families owned over 22 holdings larger than 100 hectares each, covering about 6,500 hectares in all, roughly 50 per cent of the village territory. Alongside the inlying estates of absentee landowners were scattered hundreds of tiny peasant holdings. About 1,700 smallholders owned but 1,400 hectares, just over 10 per cent of the territory. Between these extremes were about 270 holdings varying in size from 10 to 100 hectares and covering close to 5,400 hectares, or 40 per cent of the village area. The owners of these middle-range holdings belonged to the local upper class of Genuardo and neighboring towns. Most of them were absentee. They rented their land to peasant cultivators and shepherds either directly or indirectly by means of the *gabella*, as in the case of all large estates.

This pronounced inequality of landholding, the relatively small size of Genuardo, and its isolated location in the inland mountains are basic to an understanding of what transpired in the village in the immediate postwar years. In the second half of 1943, *mafiosi* had already reassumed management and supervision of several large estates in the territory of Genuardo. They operated under the aegis of the estate owners who, in turn, were backed by the loosely established Allied Government. The Allies had their district head-quarters at the former monastery of Santa Maria del Bosco, the hilltop mansion of the *latifondista* Adriano Mirabella. The reader will remember that in pre-Fascist days Adriano had been on intimate terms with Cascio Ferro, who was his retainer, but had let the *mafioso* down when the Fascists settled accounts with rural *mafiosi* (see p. 186). In the mid-1930s, Adriano had been *podestà* of Genuardo—the head of the local administration appointed by the central government. Yet these overt Fascist leanings did not prevent him from siding with the Allies and the Separatists, and he was appointed mayor again in July 1943. After some months he died, and his place was taken by his orphaned nephew and main heir, Giacomo, who had been brought up by his uncle (see p. 118). In the local elections of 1946, which very clearly confirmed the dominance of the landed class over the peasants, Giacomo was elected mayor and remained in office until 1952. To account for the prolonged control of estate owners in this critical phase of the history of the village requires consideration of the specific difficulties that the peasants encountered in their concerted attempts to gain control of the land.

In the course of 1945, local sections of the Communist Party and the left-wing trade union were established through the initiative of two artisans from the latifundist township of Piana degli Albanesi, a place near Palermo known for its pronounced Socialist orientation since the peasant movement of 1893. During the war the two Pianesi had worked and lived in Genuardo. The office of secretary of both left-wing organizations was assumed by a local schoolteacher, a man close to the village poor and strongly opposed to the dominant families. The three men did much to organize the peasants of their village, and in due course they were aided by returned former partisans who had fought the Fascists in the North. They sought to bring the peasants together in cooperatives and led token mass occupations of large estates. The peasant leaders of Genuardo were assisted and encouraged in their efforts, particularly the invasions of estates, by their counterparts from neighboring towns with their own followings. These towns are located on the fringe of the territory of Genuardo, and part of their population found employment there. Given these shared interests, it was quite natural for the peasants of these places to join forces to occupy particular estates.

Most of these land invasions were in fact symbolic: peaceful demonstrations on the estates by large crowds of peasants urging the implementation of the Gullo and Segni Land Acts, according to which peasant cooperatives were entitled to lease poorly cultivated estates on terms allowing the cooperative to retain 50 to 80 per cent of the produce. Several estates of the Baronessa complex, as well as various other *latifondi* belonging to landowners living elsewhere, were occupied in this way. In most cases, however, the peasants found the law on the side of the owners and their retainers, who asked for and received the intervention of the *Carabinieri* to stop the peasants from infringing on property rights. At Santa Maria del Bosco, sharecroppers were contracted on the usual systems and left with less than one-fourth of the crops. The grand cavalcade of peasant invaders marching to these estates was stopped by the *Carabinieri*, and several of the participants were arrested and convicted (cf. Sorgi 1959:629; and Rochefort 1961:107, 175). At Baronessa conditions of employment were no less harsh. Both old and new *mafiosi* had joined in partnership to supervise the estates. Favored by the food shortage and the labor surplus due to the restriction on emigration over the preceding three decades, the bargaining position of *gabelloti* and *campieri* was strong— strong enough to leave the peasant sharecroppers with one-fourth, one-fifth, or even less of their produce. The overseer in charge of the Baronessa complex, Calogero Simonetti, is reported to have said to grumbling candidate sharecroppers:

"If you don't want to accept the conditions, you can leave
and starve to death!"

Calogero belonged to one of the local *gabelloto* families
and became the overseer at Baronessa in 1926 when Edoardo
—the chief of the Adernò *cosca*—had to make his way to the
United States. In the course of time, strong tensions grew
between him and Giuseppe Livornese, who administered the
whole of Baronessa in the 1920s. Because Giuseppe suffered
from an eye disease, the sycophantic Calogero was able to
have him dismissed by slandering his effectiveness to the
estate owner while creeping into her good graces. The new
administrator who replaced Giuseppe was an outsider less
acquainted with local conditions, thus leaving Calogero much
more room for manipulation. Meanwhile, Calogero married
the eldest daughter of Aloisio Olivieri. A second daughter of
Aloisio married a brother of the village priest, and the third
daughter married Melchiore Cassini, who had remained out
of the Fascist toils. The alliance between these four families
of *gabelloti* proved to be a great advantage for Aloisio's four
sons (see Diagram 11). Assisted by their brother-in-law,
Calogero, they acquired the lease of several Baronessa estates
immediately after the war in shifting partnerships with
Melchiore and various surviving kinsmen and friends of
Edoardo. Aloisio, originally from the neighboring town of
Pietracollina, had settled in Genuardo at the turn of the
century. He married a local girl and tried twice without
much success to make his fortune in America. His part in a
cattle theft in 1915 has already been mentioned (see p. 150).
He had then returned to Sicily and tried hard to exploit a
niche of his own. His efforts were rewarded two years later
when the Spanish influenza killed a local *gabelloto* whose
sons still lacked the skills to maintain the lease of the estate.
Aloisio managed to acquire the contract through the influence of his friend Baron Francesco (see p. 136), who spoke
on his behalf to the owner in Palermo. The exploitation of
this estate enabled Aloisio, helped by his teenage sons, to
accumulate sufficient wealth to buy up one share of it in
1927. Thus the landed status and relative wealth of their
father, as well as the strategic marriages of their sisters,

provided the four Olivieri brothers with specific chances to move in as leaseholders on the Baronessa estates. As one informant summarized the patronage of their brother-in-law, Calogero: "*Un uomo fa un altro uomo.*" (A man makes another man.)

At Baronessa the Olivieris formed partnerships and larger coalitions with *mafiosi* from other towns after 1943. In this way they helped to build up a front against the landless peasants who tried to organize themselves in order to improve labor conditions and, ultimately, to get direct access to the land. The development of this basic pattern of conflicts and tensions in the inland areas should not, however, blind us to the strong and violent rivalries within the ranks of *mafiosi* themselves. To obtain the lease of an estate required the usual infighting. Some strongmen paid with their lives, as happened to two *gabelloti* (father and son) from Bisacquino. They refused to let their lease of an estate in the territory of Pietracollina pass to a powerful contestant of that place. One afternoon in early August 1946, when father and son rode home through the territory of Genuardo, they were shot dead from ambush. In the same period, a large herd of cattle, including several tens of milk cows, calves, horses, and mules, was stolen from the central estate of Baronessa by the Labruzzo band, a company of bandits named after its leader, Piddu Labruzzo, a man affiliated with the well-known Giuliano gang in northwestern Sicily.[4] The animals belonged to the estate owner and were managed by Calogero. On the day of this robbery, which took place one late afternoon in August, none of the supervisory personnel was present. They had gone off to a cattle market in Adernò. Taking advantage of the circumstance the bandits, armed and comprising about a dozen men, had little difficulty in coping with the three herdsmen, who were simply ordered to lie down and then tied. One of them still remembered the incident after twenty years, and when discussing it he sug-

---

4. Salvatore Giuliano operated from 1943 to 1950 in the area southwest of Palermo. For a good biography, see the study of the late Gavin Maxwell (1957). Cf. Pantaleone (1966:133–56, *et passim*).

gested two possible explanations. First, it might have been
"*uno scorno fra di loro,*" that is, *mafiosi* disgracing each other.
We have come across this stratagem earlier in this book. A
mafioso who fails to protect what has been entrusted to his
care ruins his reputation for toughness and honor, that is,
respect. Thus disgraced, he loses points vis-à-vis his peers
and rivals, who in turn may be considered as potential suc-
cessors as they prove to be more powerful retainers.[5] Second,
the raid might have been "*un accordo fra di loro,*" that is to
say, the *mafiosi* employed on and in charge of the Baronessa
estates arranged the theft themselves to show their power
over the estate owner. This particular cattle rustling was
explained in quite similar terms by a regional deputy in his
address to the Sicilian Regional Assembly some years later.
After sketching out the role of *mafiosi* on the large estates
in six communes in the inland area, he specified the impact
of those active on the Baronessa estates:

> Should we be surprised that at a certain moment in this
> area a cattle rustling of enormous proportions took place
> at the expense of the [Baronessa] owner and her kinsmen?
> No we should not because the only law that dominates in
> those localities, as long as one does not seriously change
> policy, is their law, not ours. It is the law of criminals, not
> of gentlemen, the law of semi-feudal backwardness and
> that of parasitism, not that of productivity. Reality is thus;
> I don't want to give my words here an exaggerated polemic
> or personal twist, but these are the facts. This is all that it
> is necessary to say.[6]

As long as their interests did not conflict, *mafiosi* closed
ranks to offset peasant power at the *latifondo* and to prevent
left-wing candidates from dominating the local town-council.

5. Incidents like this underscore the dynamics of power and demonstrate that power is inseparable from the changing interdependencies between human beings. Cf. Elias (1969, II: 83–84); and
Bailey, who notes that "a leader who fails to protect loses his
reputation for honour and valour, and with that gone, he cannot
keep followers and so does not have the means to stand up to
his rivals" (1969: 40).
6. Colajanni (1959: 76–78). See also Di Matteo (1967: 269–72).

The local headquarters of the Communist Party was once set on fire. Election campaigns and public meetings of the Left were frequently disturbed, once resulting in an open fight on the tiny, central *piazza* when local *mafiosi* ripped down the scaffolding from which a visiting member of the Communist Party was making a speech. At other times, left-wing speakers were simply prevented from holding a meeting on this central place and had to turn to the back streets of the village with the obvious result of a decreasing public. But even there, meetings were disturbed by thugs who threatened the audience. Apart from various sorts of intimidation, to which local authorities often turned a blind eye, *mafiosi* sought to subvert poor peasants by refusing employment to those who openly sympathized with the Left. Refusals were often framed in harsh terms. On the other hand, peasants with large families and extended kinship affiliations, a circumstance that granted them tactical power, were offered favorable conditions of employment, either on the estates or white-collar jobs in Palermo, to make them change sides together with their kinsmen. Subversion through this particular form of patronage was successful in several cases and, given the relatively small size of the village and its electorate, these proved true bloodlettings for the Left.

As mentioned before, the interests of large estate owners and their agents were backed up by the local authorities, who represented State-institutions at the village level. Most of them belonged to the same class and often to the same families that dominated the village. The post of mayor was held by Giacomo, the Baron of Santa Maria del Bosco, and the councillors were recruited from his retainers and other local *gabelloti*. The priests and schoolteachers, the physician and veterinary surgeon, the postmaster and tax-collector were all very close to or outright members of the families that controlled land. Each of them was in a position to withhold or delay specific public services. The idea that these services should be granted impersonally was completely foreign to them. In Sicily, administration and politics were and still are closely intertwined and certainly much less autonomous than in some contemporary industrial nation-states.

To obtain access to State-resources, one had to "please" the persons who administered them. In local idiom, these services were granted "for friendship" and as "favors." Left-wing peasants were emphatically excluded. The mayor is reported to have denied certificates for passports to peasant activists who wanted to emigrate to the United States. Old-age pensions were paid by the postmaster after he had "seen" (received) substantial shares of almonds, grapes, or olives according to the season in which peasants called at his office. Priests exercised control over rival, Catholic peasant organizations that weakened and split the peasant movement. Moreover, they sought to induce their parishioners to vote for the Christian Democrats, the party of the Church and, as we have seen, the party to which landowners and *mafiosi* in this area lent their support.[7] As exponents of the local elite and as members of families that owned or controlled land, priests gave a grotesque and frightening image of Communism, emphasizing its atheist orientation and refusing services to sympathizers and adherents. Priests also controlled access to schools. They were able to facilitate educational careers for children of the poor by providing the means to send them to special colleges run by the Church. Some members of the local clergy played a crucial part in the transfer of land shortly before the actual implementation of the reform. The local police, or *Carabinieri*, though foreign to the village, soon became part of the local power structure and could not but operate accordingly. At the village level, thus, a handful of families succeeded to a remarkable extent in monopolizing the means of violence, the means of production, and the means of orientation—religion, ideology, and knowledge.

At the time there were indeed few sources from which the left-wing peasant could derive support. Power domains were largely locally phrased. Isolated in his small hilltop village and alone in his work on the land, the peasant was thus largely constrained by those forces that had always dominated the inland districts. Under these circumstances, few

7. For an instructive discussion on the relationship between clergy and *mafia*, see Pecorini (1967).

peasants could afford to be as tough as Alberto, a partisan who joined the Communist resistance movement in northern Italy. Back in Genuardo, he found roughly 200 persons enrolled in the combined section of the Communist and Socialist parties. In the local elections of April 1946, this bloc netted just 369 votes out of a total of 1,377 (see Table XIV). In the course of that year, the Left succeeded in establishing a cooperative in which Alberto took an active part. His experience among the partisans in the North may have provided him with a capacity for organization. Thus mobilized, the peasants then acquired the collective lease of two estates, one of which they were able to maintain over six years. This was Piano, one of the Baronessa estates, which measured some 275 hectares, providing 120 members of the cooperative with plots ranging from one to two hectares. Each plot was individually cultivated.[8] The lease was obtained on rather favorable terms leaving the cultivators with over one-half of the crops. The other estate was abandoned after two years since no agreement on the conditions could be reached with the owner. Regarding the pressure on militant peasants, Alberto recalled:

> At the time we were confronted with various acts of intimidation from the side of those who managed and supervised *feudi*. Shortly after my return from the North, I bought a flock of sheep which I managed with my sister's husband, Tommaso. One evening we returned from the country and were driving the animals into the pen

8. This mode of operation was widespread in the South, and had a strong impact on the formulation of the agrarian reform some years later. Writes Tarrow: "The petit bourgeois goals of the peasants soon appeared in these cooperatives in their behavior with regard to the land that had been occupied. The law of 1944 specified that this land should be cultivated by the peasants either in a group, in mixed forms of cultivation, or by single peasants working separate plots of land. Of the 414,000 acres of land that had been temporarily conceded in this way, only 10 per cent was cultivated collectively; 7 per cent was worked by mixed forms of cultivation and 83 per cent was cultivated individually by the peasants. Hence the cooperatives were cooperatives in name only" (1967:282). Cf. Marciani (1966:28–29).

close to my house here at the outskirts of the village. We were accosted by two men. One of them was Melchiore Cassini; the other fellow, also from here, I was slightly acquainted with. Melchiore patted Tommaso on the shoulder and said: "We are brothers in God, are we not?" Tommaso turned around and snapped: "If you don't get out of here I'll box your ears and make you run!" We continued our work, removing the thorns from our clothes, taking care of the sheep and milking them. The two men, however, kept hanging around and Melchiore now addressed himself to me repeating the phrase "We are brothers in God." Then he started to talk about voting and he said: "You have to give your vote to ***." But I told him: "I don't like to be petted, not even by my wife. I'll give my vote to my own party and not to you." Melchiore then said: "So you refuse! Be careful though! You have got the animals and we may always meet somewhere in the country." Upon these words, I took my gun, pointed it at Melchiore, and told him: "We have already met!" The two men left. Afterwards, whenever I came across Melchiore, he was strikingly polite. He always saluted me respectfully. He surely was afraid to get involved in case I should be robbed and might turn the evidence against him. Anyhow, he never disturbed us again. In a way we were "respected."

This incident was very much an exception: few peasants took up arms as did Alberto and his companion who operated in the same violent idiom as their opponents. The municipal elections of April 1946 clearly showed the extent to which the peasants were dependent on local patrons and sided with them, thus accepting the existing distribution of power. As mentioned before, of 1,377 people who cast valid votes, 1,008 opted for the Christian Democrats while no more than 369 chose the Communist–Socialist coalition. Given the majority system of elections in force, this meant that the Christian Democrats obtained 12 out of the 15 seats in the local town council, leaving the remaining three to the left-wing opposition. The estate owner Giacomo Mirabella remained in office as mayor and as head of the administrative junta, which further consisted of four aldermen, all of them *gabelloti* or related to those who controlled large estates in the village territory. Among them were Aldo Olivieri and a brother of Calogero Simonetti (see Diagram 11). The outcome of these elections thus reflected the local distribution of resources and the range of local patronage, that is, the extent to which peasant families depended for their living upon those who controlled access to land.

The results of the first regional elections in April 1947, however, showed a quite different picture. The Communist–Socialist bloc acquired 872 votes whereas the Christian Democrats netted 356 votes out of a total of 1,528 persons who went to the polls in Genuardo. These elections were highly successful for the left-wing parties in Sicily as a whole.[9] One reason for this remarkable shift in allegiance is the lesser role of local patronage in this contest, as well as the expectations of the peasants with regard to agrarian reform: what they could not properly achieve in the village arena they hoped to attain at the level of the region.

One of the most important and serious consequences of the overwhelming victory of the Sicilian left-wing parties in the regional elections was the growing collusion between *mafiosi* and Christian Democrats. Both were in danger of losing ground to the revolutionary forces in Sicilian society, which were accepted by the central government in Rome and at least initially fuelled by the left-wing parties in the national arena. To reconquer the field and to counterbalance radical change, certain sections of the party in western Sicily turned to those elements that had always served politicians willing to grant protection and immunity in exchange for ruthless political and electoral support. Right after the regional elections in the spring of 1947 and with the national elections ahead, pockets of terror gradually spread over the inland districts.[10]

9. The Regional Assembly included 29 deputies of the Popular Bloc; 20 Christian Democrats; 9 Monarchists; 8 Separatists; and 3 Republicans among a total of 90 deputies (Di Matteo 1967:512–14).
10. In this respect, Boissevain observes: "The fact that the head of

In the course of 1946, it had become clear that Separatism —the attempt on the part of the conservative forces to constitute a proper State independent from Italy—could not work out. Early that year, the police, assisted by army units, launched a strong campaign against the bandits, many of whom had come from the dissolved Separatist army. Autonomous bandits were a nuisance not only to the State, but particularly to the landowners and their *mafiosi* retainers. The operations of the government dealt a serious blow to common banditry. In the course of a few months, ten main bands and about 200 minor criminal associations were eliminated. Hundreds of bandits were arrested or killed in the inland areas. It soon turned out that the authorities completed these actions in collusion with *mafiosi* who, in turn, used one main band—that of Giuliano in the northwestern corner of the island. *Mafiosi* acted as important informers if not directly as executioners. They had their own reasons to get rid of common bandits and converted what remained of them into political tools. In this way, the bandit chief Piddu Labruzzo, who was held responsible for the cattle raid at Baronessa mentioned before (p. 197), was forced to join Giuliano's band. The alternatives were arrest or death. The year 1946 thus marked the transition of common banditry into political banditry and, up to 1950, bandits were used as instruments in the struggle against the peasant movement and the parties of the Left.[11]

Less than two weeks after the notable advance of the "popular bloc" over the "agrarian bloc," on May 1, 1947, Giuliano's gang attacked from ambush a peaceful crowd of

---

the powerful Ministry of the Interior in Rome at the time was a wealthy Sicilian landowner can undoubtedly be advanced as one of the factors which explain the timing of these outbursts of violence, as must a concerted campaign by the Right to discredit and crush the Left. Those who wish to enforce their wishes by violence and those who were prepared to help them believed they were assured of a receptive political climate, and acted accordingly" (1966b:225).

11. See Sansone and Ingrascì (1950:105–15); Gaja (1962:304–05); Montalbano (1964a, b); and Di Matteo (1967:443–51).

peasants from three villages south of Palermo that assembled at a place in the mountains named Portella delle Ginestre to celebrate Labor Day. The shooting lasted three minutes and left 11 dead and 33 wounded. During the trial of those held responsible for this brutal assault it became clear that the gang had acted upon orders of high-ranking politicians. Their identity will probably never be ascertained. In the months following the Portella massacre, the Giuliano gang singled out the headquarters of left-wing parties and peasant trade unions in nine towns southwest of Palermo and attacked them with bombs and machine guns. In six towns, the attacks were carried out simultaneously in one single night (June 22, 1947); two persons were killed and four wounded. The band left pamphlets in these places that appealed to Sicilian youths to join Giuliano in the struggle against Communism.

These operations did much to terrorize the villagers in western Sicily. As one journal put it some years later: "With these destructive actions in which bandits and *mafiosi* were concordant and had to employ also the usual adventitious elements, the organizing and winning force of the Marxist parties was deeply neutralized in the communes of the province of Palermo, especially those in which the seats of left-wing parties and trade unions were attacked."[12]

Apart from these challenges, political homicides crippled the peasants' struggle for the land. Peasant leaders had been assassinated before. Only those who lost their lives in districts bordering on Genuardo will be mentioned here. One of the main leaders of the *Fasci* movement of 1893–1914, Bernardino Verro from Corleone (see p. 121), was gunned down in that town on November 3, 1915 by *mafiosi* whose interests were at stake when peasant cooperatives sprang up. Similar fates for similar reasons awaited the schoolteacher Lorenzo Panepinto from Santo Stefano Quisquina in May 1911 and Nicola Alongi from Prizzi in February 1920. These men were much esteemed and had considerable following. The same held good for Accursio Miraglia, secretary of the left-wing

12. For detailed accounts, see Sansone and Ingrascì (1950:135–42) and Gaja (1962:347–54).

trade union in the southern coastal town of Sciacca, who recruited peasants from several inland places and helped organize their legal occupation of large estates. Local *mafiosi* first threatened him in their usual roundabout way. Some time afterwards, on a night in early January 1947, Miraglia was assassinated. This crime, like the ones before and others soon to follow, was never punished.[13] A few weeks before the national elections of April 1948, three left-wing leaders from three different towns close to Genuardo were eliminated by *mafiosi*. On March 10, the secretary of the left-wing trade union in Corleone, Placido Rizzotto, was kidnapped and killed. (This incident is described in Chapter I.) Less than a week later, on March 16, the provincial secretary of the Christian Democrat Party, a man called Vincenzo Campo, was killed in the town of Gibellina.[14] In Camporeale, north of Genuardo, the trade union leader Calogero Cangelosi was shot dead on the night of April 2. A few days before he was killed, Cangelosi was accosted by a group of local *mafiosi* who threatened to eliminate him if he did not withdraw from politics. Earlier, the peasant leader had been approached by a local landlord who offered him employment on his farm on the condition that he leave the ranks of the Socialists.[15]

13. Cf. Sorgi (1959:627); Dolci (1963:69–85); Romano (1966:229–30, 247–49).
14. We still do not know the extent of Campo's involvement with *mafia*. Pantaleone's remarks are not especially illuminating (1966: 203–04). This incident should serve, however, to remind us that all *mafia* violence was not directed socially downwards. Rather, as Chapters V–VII illustrate, overt violence was mainly the grist of social competition among rural elites.
15. For a description of this political crime, see Sansone and Ingrascì (1950:159–61). Camporeale is known as a particularly violent place. In this town of about 7,000 inhabitants, located on the mountainous borders of the provinces of Palermo and Trapani, people "shoot each other like flies." Hence the nickname "*Macellaro*" (the Butcher's) that has been conferred upon the locality and is still used by people in neighboring places like Genuardo. Some maintain that "*Macellaro*" was the original name of Camporeale because many of the stolen animals in the area were concentrated and slaughtered in this relatively isolated community. The following anecdote underscores the social acceptance of

After this rapid sequence of political murders just before
the national elections, the peasant movement in western
Sicily suffered strong setbacks. Some cooperatives renounced
the estates they had been allotted, as happened in Genuardo,
Corleone, and neighboring towns. The use of sheer violence
with impunity and acquiescence from the side of the authorities did much to frighten the peasant activists and their supporters and weakened their resilience. These events helped

---

homicide. "On his journey through western Sicily at the time he
was Minister [about 1875], Minghetti visited the town of Camporeale where the priest introduced himself to him: 'I come to
recommend to you a poor young man who needs your protection.'
'Why? What does he want?' 'Nothing, only he has met with an
accident; he has killed a man' " (Alongi 1891:50).

After Cangelosi's death, at least half a dozen persons lost their
lives in the political struggle for the land and control of the town
council. Another left-wing leader of this town was killed by
mafiosi one night in the early spring of 1957. The victim was a
local school-teacher, called Pasquale Almerico, secretary of the
branch of the Christian Democrat Party in Camporeale and
mayor since 1952. He belonged to a group of young Catholic
leaders in favor of disentangling the party from the involvement
of *mafiosi*. This brought Almerico in conflict with the local
mafia. He refused their protection and opposed their admittance
to the party—though their membership was accepted by both
the clergy and the upper echelons of the Christian democrats.
Thus isolated, Almerico resigned from the office of mayor. Shortly
afterwards, he was brutally killed. On his way home from the
club, accompanied by his brother, "five cloaked men, their caps
pulled down over their eyes, converged upon them. A volley of
submachine-gun fire was followed by several pistol shots, and at
the same moment the village found itself plunged into complete
darkness by an electricity breakdown. The next day, in the post-
mortem room at the cemetery, bullets fell out of Almerico's body
'like beads off a broken rosary.' No fewer than 104 submachine-
gun bullets and 7 pistol bullets were counted" (Pantaleone 1966:
127). A few weeks before he was killed, Almerico had asked the
police for protection and had mentioned the names of the persons who should be held responsible for his eventual death.
Neither the authorities nor the party were in a position to change
Almerico's fate. His death was regarded as something inevitable,
and may illustrate the extent to which *mafiosi* were growing into
a political force in their own right. Cf. Dolci (1963:212–16);
Chilanti and Farinella (1964:69–70); Pantaleone (1966:123–28).

to circumvent the growing power of the Left in favor of
established power domains. Most notable in this respect were
the results of the national elections on April 18, 1948, in
which the Christian Democrats increased their votes by well
over 150 per cent. In Genuardo alone, this party more than
doubled its vote since the regional elections of the previous
year (see Table XIV). As we saw in Chapter IV, the struggle
for the land ended in defeat and disillusion for the peasants.
Only a part of them gained tiny, unviable farms without
adequate technical assistance or credit facilities. Though the
reform did help to break up the *latifondi*, it left ample room
for evasive operations. Of the Baronessa estates alone, hundreds of hectares escaped expropriation through sales before
the reform bill passed. Many former *gabelloti* now own
substantial farms and benefit from credits and funds provided by the State. For them as well as for several former
estate owners, land reform has meant labor saving machinery, better roads, and adequate access to their farms, the
construction of water supplies, and in general a share in the
welfare distributed by the State. As was true elsewhere, the
reform agency did not seek the cooperation of the peasants
in Genuardo and even destroyed what little organization
existed among them by expropriating the estate Piano held
in lease by the left-wing cooperative. These counterreform[16]
aspects were also clear in the rapid bureaucratic expansion
of the agency. It was just another electoral instrument in the
hands of the Christian Democrats, providing employment
for those with the right connections. In this way, the agency
had absorbed well over 2,500 employees by the end of the
1950s while less than 18,000 peasants had received allot-

16. Counterreform involves maneuvers to maintain and strengthen
the power and position of the landed elite through a policy of
sabotage that is built into the very reform program. See Feder
(1970). E.g., when Diego, son-in-law and heir of the Baronessa owner (pp. 81–82) and for several years President of
Sicilian *Regione*, proclaimed himself in favor of the land reform
and conceded the Piano estate to the Reform Board for expropriation, his conception of land reform was clearly different from
that of the peasants who saw their cooperative destroyed through
this maneuver. (See also Appendix A, case 16.)

ments, covering barely 77,000 hectares in all, even though the owners of close to 450,000 hectares had been notified that their land was to be expropriated.[17]

This particular outcome of the struggle for the land was due to several circumstances which cannot be fully discussed here. One main problem was the relative isolation of the peasants from outside sources of power. Neither the Italian government nor the Communists or Socialists were able to successfully challenge the entrenched power domains that constrained the peasants: the landless as well as the small-holders or "middle" peasantry. While *mafiosi* succeeded in establishing an effective liaison with the government in their capacity as vote canvassers, the Italian Communist Party alienated the most militant sector of the peasantry by empha-sizing a national strategy of broad electoral support appeal-ing to both peasant laborers and their employers. By following this highly ambiguous course the Party failed to consolidate the struggle for the land and to convert the peasant move-ment into a full-scale peasant revolution that might have radically changed the structure of south Italian society (Tarrow 1967:242–62). The Sicilian experience of the post-war period thus bears out Wolf's hypothesis regarding the course of peasant movements: "... the decisive factor in making a peasant rebellion possible lies in the relation of the peasantry to the field of power which surrounds it." More-over, "poor peasants and landless laborers are unlikely to pursue the course of rebellion, *unless* they are able to rely on some external power to challenge the power which con-strains them" (1969:290). Initially, the peasants derived support from both the government and the left-wing parties: the concessions of uncultivated land to peasant cooperatives are cases in point. In a later stage, however, and particularly in areas like that of Genuardo, no effective outside leadership was implanted in the movement which could have helped it penetrate the integument of the power domains that en-veloped the peasants. For the same reason, landowning and middle peasants abstained from lending support to the

17. Cf. Diem (1961:158); Rochefort (1961:111); and Tarrow (1967: 349–50).

movement and joined rival, conservative organizations which further weakened the rebellion.[18]

EXCURSUS ON VIOLENCE

The recrudescence of open violence in the inland districts during the immediate postwar years must be seen in connection with the overall development of Sicilian society, in which the power balances between landowners and peasants were shifting in favor of the latter. In Genuardo no outright political murders took place. Left-wing organizations were weak indeed and certainly less militant than in some of the larger neighboring places such as, for example, Corleone where they had good chances of taking control of local government, a condition that helps account for the high rates of homicide experienced by that town.[19] In the much smaller and relatively isolated village of Genuardo, the peasants were granted fewer power chances. In various ways and in different degrees, they were drawn into and constrained by the power domains of the landlords and their retainers. As a result, there were fewer violent class confrontations. Though less manifest, the structure of violence was no less real than in those neighboring towns. As elsewhere in Sicily's interior, the control over the means of production was closely related to control over the means of violence. People were dependent upon kinsmen, friends, and powerful protectors for sheer physical survival. To right wrongs, to settle conflicts, and to solve problems of various sorts, they could hardly rely on the police and law courts. The very fact that they only

18. It will be remembered that the rural middle classes in Sicily supported the revolt of 1860, triggered off by Garibaldi who presented an external force capable of destroying the power domains of the Bourbons (see Chapter VI). The establishment of rival organizations constitutes a powerful source of weakness in peasant movements (cf. Landsberger and Hewitt 1970:575–76).
19. Cf. Dolci (1963:25–50, 310–12). The tables presented by Dolci are not complete: they mention 62 cases of homicide over a period of 16 years (1944–1959). For the same town, Pantaleone records 154 murder cases from 1944 through 1948 without, however, specifying them (1966:114).

rarely appealed to State-institutions for protection and to settle wrongs reinforced the power domains of local private magnates. At the same time, it helped retard the development of a relatively stable and impersonal central control of the means of violence in west Sicilian society at large. The circumstance of a relatively low level of State-organization encouraged people to act on their own: there were simply no alternatives.

These conditions did not allow for the development of a strong conscience with regard to the use of physical violence. A high sensitivity against using violence or witnessing it would have meant a serious social handicap (see Appendix A). In fact, as noted earlier, persons who had a reputation for violence and who eschewed recourse to public authorities commanded respect. They were quite literally the most respected, the most honorable, the most powerful, and very often the most wealthy men of the community. Others less skilled in the realm of violence turned to them for mediation and protection. These "*accordi*" merely enhanced the honor and power of violent men.[20]

Certain expressions in everyday language reflect the part played by unlicensed violence in Sicilian peasant society.

Mafiosi were denoted as "honorable," "respected," or "qualified" persons. They were men able to "look after their own affairs" and to "make themselves respected." At issue is a code of behavior that is neatly summed up by the term "*omertà*" (from *omu*, man). According to it, a person makes

20. See Elias' model of civilizing processes (1969) and a recent enlargement of this theory (Elias 1971). Cf. Bloch (1961:145–62). Of particular interest is an article by the late Dutch historian Niermeyer (1959) dealing with the semantic shifts of the term "*honor*" in medieval Europe. Similar patterns can be observed in quite different societies. Writing on the New Guinea Highland peoples, Paula Brown comments: "Without an overriding authority to maintain peace and keep order in any group, fighting was the accepted means of dealing with disputes of all kinds. . . . Daring and success in combat brought prestige to the individual and the group" (1964:349). It can not be overemphasized that the relatively low level of violence in many "pristine" tribal societies is related to effective colonial domination or, in the absence of any overarching effective authority, to access to open resources.

himself respected by keeping silent over "crimes" witnessed, suffered, or committed. Reticence and secrecy, at times amounting to conspiracies of silence, especially vis-à-vis legal authorities, expressed the sway and range of established local power domains. Silence was enforced upon the weak: talking (*cantare*, lit.: singing) involved attempts to draw on external resources that would threaten the established balance of power. Through their manipulation of this complex cultural code and the social control it entailed, *mafiosi* tried to isolate the local population from external rival powers. People had to rely on them. To ignore the code meant an attempt to by-pass the power broker. In this way, *omertà* was structurally pervasive throughout the whole community, albeit in varying degrees. It is important to see the code not in isolation, but as an aspect of the real interdependencies between people who formed the community. *Omertà* was not something abstract, floating in the air so to speak, reinforcing or influencing actual behavior. On the contrary, as I hope has been made clear, it constituted a very concrete and real part of the behavior of people who depended on each other in specific and fundamental ways.

When *omertà* is envisaged as a structural part of the power domains of *mafiosi* as brokers, we may understand their specific connivance with public authorities. Like power brokers elsewhere, *mafiosi* wielded power in two spheres: their actual control in either sphere depended upon their success in dealing with the other (cf. Adams 1970:320–21). Far from replacing the State or constituting a State within a State as has been so often believed, *mafiosi* depended on the State since their local and regional power domains existed only by virtue of their access to the larger domains of the State. The concepts of political middleman and power broker prove particularly helpful in understanding this symbiosis. The very articulation of *mafiosi* with public authorities and national politicians rendered any State-based action or reform against them abortive.[21] This configuration of which *mafia* is an essential part has only recently taken a different course. It is to this development that we turn in the next and last chapter.

21. Cf. Marino's critique on Franchetti (1964:155–56).

Epilogue

"Before it was *mafia*; today it is politics."

In the previous chapters I have tried to demonstrate that the rise and development of Sicilian *mafia* must be understood as an aspect of the long-term processes of centralization and national integration of Italian society. Its vicissitudes in places like Genuardo were structurally concomitant with the gradual transformation of a feudal, dynastic State-society into that of a nation-State.[1] The violent operations of *mafiosi* marked an early stage in the development of the Italian nation. The interdependence between its regions and various social strata was still only very rudimentary, particularly in the predominantly agrarian South where noble landowners, though formally deprived of their social privileges, long retained a large measure of local and regional autonomy. The relative isolation of these levels and spheres on the one hand, and the growing impact of State-institutions on the other, provided ambitious and cunning rural entrepreneurs with

---

1. This transition is still poorly understood. More often than not, states and nation-states have been studied statically, in terms of "systems" and "ideal types," rather than in terms of their structured transformation and development over time. Even those scholars whose investigations are guided by a long-term historical perspective are primarily concerned with formal definitions, attributes, and reified abstractions. They often speak of "the State" as if it emerged full-blown with all its attributes and armor, like Pallas Athena from the head of Zeus. (This is true even of the most able writers, such as Bendix [1969] and Passerin d'Entrèves [1967.] Useful insights on the importance of changing power relations between different social groups in the process of State-formation can be gained from Elias' study of Western European societies (1969, vol. II).

specific power chances. As the main agents of expanding commercialization and monetization, leaseholders, cattle breeders, estate guards, merchants, millers, and waggoners succeeded in establishing control over the precarious links that tied the peasant to the larger society and the framework of the State. The gradual and violent rise of a rural middle stratum, the growing proletarianization of the peasantry, and the obsolescence of certain sectors of the landowning aristocracy were structurally connected with the dynamic of *mafia*. The upward mobility of peasant and rural entrepreneurs thus reflected significant changes in the distribution of power and in the nature of social inequality itself. Since *mafiosi* preserved local and regional isolation and remained closely tied to the rent-capitalistic structure of the large estates, which formed one of their main sources of power, the State in reaching this hinterland had no alternatives but to operate through them. This condition further strengthened the power domains of *mafiosi* which, in turn, helped to restrain and weaken the impact of State-institutions in western Sicily.

In the absence of a relatively impersonal central control over the means of violence, the notion of a State or nation with which people could identify themselves remained completely unknown. Long after the Unification of Italy in 1861, people saw themselves primarily as subjects of and identified themselves with powerful local and regional strongmen, called *pezzi grossi*, upon whom they in fact depended for their living and security. They were treated as subjects of these magnates and behaved accordingly.[2] Growing demo-

2. It has been argued that these patron–client configurations are structurally related to a specific orientation towards the supernatural world in which the cult of Saints stands out as a dominant element: "... it is obvious that religious and political patronage reinforce each other. Each serves as a model for the other.... This parallel was drawn for me by the Archpriest of Leone as he sought to explain the spiritual role of saints. He noted that just as you would not think of approaching a cabinet minister directly, but would work through some influential friend who could introduce you to the local deputy who could then state your case to the minister, so too must you not approach God directly. You must work through your patron saint who, being closer to God

cratization as exemplified in the extension of the franchise and the rise of political mass parties, increasing bureaucratization and expansion of government activities—processes which cannot be understood without taking account of the industrial and urban development of northern Italy—hardly posed a threat to Sicilian mafiosi and their entrenched power domains. Government-sponsored reforms and interference with the very conditions that generated *mafia* often merely helped to enlarge the scale on which *mafiosi* operated. They found and to a certain extent dominated the new channels to reach the sources of power that opened up at the regional and national level. Their inroads into the framework of the Christian Democrat Party and that of the expanding regional administration are cases in point.

One cannot say that *mafiosi* completely monopolized access to State resources, that, in other words, the violent broker could never be by-passed. *Mafiosi* were and still are undoubtedly by-passed occasionally, both inside and outside the political parties in power in Palermo and Rome. But given the failure of the left-wing parties to entrench themselves in western Sicily and to establish a rival organizational framework that could have adequately articulated local demands on regional and national levels, alternative roads remain much less effective and at times and on certain occa-

---

than you, is in a better position to persuade Him to heed your prayers" (Boissevain 1966a : 30–31). Boissevain notes the less pronounced role of these cults in Catholic countries in northern Europe where patron–client ties are likewise less important. The argument can be pushed one step further: these interrelations cannot be fully understood without considering the different stages of State-formation in southern and northern European Catholic societies. That is to say, where people have reached or are in the process of reaching adequate access to the State and can meaningfully identify themselves with the idea of a nation, they will tend to de-emphasize the cult of saints while underscoring the elements of a Christian commonwealth and specific Christian virtues as civic virtues. On the other hand, where states have not assumed the features of nation-states, or are only in the first phase of this process, as was and still is the case in southern Italy, people will be more receptive to the elements of personal power as expressed in both secular and religious realms.

sions even hazardous. Though the *mafioso* or *'ntisu*,[3] as he is often called, is still a familiar figure, this holds particularly true for the expanding urban milieu, most notably the city of Palermo and its immediate surroundings, and less so for the inland countryside. Why?

"*Prima c'era la mafia; adesso c'è la politica.*" (Before it was *mafia*; today it is politics.) This slightly opaque and ambiguous statement was made to me by a local man of about 40 resident in Palermo who was married to the daughter of one of the Cassinis and had been employed by the Agrarian Reform Board since the early 1950s. Upon closer inspection, however, these few words neatly summarize the events of recent structural changes in western Sicily. Though today there still are certain persons in the Genuardo countryside who "*vivono alle spalle altrui*" (lit.: live on the backs of others),[4] as one informant put it, it is only by twisting the imagination that one can still speak of something like "the *mafia* of Genuardo." As noted before, several *mafiosi* are established on commercially oriented farms of their own and are largely out of circulation as middlemen; others have simply left the area in search of new, more promising pastures.[5] There are a number of very powerful reasons why over the past decade or so *mafiosi* have been retreating from their position as power brokers in the inland districts.

First, the gradual disintegration of most of the large estates from the late 1940s onwards involved the disappearance of the traditional figures of *gabelloti* and *campieri*. Their homeland changed face. With the shifts in the distribution of land, the problems of management and supervision as well as the specific tasks of mediation and control vanished. Since agricultural techniques remained largely archaic, the transi-

3. From *sentire* (to listen); *'ntisu* (It.: *inteso*), listened to, a man who is listened to, a man whose word is accepted (*sua parola passa*). Implicit is the notion of respect based on a reputation for violence.
4. From *spalla*, shoulder or back.
5. The expression "*cercare pascoli nuovi*" (to look for new pastures) underscores the importance of herding and livestock breeding to capital accumulation at large. Hence the extension of the meaning attached to the term "*pascolo*."

tion from large landholdings to small and middle-range holdings severely restricted the number of big herds of cattle and sheep. This condition, too, involved a decrease of opportunities for *mafiosi* to assert themselves, just as it took away specific problems of control. The redistribution of land thus directly affected the relationships between the rural classes. Apart from the gradual disappearance of brokers between owners and cultivators and the less pronounced role of herdsmen, peasants and landowners became, in a way, less dependent upon each other. The latter, in most cases former leaseholders and estate guards, had less land and, quite apart from the impact of labor-saving machinery which some of them introduced on their farms, required fewer farm hands. A growing number of rural cultivators were provided with some land of their own, which gave them a measure of self-sufficiency hitherto unknown. Landless and land-poor peasants remained dependent upon landowners. But even people belonging to these categories succeeded in strengthening their bargaining position with respect to the landowners, since their number had decreased while the number of people to whom they could turn for employment had grown. Furthermore, the construction of roads, farms, and cottages provided additional employment. To an extent, peasant incomes were supplemented by a number of provisions regarding pensions and social security, though adequate access to these and other State resources, most notably the various contributions for agriculturalists to improve their farms, required personal links of friendship with those able to grant "favors" or to facilitate bureaucratic operations. For these reasons, *mafiosi* established as landowners had fewer sources of leverage over the peasantry than ever before. With the *latifondi* broken up, their former power domains were seriously weakened if not altogether swept away. Eventually, three surviving members of the Cassinis left Genuardo and retired to other towns. Two of their in-laws were employed by the Land Reform Board, but never acquired positions of dominance in public boards as has been described for old and new *mafiosi* in the neighboring towns of Camporeale and Corleone (Pantaleone 1966:113–28).

A second important condition that weakened control by *mafiosi* over the local population regards the rural exodus to the industrial North. The impact of migrant labor became tangible in the area from about 1960 onwards and reinforced the trend sketched above, in that increasing numbers of peasants severed their ties with local employers and, more generally, with the local organization of production by moving to industrial regions in northern Italy, Switzerland, Germany, and France. In 1967, out of a total resident population of slightly over 2,500 people, well over 500 persons, the largest part of them males between 18 and 45, had been or still were involved in migrant labor. There is no such thing as the "typical" migrant laborer. The unemployed and precariously employed left first. A second wave drew away smallholders who depended upon cheap casual labor and could not cope with sharply rising wages.[6] A third category involves unskilled sons of relatively well-to-do peasants. They have left less for "necessity" and more for "curiosity," as it is put, but also because they see no real prospect in local farming which cannot compete with more industrial forms of agriculture. Lacking professional qualifications, there are indeed few reasons for them to stay in a village whose social life has been crippled by emigration. Like their qualified age-mates awaiting white-collar employment, they describe Genuardo as a "dead village": *"Qui non c'è niente. C'è da morire!"* (In this place there is nothing to do but die.)

Migrant labor not only appeals to men. Scores of women have left with husbands, fathers, or brothers. In fact, those who had nothing but their arms to work with (lit.: *braccianti*, the landless laborers) have left, taking their families with them. This pattern is rare among smallholders, who usually leave their wives and children home in the village, sending money every month and working part of the year on the land. It is significant that the few smallholders who have left with their families are strongly criticized in the village.

6. Daily wages of casual laborers quadruplicated between the late 1950s and the early 1960s (from less than 1,000 *Lire* to about 3,000 *Lire*). Annual salaries of herdsmen increased from roughly 300,000 *Lire* to about one million *Lire*.

They are considered failures and, hence, their migration is less "legitimate." Remittances vary greatly as do the ways in which earnings are spent. Some buy up land, a house, or a shop and repair and modernize their home. Others invest in the education and careers of their children. Still others, especially unmarried young men, spend most of their money abroad, and in fact, they visit Genuardo infrequently. There are a few cases of young men who have left never to return. Migrant laborers also differ according to employment and housing conditions they find in the North. Some change employer on every trip. On my way back to Holland, I visited 14 migrant laborers from Genuardo on the outskirts of a south German town. They were contracted by a building-company that laid them off in winter. Lodged in a provisional caravan, they "were camping like gypsies," as they put it. On the other hand, there are some who have been working for years in the same place and at the same plant. Some older shepherds have returned after a few months. Apart from the *braccianti*, who left nothing behind, and the very young, those who cannot bring their wives and children with them consider migration a *sacrificio*.

Notwithstanding these varieties in migrant labor and migrant laborers, some basic patterns emerge clearly. Most Genuardesi abroad live near the border between Switzerland and Germany. Recruitment has taken place along links of kinship and friendship in most cases; kinsmen and friends abroad forming a kind of bridgehead for those still in Sicily. Few have completely cut their ties with the village. Even those who have not returned for years still own property in Genuardo. The money sent to the village (in 1966 a monthly average of about ten million *Lire* through the local post office alone) is largely spent on consumer goods. The moribund state of agriculture hardly permits alternative, more productive modes of investment. There are indeed few reasons to expect that remittances and the exodus of the labor force will help transform the anachronistic agrarian structure. Migrant labor, itself a temporary phenomenon, can only have temporary, short-term effects on the village structure. Sheer poverty has disappeared, and living standards have been raised considerably. But these are quite different from the transformation of the local organization of production. For one thing, such structural changes require the presence and involvement of the very people who are now leaving. To the extent that migrant laborers invest in land, they increase fragmentation and thus contribute to the marginal character of the zone, obstructing the consolidation of small holdings into larger units that would constitute a more viable form of agriculture. Also, by relieving the area of internal pressures for fundamental change, the labor exodus reinforces the marginality of the zone with respect to the industrial North.

It has been argued that backward areas like that of Sicily's interior are unlikely to be transformed by migrant labor to industrial regions, since it is the specific articulation of these structurally different zones to one another that precludes the development of new productive forms in the periphery.[7] This asymmetric symbiosis, clearly reminiscent of colonial situations, finds expression in both labor migration and prevalent modes of capital investment. The impact of emigration on Genuardo cannot fully be discussed here. Suffice it to note that, for the moment, industrial employment in the North provides the largest part of the local labor force with effective means to bypass *mafiosi*.[8]

A third circumstance that has reduced the prominence of local strong men in the area of Genuardo is the decreased competition for local resources. Fewer resources require control by violence. Furthermore, with the disappearance of unemployment and precarious employment, candidates for violent jobs are harder to find. As elsewhere in Europe, mountain and hill farming is becoming increasingly obsolete vis-à-vis industrial and heavily capitalized forms of agriculture.[9] Cheap labor is disappearing: even those established on

7. See the insightful essay by Schneider, Schneider and Hansen (1972). Cf. Pizzorno (1966:64–66); Cinanni (1970); Weingrod and Morin (1971:320–24).
8. For the relationship between *mafia* and migration in Camporeale, see Galtung (1962:433).
9. See Franklin's study on the waning of peasant farming in Europe (1969), and Bailey (1971).

medium-sized, commercially oriented farms cannot ignore the "price-cost squeeze" that hovers over the zone. Those who operate substantial farms must compete with other European farmers—co-members of the E.E.C.—who produce more, and less expensively. To a certain extent, the big landowners in Genuardo manage to make the grade because of government support. Mountain farming, especially, receives substantial benefits, at least on paper: mainly those with the right connections succeed in mobilizing credit and subsidies to transform their farms. Access to State resources is what counts today. Without it, local resources would be inconsequential. For example, Pietro Olivieri's farm is heavily subsidized. As we have seen before (p. 81), it covers roughly 135 hectares of the former Baronessa estates and is located in the mountains, some 15 kilometers northwest of the village. Here only pastures and wheat fields strike the eye. But Pietro has also about 200 milk-cows and an equal number of goats, which require additional pastures in certain periods of the year. The capital value of the land, farm house, and animals amounts to over 600 million *Lire*. The labor force includes eight herdsmen, who are annually employed and have salaries of about 800,000 *Lire* each. Every year some 50 hectares are sown and produce about 500 quintals of wheat worth slightly over four million *Lire*. The animals are milked during only part of the year and produce milk and cheese, which brings in over five million *Lire*. About 40 calves are born yearly, representing about eight million *Lire*. Taxes absorb slightly over one million *Lire*. The farm thus makes a gross profit of about 18 million *Lire*, but leaves its operator with much less than half if we consider expenditures regarding the lease of additional pastures, transport, maintenance and depreciation of agricultural machinery, equipment, and animals, and additional cost of labor during the harvest. As a sideline, Pietro holds an adjoining estate in *gabella* with his brother Aldo. Together with others, he runs the local mill. Pietro has two children. They are in their mid-twenties. Both have university degrees. Farmers like Pietro complain about the rising costs of labor. As one of them observed: "This emigration increases the cost of labor. The government should stop the emigration or, at least, restrict it thoroughly in order that each peasant may leave just for a year or so to pay off his debts and set up a house of his own. Thereafter, he should return and be forced to stay here."

It is obvious that not only the costs of labor are at issue here. We are dealing with the decline of a rural elite. With the peasants gone, peasant entrepreneurs cum landowners have lost a precious following—the power base that enables them to exert control at the regional and national level. They command fewer votes and thus have less leverage to operate effectively through the party network to obtain funds and to provide kinsmen, friends, and clients with the means to improve their conditions. This demonstrates the extent to which former *mafiosi* themselves now depend on power brokers who operate in higher echelons of political parties and the administration. Land is rapidly losing its significance as a power resource. Control over land no longer corresponds neatly to control over men. People like Pietro recognize the shift from *"mafia"* to "politics," in the apt words of our informant. They complain about what they call "dishonest politicians" for whom they canvassed votes in former days and who have let them down. Dishonest or not, politicians depend on votes and look for people who can provide them, preferably blocs of votes. Those entrenched in the network of one of the political parties in power or employed in the higher ranks of the regional administration are able to "make a recommendation," to mobilize State funds for "development," or to provide employment. They are the new patrons, or *pezzi grossi*, capable of attracting a considerable local following that supplies them with votes and, hence, with the means to enter the regional and national arena.

The rise of these new power brokers is exemplified in the competition for the position of mayor in Genuardo. In the local elections of 1964, a Socialist party activist, employed in one of the departments of the Sicilian regional government, beat his Christian Democrat opponent, a civil servant in the office of the mayor of Palermo. Originally from Genuardo, both men studied at the University of Palermo (only the

Socialist got a degree) where they have lived ever since. Both candidates are seen and present themselves as persons who are in a position to grant favors. In exchange for political support, they promise and sometimes can provide employment in private and public agencies in Palermo or elsewhere, agricultural funds and credits, licenses, and public work projects for the village. What makes them successful as power brokers are skills in social maneuvering: provision of benefits for the right men—those with extensive kinship affiliations, persons who have a clientele of their own. In this way, which by no means requires the use of violence, they build up local power domains that serve them in their dealings with the larger domain. The amplification of friendship networks and the maintenance of some measure of control over them are painstaking procedures which require time. The present mayor, who was 28 years when he was elected in 1964, carefully prepared his campaign after losing one round in the local arena in 1960. Unlike his Christian Democrat opponent, who was closely linked to the local and regional establishment and who refrained from any campaigning himself, the Socialist candidate had to forge his own following. Though he could draw on the left-wing minority as well as on several young unemployed professionals and disappointed elements in the opposite camp, he had to foster friendship and confidence and to make clear that he was in a position to articulate local demands more adequately than the Christian Democrats had done over the past 16 years. The Socialist–Communist electoral victory involved 771 votes out of a total of 1,356 valid returns. The mayor's control over these local votes, or at least part of them, serves as leverage that enables him to exert pressure on party members in the larger arena. Some of them administer and control development funds allocated by the State to the department of the regional government run by the Socialists. These regional politicians depend on people like the Genuardo mayor in regional and national elections. It is very much in their interest to meet some of the demands of their clients. To neglect them would amount to sawing off the branch they sit on. In fact, over the past few years, substantial funds for public works have been allocated to Genuardo, providing work for a number of people. In a similar vein, some young professionals have been "*sistemato*," that is, provided with permanent employment through the brokerage of the mayor. So we have come full circle.[10]

Like their *mafiosi* counterparts before, the new power brokers connect different categories of people who depend on one another but who cannot establish direct effective relationships. As far as Genuardo is concerned and as far as one can tell, their mediation between votes and State-resources does not require the use of violence or intimidation. Party patronage in this area has outstripped violent forms of brokerage and meets the general characteristics of modern politics in southern Italy which, according to one observer, amounts to "the judicious manipulation of blocs of votes through the allocation of economic development projects from the state" (Tarrow 1967:331). On a lower rung, just below that of the power brokers, and in urban rather than in rural areas, certain people still engage in violent competition for building contracts, the control over markets and transport, and the organization and supervision of labor at large. Instances of prepotence and intimidation occasionally take place in Genuardo. These incidents, however, pale before organized violent operations in urban centers like Palermo.[11] In villages and towns as small and predominantly agricultural as Genuardo, where life largely depends on the outside resources of State welfare and remittances from migrant labor, the scarcity of local spoils sets strong limits on violent forms of competition. For one thing, Genuardo lacks local contractors of any stature. Much of the house building is done by local masons and partly by the people themselves. They can hardly meet the great demand. The larger projects mentioned before and the construction of roads in the coun-

10. In the local elections of 1969, the mayor was re-elected.
11. For a description of violent control over markets and building areas in the 1950s and early 1960s, see Pantaleone (1966:167–79) and Poma and Perrone (1964:103 ff.). Sciascia's narrative (1961) on the *mafia* of an inland town is of particular interest, quite apart from its unusual literary value.

try are carried out by building companies from other places. Nothing could be ascertained about the extent, if any, of their infighting. Acts of intimidation occur on a small scale and are not connected with any comprehensive network of violent entrepreneurs as in former days. We hear of cases in which payment is withheld for work done and of people who succeed in getting on the payroll of the public work projects without doing any substantial work. Like the occasional thefts of animals and acts of violence and intimidation, these operations remain isolated events. If they reveal a pattern at all, it is that violence pays much less than it ever did. What invites control are votes. To weld them together in the Genuardo area requires qualifications other than physical force.

There are thus several reasons that explain the retreat of *mafiosi* as violent power brokers from the social life of Genuardo. It has been often argued, though less often clearly demonstrated, that during the last two decades *mafiosi* have been moving from the countryside to the city, from the inland *feudi* to the urban markets and building areas, as well as into the organizations of public administration.[12] Insofar as this may be true, and the recent history of Genuardo shows this process very clearly, it is largely in a figurative sense that one can speak of a "movement" from the hinterland to the capital city of Palermo. There is indeed little evidence for an actual migration of former *gabelloti* and estate guards —the backbone of the rural *mafia*—from the country to the city. With the possible exception of people like Luciano Liggio, who was still a teenager when he assumed the lease of the Strassate *feudo* in the territory of Corleone at the end of the war, few *mafiosi* from the inland zone have become successful in urban ventures. In Genuardo, few *mafiosi* moved at all, and those who did, like three members of the Cassinis, have not succeeded in exploiting a substantial niche elsewhere.

This seems to be a general pattern. *Mafiosi* depend very

12. E.g., Renda (1956:218–20); Romano (1966:325–26); and Pantaleone (1966:167–68).

much on personal relations with a local clientele—their "home farm" so to speak—whose growth takes time. Their power domains are locally phrased, and it is precisely their control over a distinct locality that enables them to influence higher levels of society as power brokers. When not forced by circumstances, established *mafiosi* have little reason for moving.[13] Well-known chiefs like Vito Cascio Ferro, Calogero Vizzini, and Giuseppe Genco Russo lived most of their lives in such places as Bisacquino, Villalba, and Mussomeli. The semi-literacy of these prominent rural *mafiosi*, which has so often puzzled observers of the Sicilian scene who are used to and hence expect certain standards of literacy among influential political figures, is wholly consonant with, and incomprehensible apart from, their parochial locus.

The so-called "movement" of *mafiosi* from rural to urban areas in the 1950s should therefore be understood in a special sense. On the one hand, it involved a gradual decline of violent forms of mediation in the inland areas. On the other hand, it showed a proliferation of violence in urban centers, most notably Palermo and the adjoining zones of this city. Regarding the continuity of *mafia*, for which I found little evidence in Genuardo, one should look at the penetration of relatively young, professional kinsmen and friends of established rural *mafiosi* of an older generation into the organs of the regional administration. Though these civil servants are not necessarily *mafiosi* themselves, there are good reasons to assume that many of them are highly sensitive to pressure from *mafiosi* to their home towns, as well as in their new residence where gangsterlike groupings are in a position to ask and obtain favors.[14]

The transition from *mafia* to politics, the process that has

13. Placed in a strange environment, *mafiosi* have their wings clipped. Hence the legal measure of *domicilio coatto*, (forced residence in a given place) to which several of them have been recently subjected.

14. For brief notes on this development, see the articles of Lino Jannuzzi (1965a, 1965b, 1971). There is nothing new about these incursions and collusions, save for the larger scale on which they are now tangible. We thus find growing bureaucratization without a corresponding extension of central control.

been described as the *"politicizzazione"* of both old and newly established public offices, has been investigated by a Parliamentary Commission since 1963. As far as one can tell (no substantial accounts were available at this writing), the Commission has primarily dealt with the phenomenon of *mafia* in urban centers, specifically Palermo, the locus of the regional government.[15] It is to be noted that the Anti-*Mafia* Commission employs a fairly broad notion of *mafia* that includes various forms of corruption, not just the specifically violent incursions into the framework of the State that have been the subject of this book. Interviewed by a Palermo newspaper in the summer of 1966, Donato Pafundi, then president of the Commission, described the phenomenon in the following terms:

> The *mafia* in Sicily is a "mental condition" pervading everything and all sorts of people on every level. The *mafia* ended up in the blood, in the most hidden structures of society. Above all, it is to be found in the atavistic distrust of the law and, for that reason, in the disregard of the law which among Sicilians assumes the characteristics of an epidemic voluptuousness. It is a mentality harboring in proprietors, peasants, magistrates, local authorities, the police, everywhere. It is impossible to identify, to dissect, to separate the collusion with the *mafia*. Because, as I have said, it enters in all the houses, through the door as well as through the window. Hence the *omertà* which is fortunately suffering the first flaws, the first cracks. . . .
>
> Do you know that the apparatus of the public forces to maintain law and order in Sicily is the most complete and the most extensive in Italy? But for the *mafia* it is of no use. As I have said before, it is a mental condition that bewitches, enchants, contaminates—you may choose the appropriate term for yourself—it instills everywhere also

15. Its investigations cover markets; regional, provincial, and communal administration (the so-called *enti locali*); the administration of justice; and banks. See Pantaleone (1969). In the summer of 1963, six persons from Genuardo were interrogated by the local *Carabinieri* and had to account for their sources of income, but this did not lead to arrests and exiles as happened elsewhere.

in those strongholds, like the Magistracy, that should be unassailable and vaccinated against the *mafia*.[16]

If *mafia* is as pervasive as suggested by Senator Pafundi, comprising all instances of corruption and illegality, one cannot reasonably expect that the Anti-*Mafia* Commission will be able to complete its task, that is, "to report to Parliament on the most suitable remedy." Indeed, after almost ten years of study, in the spring of 1972 the Commission has concluded in its extensive report that *mafia* by its very nature defies any remedy. All public agencies that would take action are rendered ineffective, since they are in varying degrees intertwined with *mafiosi* and their protectors. Sicilian *mafia*, understood as *the collusions themselves* rather than as something separate from them (a common but fallacious conceptualization), presents itself as an effective force in present-day Italian politics, reflecting the stage of development of Italian society at large. Corruption, and *mafia* for that matter, are inherent parts of societies in a relatively early phase of State-formation. Can one ask Sicilians to act as citizens when most of them still are and consider themselves as subjects of powerful local and regional magnates upon whom they depend for protection and making a living? Under the present conditions, the State can only remove the most out-

16. "La mafia in Sicilia è uno 'stato mentale,' pervade tutto e tutti, a tutti i livelli. La mafia è finita nel sangue, nelle strutture più riposte della società. Sta soprattutto nell'atavica sfiducia nelle leggi e perciò nel non osservarle, che nei siciliani assume un carattere di voluttà epidermica [sic]. E' una mentalità che alberga nei possidenti, nei contadini, nei magistrati, nelle autorità locali, nella polizia, dappertutto. La collusione con la mafia non è possibile individuarla, sezionarla, separarla. Perché come abbiamo detto, entra in tutte le case, dalla porta come dalla finestra. Di qui l'omertà che per fortuna sta subendo le prime incrinature, le prime fenditure ...

"Lei sa che l'apparato delle forze d'ordine pubblico in Sicilia è il più completo e grande d'Italia? Ma per la mafia non serve. Come le ho detto prima, uno stato mentale, che ammalìa, affascina, contagia—scelga lei il termine—si insinua dappertutto anche in quelle roccaforti, come la Magistratura, che dovrebbero essere imprendibili e vaccinate contro la mafia." Interview, *Giornale di Sicilia*, August 6, 1966.

standing symptoms of *mafia* and corruption. It is to mis-understand these conditions and the specific stage of de-velopment of Italian society, to ask for and expect more substantial forms of short term intervention. By comparison, Wertheim notes the Sisyphean proportions of the fight against corruption in the new non-socialist Asian states: "All such measures of stricter supervision fail because of their negative approach: they merely combat undesirable symp-toms. The root of the evil is the lack of a . . . spiritual involve-ment in its task in society, on the part both of the officials and of the whole community" (1964:130). What here is called "the root of the evil," however, is nothing but corruption or symptoms of corruption themselves. Though Wertheim men-tions the Chinese example as being instructive (which it certainly is), he does not make clear what specific type of change had taken place that enables people to encourage a positive approach in all public servants or to carry through sharp measures against deviations. Attitudes towards the government and involvement in tasks in society on the part of the people who form it will only change with changes in the society at large. Only by studying these interrelations and seeing them as aspects of the distribution of power and the division of labor in society will we get beyond the mere description of corruption and help account for its genesis, development, and decline. Furthermore, to see corruption as something which is morally bad needlessly burdens the task of analysis. It suggests that there are evildoers who can be punished. We must expect, however, that people who act in particularistic and corrupt ways in not making a clear dis-tinction between public and private affairs have few other options. They are part of societies in which the distribution of power is far more uneven than in certain nation–State societies where people can, quite apart from personal merits, afford to be "honest." In some contemporary European societies, and perhaps also in present-day China, we are con-cerned with a growing functional interdependence between regions, between social strata, and between governments and governed. These interrelations have, in the words of Elias, become "sufficiently great and sufficiently reciprocal for none of them to be able to disregard completely what the others think, feel or wish" (1972).

As the present essay has sought to make clear, the retreat of *mafiosi* from certain zones in Sicily's interior during the past decades is connected with the largely unplanned but structured processes of outward labor migration and the gradual obsolescence of peasant farming, rather than a fundamental transformation of the tragic conditions underlying the lives of the people portrayed in this book.

APPENDICES

Appendix A

The following cases further demonstrate the relatively high level of socially permitted physical violence and corresponding low level of revulsion against using it or witnessing it. They also illustrate the extent to which power domains were locally phrased and rendered the overarching authority of the State largely nominal.

1. In May 1944, a peasant from the neighboring town of Salaparuta, who owned land in the territory of Genuardo, killed two bandits near his cottage in the country. They had sent him extortion letters and came to take the money. The peasant was not tried since he had been threatened and had acted in self-defense.
2. In November 1945, unknown bandits attacked and robbed three wayfarers along the road to the village, killing one of them.
3. During another holdup, in the wooded upper reaches of the village territory, of a group of mounted peasants returning from their fields one late afternoon in November 1946, one peasant was shot dead. Upon the bandits' order to dismount, lie down, and leave them his mule, he had reached for his gun. (He was a skilled marksman and could not stand being forced at gunpoint.) The perpetrators remained unknown.
4. As discussed above (p. 197), in August 1946, two *mafiosi* from Bisacquino were killed by rivals in a dispute over the lease of an estate in the bordering commune of Pietracollina.

5. For reasons of vendetta, the particulars of which are lacking, an outlaw from a neighboring town was shot dead by unknown *mafiosi*. His body was thrown into the river Belice, where it was found one day in early April 1947.

6. In the same period a brother of Saverio Tortochetti, killed by the local *mafia* in 1921 (see pp. 159–60), was kidnapped by bandits and carried off to a secluded place in the country. His family, rather well-off and, as we have seen, not involved in the *mafia* network, was informed of the kidnapping and told to pay ransom. Things worked out in an unexpected way when a patrol of *Carabinieri* accidentally walked into the mountain cave where Tortochetti had been placed to await his fate.

7. Pertaining to the same period is an unverified and probably apocryphal story about Simone Cassini, one of the local *mafiosi* prominent shortly after the war (see Diagram 11). Alone in the country, Simone was surprised by two bandits who ordered him to dismount and hand over his two mules. Simone could not but comply, and he is reported to have said on that occasion: "Also from me you have to steal?" He did not, however, simply accept his loss and informed his "friends" in neighboring places about what had happened. Some days afterwards, his two mules were found grazing near the place where they had been stolen. Not far from there sprawled the disfigured corpses of the two bandits.

8. In the spring of 1947, Giorgio, a well-to-do peasant, was kidnapped and sequestered by bandits who, upon his promise to pay them, released him. Giorgio, however, did not keep his word, and some weeks passed during which the incident was almost forgotten. In the meantime another extortion letter, which only later proved to be from another party, reached Giorgio, who then applied to his brother's wife's father, a shepherd *mafioso* and still a respected old-timer, who discussed the matter with his "friend" Leonardo, another shepherd. Both had been active in the local *cosca* before the Fascist roundups. They were *amici di lasagni,* that is, very close

friends.[1] Leonardo had pasture land in lease near the place where the money had to be taken and arranged to be there with his sheep at the time stipulated in the letter, a coincidence that would not raise the suspicion of the extortionist whose identity could then quite easily be ascertained. When the author appeared he turned out to be Stefano, one of the local poor. Leonardo drew near with his sheep to enter in a casual conversation. He then took hold of Stefano and gave him a terrible thrashing with his stick. Leonardo merely "let his victim live," as one informant observed. People like Leonardo and his friend did not allow dilettantes to enter the field of extortion. When letters were to be written, they would pen them.[2]

Some weeks later, at the end of May, one of the local millers discovered the body of a drowned man at the bottom of his country mill-well. Closer inspection revealed it to be that of Giorgio. Investigations disclosed that Giorgio had fallen victim to the bandits whom he had originally promised to pay. The bandits had returned and captured the unsuspecting Giorgio at the outskirts of the village. They set off to the country mill. Giorgio was tied, his pockets filled with stones, and flung into the well.

9. In July 1950, a peasant laborer from Genuardo, who gleaned the stubbles of the Moli estate, got into trouble with the *campiere* charged with the supervision of this estate. The latter tried to make the peasant leave. This gave rise to a heated argument on the right of gleaning. The peasant made clear that he would discuss the issue with the landowner himself in order to straighten things out. This enraged the *campiere*, who took his gun and killed his unarmed opponent. The man was arrested but

1. *Amici di lasagni.* From *lasagna*, but here meaning the place where people eat together at the country mill.
2. Cf. Hobsbawm's observation on the distinction between *mafia* and banditry: "*Mafia* maintained public order by private means. Bandits were, broadly speaking, what it protected the public from" (1959:40).

released after a month or so, since it was argued that he had shot him in self-defense. According to some inform- ants who witnessed the incident, the peasant had not actually threatened the *campiere* but merely moved his arms to sustain his point in the argument.

10. One Sunday morning in December 1950, two *lupara*-shots[3] killed Gaspare, a cobbler, at the front porch of his house. The news of this murder was allegedly greeted with wide approval in the village. Gaspare was con- sidered *cattivo* (bad), a man who needlessly bothered and nagged other people, including his wife and children whom he terrorized. But the reason for his murder was an affair he had with a recently married woman. They had maintained relations long before her marriage. People say that her husband did the killing. Her father gave himself up to spare his son-in-law. He was tried and spent about three years in prison. Shortly after the incident, the girl and her husband moved to Palermo.

11. One night in July 1952, an old shepherd was shot dead on the threshold of his farmhouse. It appeared that the murderer had called for him from the outside and then waited to kill his victim. This homicide was brought into connection with the fact that the shepherd had accused various persons during the Fascist roundups in the late 1920s. The long time lag may explain the imprudence of the shepherd. The author of this vendetta remained un- known.

12. At the end of November 1952, a sharecropper from Bis- acquino was killed by *lupara*-shots. He had sent extortion letters.

13. On a rainy morning in March 1956, on pasture land just above the village, two *lupara*-shots ended the life of the shepherd Leonardo, the man who so mercilessly pun- ished Stefano (see case 8). Suspicion fell on another shepherd, Biagio, a former partner of Leonardo. Some time before they had broken off their partnership after

---

3. *Lupara*, lit. wolf-shot. A cartridge loaded with large leaden balls. When fired, the shot has a specific spread effect, thus enlarging the chance of hitting the mark.

having discords. Biagio remained a full year in detention before he was released for lack of evidence. Many people believed him innocent. Some informants traced a relationship between Leonardo's death and his violent action against Stefano, whose brother emigrated shortly afterwards. This man, who later returned to the village, was never charged.

14. (Time: about 1955.) Vincenzo, a waggoner, had sexual relations with Paola, a servant girl employed at his parental home, but refused to marry her as is customary. He left the village and stayed with "friends" in several places in other provinces. His occupation facilitated these continual moves. Paola became pregnant and sought to get her way by means of force. She addressed herself to her maternal uncles, known *mafiosi* in a town south of Palermo. They sent a "friend" to Vincenzo, who was thus forced to return to Genuardo. After some time, shortly before the birth of his daughter, he married Paola.

15. (Time: the 1950s.) Giuseppina was married to Pietro. Both belong to the village poor. After she had two daughters by him, their relationship cooled. Luigi, belonging to a well-to-do family, returned to the village after the war. After completing his studies at the university, he acquired a prominent position in the village. He was and still is well-known in the area. In the course of time, Luigi established a relationship with Giuseppina. His visits to her home evoked general criticism. Luigi ignored this. The liaison did not lead to retaliation from the side of Pietro or Giuseppina's grown-up brothers, though people expected this to happen. Eventually, Luigi and Giuseppina went to live together. Acting thus, Luigi staked his own honor as well: taking responsibility for Giuseppina, he now fully shared in her shame. Afterwards, a son was born and when Pietro died, both married formally. Social criticism did not calm down. Yet, Luigi's prestige, influence, and personality counter-balanced the affair pretty well. The position of Giuseppina's brothers was equivocal. In the beginning they threatened Luigi; later on they gradually came to terms with him,

for they understood that it was very much in their interest to do so. Luigi was a powerful patron, able to mobilize energetic and dangerous allies—specifically *mafiosi* from other towns with whom he was on intimate terms. Through his influence, Luigi was able to get work for them (they were truck drivers). So they made the best of a bad bargain. They were certainly not ostracized. Some people, however, still refer to them as "men with golden horns."[4] As the proverb says: Horns are like teeth: when they come in they are painful, but when they are growing they help you eating. This epitomizes the power and pragmatic aspects of honor and values so often neglected in discussions of the subject by social scientists.[5]

16. (Time: about 1959.) Giovanni and Maria, both about eighteen years old, met regularly in the church where the boy assisted the verger. They had sexual intercourse, and Maria informed her father about it. When Giovanni was asked to marry the girl, he refused: she might have extended her favors to other men as well. This appeared to be untrue, though the coquettish ways of the girl earned her the reputation of a *civetta* (flirt) which weakened her cause. Another reason for refusal, from the side of the boy's family, was a difference in social position. Maria's father was a landless laborer (and son of one of the casual laborers involved in the 1915 rustlings [see pp. 148–49]), while Giovanni was from an artisanal background. Furthermore, Giovanni was not really in love with the girl. The priest opted for his protégé. He nursed a grievance against Maria's father, who had offended him after the priest had mediated in the expropriation of the Piano estate held in lease by the left-wing cooperative of which Maria's father was a member. Thus pressed, his honor at stake, the man turned to *mafiosi* from a

4. Horns (*corna*) are the stigmatized attributes of the cuckold (*cornuto*), the man who fails to control the sexual activities of the women he is socially committed to. For an instructive discussion on this subject, see Pitt-Rivers (1961:116; 1965:46 ff.).
5. See, however, John Davis' recent analysis of honor in southern Italy (1969).

neighboring village and showed himself ostentatiously with them in public. With this move he indicated how far he was willing to go. At this point Luigi (see case 15) intervened and succeeded in pursuading the priest to climb down. Shortly after this encounter Giovanni and Maria married. In the 1960s they emigrated to Germany. They did not get along very well together. Their marriage, forged through intimidation, was, upon request of Giovanni, eventually dissolved by the Church.

17. The estate owner Giancarlo wanted to dismiss his *gabelloto* and consequently came at loggerheads with him. In collusion with a close friend of Giancarlo, the *gabelloto* hired two cutthroats to kill the estate owner. This was accomplished at the end of April 1959 at Giancarlo's country house along the western borders of the Genuardo territory. Afterwards, the accomplice killed one of the assassins. In the end, the offenders—all of them from a neighboring town—were arrested, tried, and convicted.

18. On account of his involvement in cattle raids, one of them at the expense of the Tortochettis, a cowherd from Bisacquino was killed by an hired assassin in April 1960 at the estate Moli. It was assumed that the man was eliminated by order of the thieves, who feared that their accomplice might talk.

19. On the night of July 20, 1962, poachers from a town in the province of Agrigento drove their car onto the Santa Maria del Bosco estates to shoot rabbits. They were disturbed in their hunting efforts by the owner Giacomo (the former mayor of Genuardo [see Chapter VIII]) who fired his Winchester from his window in their direction; killing one poacher (a university student). Giacomo was tried for manslaughter and condemned to ten months' imprisonment by the Court of Appeal in October 1965.

Apart from these cases of homicide and other forms of violence in the period from 1944 through 1962, the territory of Genuardo was afflicted by scores of cattle raids. Between 1950 and 1962, over 40 cases were registered by the local

Carabinieri. Though occasionally some of the stolen animals were found, in only two cases could the rustlers be identified and tried. To obtain an idea of the organization required to carry out a successful rustling as well as to make clear the difficulties in coping with cattle thieves, three cases will be looked at more closely.

1. The three brothers Angelo, Fortunato, and Federico Occhipinti, all of them married as of 1966, run a farm of about 30 hectares roughly seven kilometers west of the village. The land was bought by their father in the early 1920s. The farmhouse on it has been rebuilt (with 36 per cent of the cost paid by the regional government). It includes stables, barns, and hayloft. An additional 20 hectares are held in lease as pasture land for the cows and sheep. They employ two boys for tending the flocks and one tractor driver for plowing and mowing. The Occhipinti brothers also have a large house in the village where they stay permanently. The three families live next to each other in the house, but each forms an independent household. They have a car, which they use to go to their farm and back every day, though one of them stays there during the night. They descend from a *gabelloto* family: their maternal grandfather was Giacomo Cassini (see Diagram 7). As the eldest, Angelo, remarked: "My grandfather belonged to the well-to-do-families at the time. In the *circolo* [club] he was approached by the laborers, who queued up at the *piazza* to ask for contracts. Times have been changing. Now we have to beg the laborers, otherwise they won't come. This has been true since people have been leaving for Germany."

On the night of September 19, 1957, Fortunato was driving the herd of 20 cows back to the farmhouse on horseback. But before he arrived there, his way was blocked by two men on foot who came down the road, and while still some distance away, they asked for matches. Fortunato ignored them. They said: "Don't you recognize us? We have been around here at the harvest!" Fortunato answered: "I don't know anybody!" And, understanding that the two men were up to no good, he spurred his horse on and fled, for he was unarmed. One of the men shot at him with his pistol, but missed. Fortunato's horse stumbled and fell but drew itself up again, and Fortunato succeeded in reaching the farmhouse, leaving behind the cows. He sent one of the cowherds to the village to warn his brothers and the *Carabinieri*. Though there were some people around they were not willing to help Fortunato recover the animals. They advised him to stay at the farmhouse. They said he might be killed. As it grew darker, Fortunato could see the thieves bring the cows together on a hill and take off their bells. Fortunato now and then fired a shot at them with the gun he had found in the farmhouse, but of course missed them, for they were too far away. When it was completely dark, the thieves disappeared with the animals by an unknown route.

When Fortunato's brother, Angelo, had been informed by the boy sent to the village, he contacted the local *Carabinieri* and set out with them to his farm. That evening and the next day they searched the whole area, especially the wooded parts of Genuardo, without any result. The third day, the brothers received an extortion letter in which they were promised their animals if they would bring half a million *Lire* to a cottage in the mountains. In agreement with the *Carabinieri*, one of the brothers went there while some *Carabinieri* hid nearby. They arrested an old shepherd and a boy. (While in custody the old man later died; the boy was released in the summer of the next year.) After a week, Angelo identified a cow as one of his at a butcher's in Ribera, a town south of Genuardo. In the same shop the skins of three of his animals were also discovered. The butcher was convicted for slaughtering animals illegally and he was fined 20,000 *Lire*. In July 1958, the law suit against unknown persons was closed.

It was generally believed that the raid was organized by *mafiosi* from the town of Adernò who had land next to that of the Occhipintis. Some people suggested that the three brothers were stingy with *ricotta*; in general they were not very generous towards these *mafiosi*. One informant believed that the Occhipintis were not sufficiently protected. Their mother's brother, Antonio (see Diagram 7), thought of himself as a *mafioso*, but was not considered *"omu."* He had addressed himself to his nephew's neighbors, but they said they knew nothing.

2. One night in February 1958, a flock of 140 sheep was stolen from a man called Leoluca who lived at the outskirts of the village. The animals had been driven out of the open pen near his house. Investigations by the authorities and the owner did not have any effect. They searched the triangle formed by Alcamo, Burgio, and Corleone. In January 1959, another flock of 80 sheep was stolen in similar fashion from Leoluca. After some time he received an anonymous letter that specified the whereabouts of the sheep: the present owners, place, and other details. The following morning Leoluca arrived with *Carabinieri* at the indicated place. They recovered 40 sheep, among which were animals taken in the first raid. Two men were arrested and tried. According to Leoluca: "Those who assisted the thieves were people from here and actually kinsmen of the thieves, who lodged with them on the night of the theft. The anonymous letter was written by their accomplice here in the village, who obtained part of the booty the first time, but who was left without anything the second theft. He was offended and avenged himself this way. After all, I understood who he was. In fact, I know him very well. I then bred the 40 sheep until I had about 100. Then I sold them. My grown-up children have now left for Germany."

3. One night in early April 1961, twenty-two goats, five cows, and five calves were stolen from Filippo and his father, poor goatherds living on the outskirts of the village. The same night, eleven goats returned by themselves. Filippo denounced the theft, but nothing could be ascertained about the perpetrators. It was assumed that the animals had been loaded on a truck waiting

outside the village. Filippo's mother remembered in a conversation six years later: "We know who had done it. First they were our guests, so they could see the environment, how we lived, what kind of people we were, whether we had arms and were able to kill, where we had the keys, and so on. We only lack the proof. Moreover, one has to be careful: *bisogna guardare le spalle agli uomini* (one has to protect one's menfolk by not talking). They go out in the country everyday!" A second informant commented: "Certain goatherds and shepherds here are respected. The thieves look where to steal. Those with a capacity to kill are left in peace."

Appendix B

TABLE I

Population of Genuardo: 1548–1966

date	population
1548	500
1642	1,003
1701	1,763
1748	2,448
1798	3,018
1861	3,364
1871	3,201
1881	3,293
1901	2,646
1911	2,117
1921	1,911
1931	2,801
1961	2,669
1966	2,556

Source: Communal Archives

TABLE II

Distribution of land in Genuardo (1900)

landowners number	%	land hectares	%	size of property
1,052	88	1,446	10	small: less than 10 ha.
120	10	3,141	23	medium: 10–100 ha.
26	2	9,200	67	large: over 100 ha.
1,198	100	13,787	100	

Source: Private papers (1900).

TABLE III

Changes in the distribution of landed properties in Genuardo:
1843–1966

date	landed properties in hectares		
	less than 10 ha.	10–100 ha.	more than 100 ha.
1843	1,200	—	12,587
1900	1,446	3,141	9,200
1947	2,087	5,722	6,455
1966	5,568	6,079	2,015

Sources: Private papers (1843 and 1900); INEA (1947); and Communal Archives (1966).

TABLE IV

Changes in the distribution of landed properties larger than 200 hectares
(compare Table III)

date	area covered by large estates (in hectares)
1843	12,587
1910	6,982
1926	4,380
1929	4,964
1947	4,040
1966	745

Sources: Private papers (1843); Lorenzoni (1910); Castrilli (1926); Molè (1929); INEA (1947); and Communal Archives (1966).

TABLE V

Patterns of land use in Genuardo from 1852 to 1947

	1852 ha.	%	1914 ha.	%	1929/47 ha.	%
cereals	9,187	67	11,527	84	10,695	78
natural pastures	3,697	27	1,635	12	1,806	13
woods	672	5	94	1	128	1
olives, vines, and other fruits	223	1	373	2	286	2
uncultivated	*		159	1	301	2
unproductive	*		*		421	3
total	13,779	100	13,788	100	13,637	100

Sources: Private papers; *Catasto Agrario* (1935); INEA (1947).
* No data specified.

TABLE VI
Animals belonging to people living in Genuardo (1900–1966)

	animals number		owners number	
	1900	1966	1900	1966
mules	316	± 500	216	± 400
horses	113	± 20	79	± 15
donkeys	163	2	151	2
oxen	108	—	24	—
cows	193	1,775	42	102
sheep	3,810	4,573	9	24
goats	103	565	7	7

Sources: Private papers; Communal Archives; interviews.

TABLE VII
The pattern of landholdings in Genuardo (1930)

size of holdings (hectares)	number of holdings	area covered (hectares)
0.25–50	—*	5,125
50–100	13	939
100–200	19	2,773
larger than 200	8	4,380

Source: Castrilli (1926:235); cf. *Catasto Agrario* (1935).

* Not specified by Castrilli. The *Catasto Agrario*, which refers to the situation as existing in March 1930, mentions a number of 470 *aziende agricole* (farms) smaller than 50 hectares. Yet this is hardly an appropriate term, since many so-called *aziende*, especially the smaller ones (of which 107 were smaller than one hectare and 130 between one and three hectares), consisted of several fragmented and widely scattered holdings. In this category, compact holdings and viable farms were rare.

TABLE VIII
Labor force at Baronessa (1902)

Personnel	tot.	lire	horses	sheep	Annual Payment						land cultivated (hectares)
					cheese and ricotta (kg.)	wine (lt.)	bread (kg.)	pasta (kg.)	olive-oil (kg.)	beans (kg.)	
overseer	1	525	1	—	12	264	608	12	6.4	112	5¼ wheat beans 1.3‡
field guard	5	225	½	—	12	264	608	12	6.4	112	5¼ wheat beans 1.3
bookkeeper	1	225	½	—	12	264	608	12	6.4	112	5¼ wheat beans 1.3
storekeeper	1	225	½	—	12	264	608	12	6.4	112	5¼ wheat beans 1.3
oxen driver	2	225	½	—	12	264	608	12	6.4	112	5¼ wheat beans 1.3
mule driver	2	225	½	—	12	264	608	12	6.4	112	5¼ wheat beans 1.3
hired hand	15	190	—	—	12	192	608	10	6.4	112	— beans 0.16
cheesemaker	1	127.5	½	50*	—	192	584†	—	6.4	—	—
shepherd	6	115	½	25*	—	115	512*	—	6.4	—	—
shepherd boys	5	70	—	—	—	—	512	—	—	—	—

* In *società* (partnership) with the *gabelloti*. The latter took all the milk; the cheesemaker obtained one-third of the lambs.

† Not included 146 kg. for dogs.

‡ Liters—sown.

TABLE IX

Flocks herded on the Baronessa estates between September 1920 and August 1921

estates	size in hectares	sulla-plots in hectares	owners of cattle and flocks	home town	cattle	sheep	land use
Zotto	380	19	Baronessa	Genuardo	—	500	pasture
Zotto		15	Leonardo	Villamaura	23	320	pasture
Zotto		15	Baronessa	Genuardo			pasture
Zotto			Leonardo	Villamaura			pasture
Zotto		68	Nicola	Corleone	20	330	pasture
Zotto		5	Baronessa	Genuardo			hay
Zillo	126	38	Michele	Burgio	30	408	pasture
Zillo		42	Giovanni	Genuardo	23	460	pasture
Ponte	134	13	Baronessa	Genuardo			pasture and hay
Ponte		20	Baronessa	Genuardo			hay and seed
Rello	375	25	Antonio	Adernò	24	620	pasture
Rello		64	Luigi	Genuardo	40	500	pasture
Rello		62	Pietro	Genuardo	23	250	pasture
Rello		5	Baronessa	Genuardo			hay and seed
Rocca*	60		Rosario	Prizzi	25	1,000	natural pastures
	1,075	391			208	4,388	

* This small estate, located in the mountains, was not cultivated with *sulla*, but consisted of natural pastures.

TABLE X

Land use and division of labor at Baronessa according to Buttazzoni (1939). Numbers refer to hectares

fields	wage-labor	sharecropping	lease	total
cereals	78	786	—	864
sulla	270	—	—	270
beans	21	15	—	36
fallow	123	—	—	123
natural pastures	553	—	200	753
olives a.o. trees	54	—	—	54

TABLE XI

Animals employed at Baronessa according to Buttazzoni (1939)

animals	Baronessa	outsiders	total
oxen and cows	117	—	117
horses	15	9	24
mules	12	60	72
sheep	402	798	1,200
goats	144	102	246

TABLE XII

*Changes in the distribution of landed properties in
Genuardo: 1947–1966*

categories	area covered hectares		properties numbers	
	1947	1966	1947	1966
less than 0.5 hectares	145	121	970	406
0.5–2	507	784	475	706
2–10	1,435	4,663	329	921
10–50	3,155	4,726	144	240
50–100	1,567	1,333	24	19
100–200	2,415	1,276	16	9
larger than 200 hectares	4,040	745	6	1
	13,264	13,648	1,964	2,302

Sources: INEA (1947); Communal Archives (1966).

It is necessary to recognize that reliable data on this subject are difficult to obtain. To gather them would have required much more time than I had at my disposal. The archives to which I was permitted access were neither complete nor up-to-date. The bulk of cadastral listings embrace several names each. For this reason, the problems of fragmentation are often more significant than the mere number of holdings suggests.

TABLE XIII

Division, sale, and expropriation of the Baronessa estates from 1946 onwards

estates	size	latifundist kin group	ownership outsiders	reform
Zotto	380	180	200	—
Rizzo	121	90	31	—
Bovaro	263	—	263	—
Rello	376	60	215	101
Rocca	61	—	61	—
Zillo	126	80	46	—
Sassone	341	273	—	68
Ponte	135	—	94	41
Piano	275	45	—	230
hectares	2,078	728	910	440
%	100	34	41	25

TABLE XIV

Elections in Genuardo: 1946–1948
(total valid votes)

Arena	Date	DC	PCI/PSI	Total
Town council	April 7th 1946	1,008	369	1,377
National Assembly	June 2nd 1946	669	405	1,301
Regional Assembly	April 20th 1947	356	757	1,435
National Assembly	April 18th 1948	881	398	1,533

Source: Le Elezioni in Sicilia (1956).

Appendix C

Diagram 1
The Jaconis : *gabelloti* and professionals.

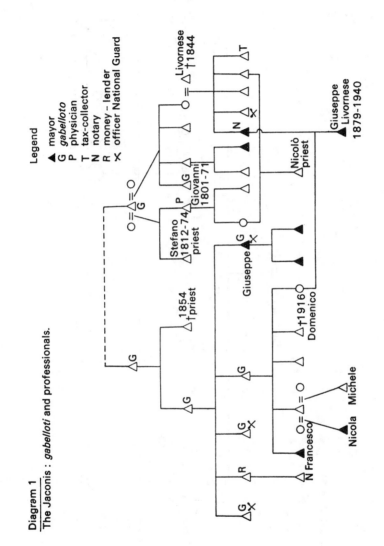

Legend

▲ mayor
G *gabelloto*
P physician
T tax-collector
N notary
R money - lender
✕ officer National Guard

Diagram 2

Latifundist kin group Vassallo

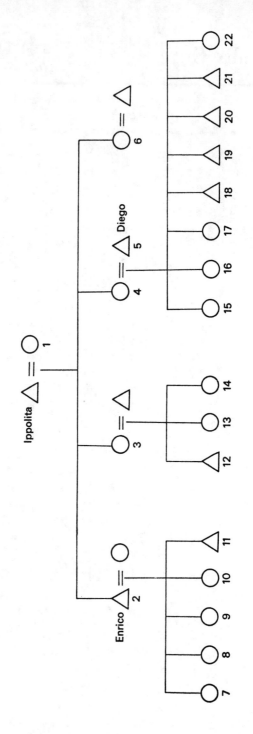

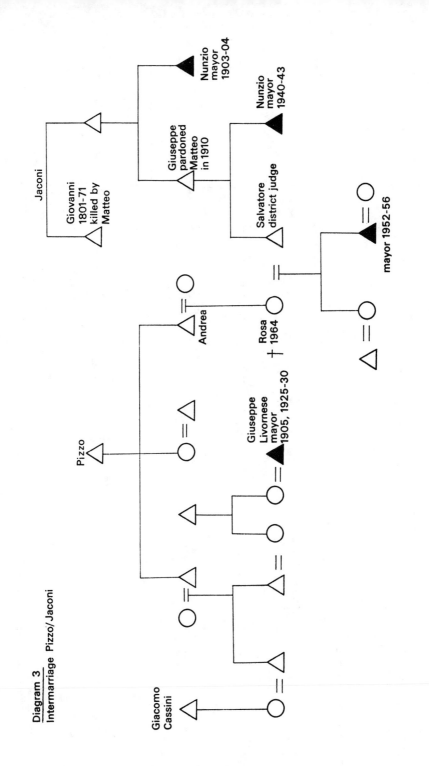

Diagram 3
Intermarriage Pizzo/Jaconi

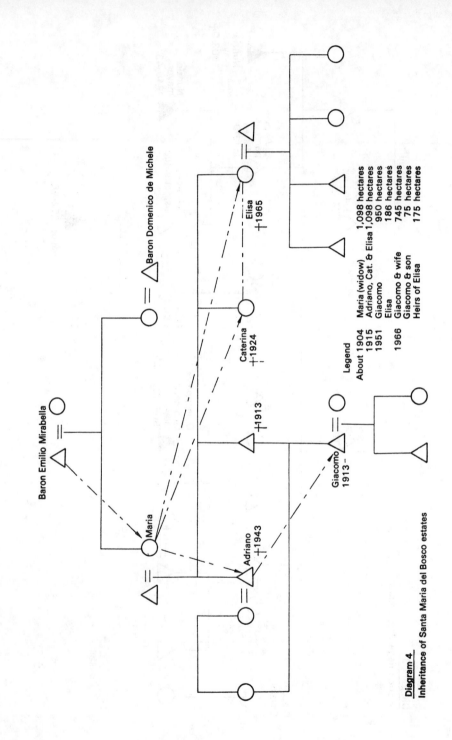

Baron Emilio Mirabella

Baron Domenico de Michele

Maria

Adriano
†1943

Giacomo
1913–

Caterina
†1924

Elisa
†1965

†1913

Legend

About 1904	Maria (widow)	1,098 hectares
1915	Adriano, Cat. & Elisa	1,098 hectares
1951	Giacomo	950 hectares
	Elisa	186 hectares
1966	Giacomo & wife	745 hectares
	Giacomo & son	75 hectares
	Heirs of Elisa	175 hectares

Diagram 4

Inheritance of Santa Maria del Bosco estates

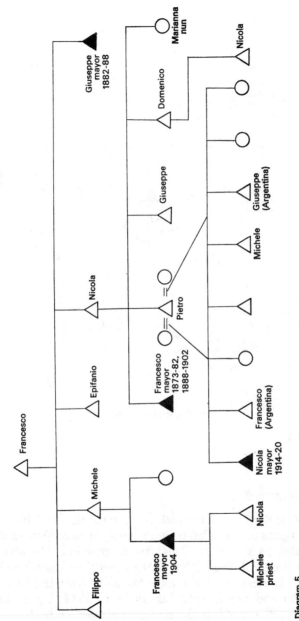

Diagram 5
Section of the Jaconis

Diagram 6

The Selvinis

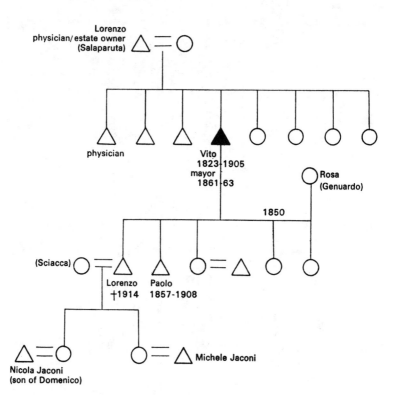

Note to Diagram 6

When Vito settled in Genuardo, he bought up land for his two sons, Lorenzo and Paolo, who later on managed additional estates as *gabelloti*. Paolo never married. He had a mistress in a neighboring town (not uncommon among well-to-do *civili*). Lorenzo took the local tax-office from the Livornesi in 1895 and ran it until his death in 1914. Up to the present, this office is still in the hands of his descendants.

Diagram 7
The Cassinis : *gabelloti*

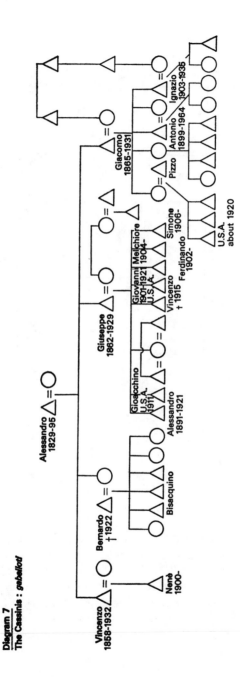

Diagram 8
Composition of the core of the Adernò *mafia*

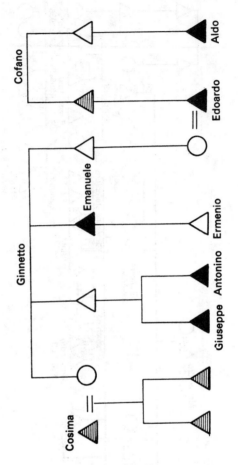

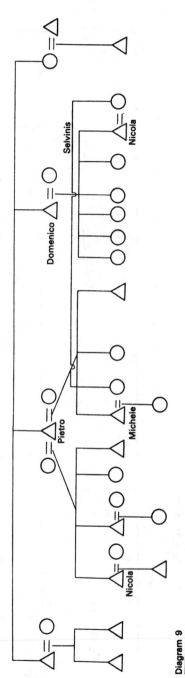

Diagram 9

Section of the Jaconis (about 1914)

Diagram 10
Section of the Cassinis

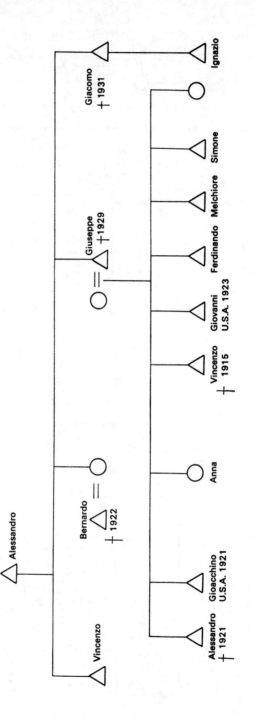

Diagram 11
The Olivieris : *gabelloti*

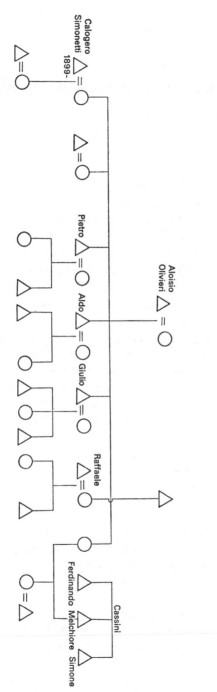

Glossary of Sicilian and Italian Words

abigeato	Cattle rustling
amministratore	Steward on large estate
aratro	Wooden, iron-tipped plow drawn by oxen or mules
azienda	Farmstead
burgisi	Smallholders ("middle peasants")
cacocciula	Local clique of *mafiosi* (see *cosca*)
campiere	Armed, mounted field guard on large estate
campierato	Area controlled by a *campiere*; task of surveillance; also: tribute collected from peasants working in the area
cantina	Plant for processing grapes into wine
Carabinieri	Local detachment of the national police force (part of the Italian Army)
chiusura	Enclosure
circolo	Local club for adult males
civili	Gentlemen
civiltà	Civility
compare (*cumpa'*)	Co-parent
contadino	Peasant
corona	Area of intensive cultivation immediately surrounding the village
cosca (pl.: *cosche*)	Local clique of *mafiosi*
cuccia	Enforced tribute
curatolo	Chief herdsman; foreman of the shepherds tending the estate herds; cheesemaker

enfiteusi	Emphyteusis, copyhold "Under emphyteusis land is given with the obligation of paying rent and maintaining the property. Unlike the metayer [sharecropper], in which the land always remains in the hands of the original owner, emphyteusis may terminate in full ownership for the tenant. Land held in emphyteusis may be inherited" (Pitkin 1960:171).
fiera	Local market
frane	Landslides
feudo (pl.: *feudi*)	Large estate (originally a fief), and used in ordinary language to designate a large estate
gabella	Lease of an estate, usually of six years' duration
gabelloto (*gabellotto*)	Leaseholder
girato	Area of intensive cultivation around a *masseria*
guardiania (*guardianeria*)	see *campierato*
latifondo	Large landed estate
lupara	From *lupo*, wolf; sawed-off shotgun; a specific mode of killing a man, i.e. with a *lupara*
mafioso	Violent entrepreneur, middleman
maggese	Fallow
mandria	Herd of cattle or sheep
masseria	Farm; as an ecological unit of land and animals; farm building
metateria	Sharecropping
metatiere	Sharecropper
mezzadria	Sharecropping
mezzadro	Sharecropper

omertà	From *umo*, man; code of honor. "... the attitude which assumes that recourse to legal authority in cases of persecution by private enemies is a symptom of weakness, almost of cowardice. It is an exaggeration of the sentiment, more or less common in Latin countries, that appeal to law against offenses involving personal insult, for instance adultery, is unmanly and that the duel is the proper means of recovering lost honor. Sicilian circles affected by mafiist psychology held that many offenses must be avenged by personal action or by that of relatives and friends. Common theft, for example, was considered a sign of lack of respect indicating that the thief did not fear vengeance" (Mosca 1933:36).
paese (*paisi*)	Village, town
padrone	Patron, boss, employer
partito	Party
pezzo grosso	Big shot
pizzu	Enforced tribute (see *cuccia*)
ringrano	Stubble field; field in which grain is sown for a second consecutive year
società	Partnership of entrepreneurs; society
soprastante	Overseer on a large estate
sulla	Fodder crop. *Hedysarium coronarium*, a perennial legume indigenous to the Mediterranean, is the most important soil-renewal and fodder crop. The variety here concerned reaches heights between one and two meters
uomo di fiducia	Man of confidence; retainer
usi civici	Common use rights on *feudi*
villano (*viddanu*)	Peasant, countryman (pejorative)

Bibliography

Adams, Richard N.
1966 Power and Power Domains. *América Latina*, 9:3–21.
1970 Brokers and Career Mobility Systems in the Structure of Complex Societies. *Southwestern Journal of Anthropology*, 26:315–27.

Alongi, Giuseppe
1887 *La Mafia nei suoi Fattori e nelle sue Manifestazioni. Studio sulle Classi Pericolose della Sicilia.* Torino: Fratelli Bocca Editori.
1891 *L'Abigeato in Sicilia. Studii di Patologia Sociale.* Marsala: Tip. di Luigi Giliberto.

Anonymous
1879 *I Masnadieri Giulianesi: Ultimo Avanzo del Brigantaggio in Sicilia.* Palermo: Tip. del Giornale di Sicilia.

Bailey, F. G.
1966 The Peasant View of the Bad Life. *Advancement of Science*, 23:399–409.
1969 *Stratagems and Spoils. A Social Anthropology of Politics.* Oxford: Basil Blackwell.
1971 (Ed.), *Gifts and Poison: The Politics of Reputation.* Oxford: Basil Blackwell.

Barnes, J. A.
1968 Networks and Political Process. In: Marc J. Swartz (Ed.), *Local-Level Politics. Social and Cultural Perspectives.* Chicago: Aldine Publishing Company.

Barth, Fredrik
1959 *Political Leadership Among the Swat Pathans.* London: The Athlone Press.
1963 *The Role of the Entrepreneur in Social Change in Northern Norway.* Oslo: Universitetsforlaget.

Barzini, Luigi
1965 *The Italians.* New York: Bantam Books, Inc.
Bendix, Reinhard
1962 *Max Weber. An Intellectual Portrait.* London: Methuen.
1969 *Nation-Building and Citizenship. Studies of Our Changing Social Order.* Garden City, New York: Anchor Books.
Bloch, Marc
1961 *Feudal Society.* Tr. L. A. Manyon. Chicago: The University of Chicago Press.
Blok, Anton
1966 Land Reform in a West Sicilian Latifondo Village: The Persistence of a Feudal Structure. *Anthropological Quarterly,* 39:1–16.
1969a South Italian Agro-Towns. *Comparative Studies in Society and History,* 11:121–35.
1969b Variations in Patronage. *Sociologische Gids,* 16: 365–78.
1969c Mafia and Peasant Rebellion as Contrasting Factors in Sicilian Latifundism. *Archives Européennes de Sociologie (European Journal of Sociology),* 10:95–116.
1972 The Peasant and the Brigand: Social Banditry Reconsidered. *Comparative Studies in Society and History,* 14:495–504.
1973 Coalitions in Sicilian Peasant Society. In: Jeremy Boissevain & J. Clyde Mitchell (Eds.), *Network Analysis. Studies in Human Interaction.* The Hague: Mouton & Co.
Bobek, Hans
1962 The Main Stages in Socio-Economic Evolution from a Geographical Point of View. In: Philip L. Wagner and Marvin W. Mikesell (Eds.), *Readings in Cultural Geography.* Chicago: The University of Chicago Press.
Boissevain, Jeremy
1966a Patronage in Sicily. *Man,* 1:18–33.
1966b Poverty and Politics in a Sicilian Agro-Town. *International Archives of Ethnography,* 50:198–236.

Bibliography 269

1968   The Place of Non-Groups in the Social Sciences. *Man*,
        3:542–56.
1973   *Friends of Friends. Networks, Manipulators and Coa-
        litions.* Oxford: Basil Blackwell.
Braga, Giorgio
1967   Questioni di Sociologia. *Aggiornamenti Sociali*, 18:
        295–306.
Brancato, Francesco
1956   *Storia della Sicilia Post-Unificazione. La Sicilia nel
        Primo Ventennio del Regno d'Italia.* (Parte Prima).
        Bologna: Cesare Zuffi Editore.
Braudel, Fernand
1966   *La Méditerranée et le Monde Méditerranéen à l'Époque
        de Philippe II.* Paris: Librairie Armand Colin. 2 vols.
        Second Edition.
Brenan, Gerald
1950   *The Spanish Labyrinth. An Account of the Social and
        Political Background of the Civil War.* Cambridge:
        Cambridge University Press. Second Edition.
Brown, Paula
1964   Enemies and Affines. *Ethnology*, 3: 355–56.
Buttazzoni, Guido
1939   Lineamenti Economici e Storici della Proprietà Fon-
        diaria in Sicilia. *Bonifica e Colonizzazione*, October,
        854–66.
Cahen, Claude
1940   *Le Régime Féodal de l'Italie Normande.* Paris: Lib-
        rairie Paul Geuthner.
1960   Réflexions sur l'Usage du Mot de "Féodalité." A Pro-
        pos d'un Livre Récent. *Journal of the Economic and
        Social History of the Orient*, 3:2–20.
Campbell, J. K.
1964   *Honour, Family and Patronage. A Study of Institu-
        tions and Moral Values in a Greek Mountain Com-
        munity.* Oxford: Clarendon Press.
Candida, Renato
1960   *Questa Mafia.* Caltanissetta–Roma: Salvatore Sciascia
        Editore. Second Edition.

270   *Bibliography*

Caro Baroja, Julio
1963   The City and the Country: Reflexions on Some
       Ancient Commonplaces. In: Julian Pitt-Rivers (Ed.),
       *Mediterranean Countrymen. Essays in the Social An-
       thropology of the Mediterranean.* Paris–The Hague:
       Mouton & Co.
Castrilli, Vincenzo
1926   Il Latifondo in Sicilia. *La Riforma Sociale,* 37:220–38.
Chilanti, Felice and Mario Farinella
1964   *Rapporto sulla Mafia.* Palermo: S. F. Flaccovio Editore.
Cinanni, Paolo
1970   *Emigration und Imperialismus. Zur Problematik der
       Arbeitsemigranten.* München: Trikont Verlag.
Cobb, Richard
1969   A *Second Identity: Essays on France and French His-
       tory.* London: Oxford University Press.
1970   *The Police and the People: French Popular Protest
       1789–1820.* Oxford: Clarendon Press.
1972   *Reactions to the French Revolution.* London: Oxford
       University Press.
Colajanni, Pompeo
1959   Chi sono i Mafiosi? (Discorso sull'Ordine Pubblico
       nella Prima Legislatura dell'Assemblea Regionale,
       November 22, 1949.) In: Matteo G. Tocco (Ed.), *La
       Mafia. E' un Problema di Polizia?* Palermo: Quaderni
       di Sala d'Ercole.
Cutrera, Antonio
1900   *La Mafia ed i Mafiosi.* Palermo: Edizioni Reber.
D'Alessandro, Enzo
1959   *Brigantaggio e Mafia in Sicilia.* Messina-Firenze: Casa
       Editrice G. D'Anna.
Damiani, A.
1885   *Atti della Giunta per l'Inchiesta Agraria e sulle Con-
       dizioni della Classe Agricola.* Vol. XIII. Roma.
Davis, J.
1969   Honour and Politics in Pisticci. *Proceedings of the
       Royal Anthropological Institute of Great Britain and
       Ireland,* 69–81.

De Stefano, Francesco and Francesco Luigi Oddo
1963 *Storia della Sicilia dal 1860 al 1910.* Bari: Editori Laterza.

Dickinson, Robert E.
1955 *The Population Problem of Southern Italy. An Essay in Social Geography.* Syracuse: Syracuse University Press.

Diem, Aubrey
1961 *Land Reform and Reclamation in Sicily.* Ph.D. dissertation. Ann Arbor: The University of Michigan.
1963 An Evaluation of Land Reform and Reclamation in Sicily. *Canadian Geographer,* 7: 182–91.

Di Matteo, Salvo
1967 *Anni Roventi. La Sicilia dal 1943 al 1947. Cronache di un Quinquennio.* Palermo: G. Denaro Editore.

Dolci, Danilo
1963 *Waste. An Eye-Witness Report on some Aspects of Waste in Western Sicily.* Tr. R. Munroe. London: Macgibbon & Kee.

Elias, Norbert
1969 *Über den Prozess der Zivilisation. Soziogenetische und psychogenetische Untersuchungen* [1939]. Bern–München: A. G. Francke Verlag, 2 vols. Second Edition.
1970 *Was ist Soziologie?* München: Juventa Verlag.
1971 The Genesis of Sport as a Sociological Problem. In: Eric Dunning (Ed.), *The Sociology of Sport. A Selection of Readings.* London: Frank Cass & Co.
1972 Processes of State Formation and Nation Building. *Transactions of the 7th World Congress of Sociology.* Varna, September 1970, Band III. Sofia: International Sociological Association, pp. 274-84.

Elias, Norbert and Eric Dunning
1971 Dynamics of Sport Groups with Special Reference to Football. In: Eric Dunning (Ed.), *The Sociology of Sport. A Selection of Readings.* London: Frank Cass & Co.

Elias, Norbert and J. L. Scotson
1965   *The Established and the Outsiders. A Sociological Enquiry into Community Problems.* London: Frank Cass & Co.

Feder, Ernest
1970   Counterreform. In: Rodolfo Stavenhagen (Ed.), *Agrarian Problems & Peasant Movements in Latin America.* Garden City, New York: Anchor Books.

Fél, Edit and Tamás Hofer
1969   *Proper Peasants. Traditional Life in a Hungarian Village.* Chicago: Aldine Publishing Company.

Firth, Raymond
1963   Bilateral Descent Groups. An Operational Viewpoint. In: I. Schapera (Ed.), *Studies in Kinship and Marriage Dedicated to Brenda Z. Seligman on her 80th Birthday.* Royal Anthropological Institute Occasional Paper No. 16.

Fortune, R. F.
1963   *Sorcerers of Dobu. The Social Anthropology of the Dobu Islanders of the Western Pacific* [1932]. New York: E. P. Dutton & Co.

Foster, George M.
1965   Peasant Society and the Image of Limited Good. *American Anthropologist,* 67:293–315.
1966   Reply to Kaplan, Saler, and Bennett. *American Anthropologist,* 68:210–14.

Franchetti, Leopoldo
1925   *La Sicilia nel 1876. Condizioni Politiche e Amministrative* [1877]. (Libro Primo) Firenze: Vallecchi Editore. Second Edition.

Frank, Andre Gunder
1967   *Capitalism and Underdevelopment in Latin America. Historical Studies of Chile and Brazil.* New York and London: Monthly Review Press.

Franklin, S. H.
1969   *The European Peasantry. The Final Phase.* London: Methuen & Co.

Freeman, J. D.
1961   On the Concept of the Kindred. *Journal of the Royal Anthropological Institute*, 91:192–220.

Friedrich, Paul
1965   A Mexican Cacicazgo. *Ethnology*, 4:190–209.
1968a The Political Middleman. In: Marc J. Swartz (Ed.), *Local-Level Politics. Social and Cultural Perspectives* Chicago: Aldine Publishing Company.
1968b The Legitimacy of a Cacique. In: Marc J. Swartz (Ed.), *Local-Level Politics. Social and Cultural Perspectives*. Chicago: Aldine Publishing Company.
1970   *Agrarian Revolt in a Mexican Village.* Englewood Cliffs, New Jersey: Prentice Hall, Inc.

Gaetani D'Aragona, G.
1954   A Critical Evaluation of Land Reform in Italy. *Land Economics*, 30:12–20.

Gaja, Filippo
1962   *L'Esercito della Lupara. Baroni e Banditi Siciliani nella Guerriglia contra l'Italia.* Milano: Area Editore.

Galtung, Johan
1962   Componenti Psico-Sociali nella Decisione di Emigrare. In: Autori Vari, *Immigrazione e Industria.* Milano: Edizioni di Comunità.

Ganci, M.
1954   Il Movimento dei Fasci nella Provincia di Palermo, *Movimento Operaio*, 6:817–92.

Garufi, C. A.
1946–47, Patti Agrari e Comuni Feudali di Nuova Fondazione in Sicilia dallo Scorcio del Secolo XI agli Albori del Settecento. Studi Storico-Diplomatico. *Archivio Storico Siciliano*, Serie III, 1:31–111 and 2:7–131.

Geertz, Clifford
1963   *Agricultural Involution. The Process of Ecological Change in Indonesia.* Berkeley: University of California Press.

Genovese, Nicolo
1894   *La Questione Agraria in Sicilia. Cause e Rimedi.* Milano: Libreria Ed. Di Giuseppe Palma.

274 *Bibliography*

Genuardi, Luigi
1911   *Terre Comuni ed Usi Civici in Sicilia Prima dell'*
       Abolizione della Feudalità. Studi e Documenti.
       Palermo: Scuola Tip. "Boccone del Povero."
Govone, Uberto
1902   *Il Generale Giuseppe Govone. Frammenti di Memorie.*
       Torino: Francesco Casanuova Editore.
Grieco, Ruggero
1964   Perchè il Fascismo Combatte la Mafia. In Nando
       Russo (Ed.), *Antologia della Mafia.* Palermo: Il Punto
       Edizioni.
Hall, John W.
1962   Feudalism in Japan—A Reassessment. *Comparative*
       Studies in Society and History, 5:15–51.
Hess, Henner
1970   *Mafia. Zentrale Herrschaft und lokale Gegenmacht.*
       Tübingen: J. C. B. Mohr.
Hobsbawm, E. J.
1959   *Primitive Rebels. Studies in Archaic Forms of Social*
       Movement in the 19th and 20th Centuries. Manches-
       ter: Manchester University Press.
1969   *Bandits.* London: Weidenfeld & Nicolson.
1972   Social Bandits. A Comment. *Comparative Studies in*
       Society and History, 14:504–07.
Honigmann, John J.
1970   Rationality and Fantasy in Styrian Villagers. *Anthro-*
       pologica, N.S. 12:129–39.
Jannuzzi, Lino
1965a I Nomi della Mafia. *L'Espresso,* April 4th.
1965b I Grandi Protettori. *L'Espresso,* April 11th.
1971   Vostro Onore. *L'Espresso,* May 16th.
Johnson, Chalmers
1968   *Revolutionary Change.* London: University of London
       Press.
Kaplan, David and Benson Saler
1966   Foster's "Image of Limited Good": An Example of
       Anthropological Explanation. *American Anthropolo-*
       gist, 68:202–05.

La Mantia, Giuseppe
1904   *I Capitoli delle Colonie Greco-Albanesi di Sicilia dei Secoli XV e XVI.* Palermo: Tip. A. Giannitrapani.

Landsberger, Henry A.
1969   The Role of Peasant Movements and Revolts in Development. In: Henry A. Landsberger (Ed.), *Latin American Peasant Movements.* Ithaca and London: Cornell University Press.

Landsberger, Henry A. and Cynthia N. Hewitt
1970   Ten Sources of Weakness and Cleavage in Latin American Peasant Movements. In: Rodolfo Stavenhagen (Ed.), *Agrarian Problems & Peasant Movements in Latin America.* Garden City, New York: Anchor Books.

Lorenzoni, Giovanni
1910   *Inchiesta Parlamentare sulle Condizioni dei Contadini nelle Provincie Meridionali e nella Sicilia.* Vol. VI. Roma: Tipografia Nazionale di Giovanni Bertero.

McDonald, J. S.
1956   Italy's Rural Social Stucture and Emigration. *Occidente,* 12:437-56.

Mack Smith, Denis
1950   The Peasants' Revolt of Sicily in 1860. In: *Studi in Onore di Gino Luzzatto.* Vol. III. Milano: Giuffre Editore.
1959   *Italy. A Modern History.* Ann Arbor: The University of Michigan Press.
1965   The Latifundia in Modern Sicilian History. *Proceedings of the British Academy:* Vol. LI. London: Oxford University Press.
1966   Preface to the English Edition. Michele Pantaleone, *The Mafia and Politics.* London: Chatto & Windus.
1968a *A History of Sicily: Medieval Sicily (800–1713)* and *Modern Sicily (After 1713).* 2 vols. London: Chatto & Windus.
1968b (Ed.), *The Making of Italy 1796–1870.* New York: Harper & Row.

276 *Bibliography*

Marciani, Giovanni Enrico
1966 *L'Esperienza di Riforma Agraria in Italia.* Roma: Giuffre Editore.

Marino, Giuseppe Carlo
1964 *L'Opposizione Mafiosa (1870–1882). Baroni e Mafia contro lo Stato Liberale.* Palermo: S. F. Flaccovio Editore.

Maxwell, Gavin
1957 *God Protect me from my Friends.* London: Longmans.
1959 *The Ten Pains of Death.* London: Longmans.

Mayer, Adrian C.
1966 The Significance of Quasi-Groups in the Study of Complex Societies. In: Michael Banton (ed.), *The Social Anthropology of Complex Societies.* A.S.A. Monographs, 4. London: Tavistock Publications.

Mitchell, J. Clyde
1969 The Concept and Use of Social Networks. In: J. Clyde Mitchell (Ed.), *Social Networks in Urban Situations.* Manchester: Manchester University Press.

Mitrany, David
1951 *Marx Against the Peasant. A Study in Social Dogmatism.* London: Weidenfeld & Nicolson.

Molè, Giovanni
1929 *Studio-Inchiesta sui Latifondi Siciliani.* Roma: Tipografia del Senato del Dott. G. Bardi.

Montalbano, Giuseppe
1964a La Mafia e i Comunisti Siciliani. *Corrispondenza Socialista,* 5:126–33.
1964b Destre, PCI e Separatisti in Sicilia. *Corrispondenza Socialista,* 5:235–44.

Moore, Barrington, Jr.
1966 *Social Origins of Dictatorship and Democracy. Lord and Peasant in the Making of the Modern World.* Boston: Beacon Press.

Mori, Cesare
1933 *The Last Struggle with the Mafia.* Tr. Orlo Williams. London and New York: Putnam.

Mosca, Gaetano
1900 Che Cosa è la Mafia? *Giornale degli Economisti,* Ser. II, 20 : 236–62. Reprinted in : Nando Russo (Ed.), *Antologia della Mafia.* Palermo: Il Punto Edizione, 1964.
1933 Mafia. *Encyclopaedia of the Social Sciences.* Vol. X. New York: Macmillan.

Moss, Leonard W. and Walter H. Thomson
1959 The South Italian Family: literature and Observation. *Human Organization,* 18 : 35–41.

Navarra Crimi, Gaetano
1925 *Problemi dell'Economia Siciliana.* Siracusa: Editore S. Santoro.

Newbigin, Marion I.
1949 *Southern Europe. A Regional and Economic Geography of the Mediterranean Lands.* London: Methuen.

Niermeyer, J. F.
1959 De Semantiek van *Honor* en de Oorsprong van het Heerlijk gezag. *Dancwerc. Opstellen aangeboden aan Prof. Dr. D. Th. Enklaar ter gelegenheid van zijn 65ste verjaardag.* Groningen: J. B. Wolters.

Novacco, Domenico
1959 Considerazioni sulla Fortuna del Termine "Mafia." *Belfagor,* 14 : 2–11.
1963 *Inchiesta sulla Mafia.* Milano: Feltrinelli Editore.
1964 Bibliografia della Mafia. *Nuovi Quaderni del Meridione,* 2 : 188–239.

Paine, Robert
1970 Lappish Decisions, Partnerships, Information Management, and Sanctions—A Nomadic Pastoral Adaptation. *Ethnology,* 9 : 52–67.

Pantaleone, Michele
1966 *The Mafia and Politics.* London: Chatto & Windus.
1969 *Antimafia: Occasione Mancata.* Torino: Einaudi Editore.

Passerin d'Entrèves, Alexander
1967 *The Notion of the State. An Introduction to Political Theory.* Oxford: Clarendon Press.

Pecorini, Giorgio
1967   Chiesa e Mafia in Sicilia. Viaggio-Inchiesta fra i Cristiani dell'Isola. *Comunità*, 21:49–68.
Petacco, Arrigo
1972   *Joe Petrosino*. Verona: Arnoldo Mondadori Editore.
Pitkin, Donald S.
1959   The Intermediate Society: A Study in Articulation. In: Verne F. Ray (Ed.), *Intermediate Societies, Social Mobility, and Communication*. Proceedings of the 1959 Annual Spring Meeting of the American Ethnological Society. Seattle: University of Washington Press.
1960   Land Tenure and Family Organization in an Italian Village. *Human Organization*, 18:169–73.
1963   Mediterranean Europe. *Anthropological Quarterly*, 36:120–29.
Pitt-Rivers, Julian A.
1961   *The People of the Sierra*. Chicago: The University of Chicago Press.
1963   Introduction. In: Julian Pitt-Rivers (Ed.), *Mediterranean Countrymen: Essays in the Social Anthropology of the Mediterranean*. Paris—The Hague: Mouton & Co.
1965   Honour and Social Status. In: J. G. Peristiany (Ed.), *Honour and Shame. The Values of Mediterranean Society*. London: Weidenfeld & Nicolson.
Pizzorno, Alessandro
1966   Amoral Familism and Historical Marginality. *International Review of Community Development*, 15/16: 55–66.
Poma, Rosario and Enzo Perrone
1964   *Quelli della Lupara. Rapporto sulla Mafia di Ieri e di Oggi*. Firenze: Edizioni Casini.
Pontieri, Ernesto
1943   *Il Tramonto del Baronaggio Siciliano*. Firenze: G. C. Sansoni Editore.
1965   *Il Riformismo Borbonico nella Sicilia del Sette e dell'Ottocento. Saggi Storici*. Napoli: Edizioni Scientifiche Italiane. Second Edition.

Prestianni, Nunzio
1947 *L'Economia Agraria della Sicilia.* Palermo: Instituto Nazionale de Economia Agraria. Osservatorio di Economia Agraria per la Sicilia.

Pupillo-Barresi, A.
1903 *Gli Usi Civici in Sicilia. Ricerche di Storia del Diritto.* Catania: Niccolo Giannotta Editore.

Raffiotta, Giovanni
1959 *La Sicilia nel Primo Ventennio del Secolo XX. Storia della Sicilia Post-Unificazione.* Parte Terza. Palermo: Industria Grafica Nazionale.

Redfield, Robert
1960 *Peasant Society and Culture.* Chicago: The University of Chicago Press.

Reid, Ed
1952 *Mafia.* New York: New American Library.

Renda, Francesco
1956 Funzioni e Basi Sociali della Mafia. In: Francesco Renda, *Il Movimento Contadino nella Società Siciliana.* Palermo: Edizione "Sicilia al Lavoro."
1963 *L'Emigrazione in Sicilia.* Palermo: Edizione "Sicilia al Lavoro."

Rochefort, Renée
1961 *Le Travail en Sicile. Étude de Géographie Sociale.* Paris: Presses Universitaires de France.

Romano, Salvatore Francesco
1952 Sul Brigantaggio e sulla Mafia. In: S. F. Romano, *Momenti del Risorgimento in Sicilia.* Messina-Firenze: Casa Editrice G. D'Anna.
1959 *Storia dei Fasci Siciliani.* Bari: Editore Laterza.
1964 *Breve Storia della Sicilia. Momenti e Problemi della Civiltà Siciliana. Torino:* Edizioni RAI Radiotelevisione Italiana.
1966 *Storia della Mafia.* Verona: Arnoldo Mondadori Editore. I Record. Second Edition.

Romeo, Rosario
1950 *Il Risorgimento in Sicilia.* Bari: Laterza.

Salvioli, Giuseppe
1895 Le Latifundium Sicilien et son Mode d'Exploitation. *Le Devenir Social*, 1:449–64.
1902 Il Villanaggio in Sicilia e la sua Abolizione. *Rivista Italiana di Sociologia*, 6:371–401.
1903 Le Colonizzazioni in Sicilia nei Secoli XVI e XVII. (Contributo alla Storia della Proprietà.) *Vierteljahrschrift für Sozial-und Wirtschaftsgeschichte*, 1: 70–78.
1909 L'Origine degli Usi Civici in Sicilia. *Rivista Italiana di Sociologia*, 13:154–79.

Sansone V. and G. Ingrascì
1950 *Sei Anni di Banditismo in Sicilia.* Milano: Le Edizioni Sociali.

Sartorius von Waltershausen, A.
1913 *Die Sizilianische Agrarverfassung und ihre Wandlungen: 1780–1912.* Leipzig: A. Deichert'sche Verlagsbuchhandlung.

Schneider, Jane
1969 Family Patrimonies and Economic Behavior in Western Sicily. *Anthropological Quarterly*, 42:109–29.
1971 Of Vigilance and Virgins: Honor, Shame, and Access to Resources in Mediterranean Societies. *Ethnology*, 10:1–24.

Schneider, Peter
1972 Coalition Formation and Colonialism in Sicily. *Archives Européennes de Sociologie (European Journal of Sociology)*, 13:255–67.

Schneider, Peter, Jane Schneider, and Edward C. Hansen
1972 Modernization and Development: The Role of Regional Elites and Non-corporate Groups in the European Mediterranean. *Comparative Studies in Society and History*, 14:328–50.

Sciascia, Leonardo
1961 *Il Giorno della Civetta.* Torino: Einaudi Editore.

Sereni, Emilio
1947 *Il Capitalismo nelle Campagne (1860–1900).* Torino: Einaudi Editore.

Silverman, Sydel F.
1965 Patronage and Community–Nation Relationships in Central Italy. *Ethnology,* 4:172–89.
1966 An Ethnographic Approach to Social Stratification: Prestige in a Central Italian Community. *American Anthropologist,* 68:899–921.
1967 The Community–Nation Mediator in Traditional Central Italy. In: Jack M. Potter, May N. Diaz, and George M. Foster (Eds.), *Peasant Society. A Reader.* Boston: Little, Brown & Company.
1971 Agricultural Organization, Social Structure, and Values in Italy: Amoral Familism Reconsidered. In: Yehudi A. Cohen (Ed.), *Man in Adaptation. The Institutional Framework.* Chicago: Aldine Publishing Company.

Sonnino, Sidney
1925 *La Sicilia nel 1876. I Contadini* [1877]. (Libro Secondo) Firenze: Vallecchi Editore.

Sorgi, Antonino
1959 Quindici Anni di Lotte Contadine. *Il Ponte,* 15: 620–35.

Stone, Lawrence
1965 *The Crisis of the Aristocracy, 1558–1641.* Oxford: Clarendon Press.

Tarrow, Sidney G.
1967 *Peasant Communism in Southern Italy.* New Haven and London: Yale University Press.

Tilly, Charles
1967 *The Vendée.* New York: John Wiley and Sons.

Tomasi di Lampedusa, Giuseppe
1958 *Il Gattopardo.* Milano: Feltrinelli Editore.

Van den Muyzenberg, Otto D.
1971 Politieke Mobilisering en Geweld in Centraal Luzon (Filippijnen). *Sociologische Gids,* 18:148–60.

Van Velsen, J.
1967 The Extended Case Method and Situational Analysis. In: A. L. Epstein (Ed.), *The Craft of Social Anthropology.* London: Tavistock Publications.

282   *Bibliography*

Vöchting, Friedrich
1951   *Die italienische Südfrage. Entstehung und Problematik eines wirtschaftlichen Notstandsgebietes.* Berlin: Duncker & Humblot.

Walter, Eugene Victor
1969   *Terror and Resistance. A Study of Political Violence with Case Studies of some Primitive African Communities.* New York: Oxford University Press.

Weingrod, Alex
1968   Patrons, Patronage, and Political Parties. *Comparative Studies in Society and History,* 10:377–401.

Weingrod, Alex and Emma Morin
1971   Post Peasants: The Character of Contemporary Sardinian Society. *Comparative Studies in Society and History,* 13:301–24.

Wertheim, W. F.
1964   *East–West Parallels. Sociological Approaches to Modern Asia.* The Hague: W. Van Hoeve.

Wolf, Eric R.
1956   Aspects of Group Relations in a Complex Society: Mexico. *American Anthropologist,* 58:1065–78.

1959   *Sons of the Shaking Earth. The People of Mexico and Guatemala—Their Land, History, and Culture.* Chicago: The University of Chicago Press.

1962   Cultural Dissonance in the Italian Alps. *Comparative Studies in Society and History,* 5:1–14.

1966a   Kinship, Friendship, and Patron–Client Relations in Complex Societies. In: Michael Banton (Ed.), *The Social Anthropology of Complex Societies.* A.S.A. Monographs, 4. London: Tavistock Publications.

1966b   *Peasants.* Englewood Cliffs, New Jersey: Prentice-Hall.

1967   Closed Corporate Communities in Mesoamerica and Central Java. In: Jack M. Potter, May N. Diaz, and George M. Foster (Eds.), *Peasant Society. A Reader.* Boston: Little, Brown.

1969   *Peasant Wars of the Twentieth Century.* New York. Harper & Row.

1971 Peasant Rebellion and Revolution. In: Norman Miller and Roderick Aya (Eds.), *National Liberation. Revolution in the Third World*. New York: The Free Press.

Wolfgang, Marvin E. and Franco Ferracuti

1967 *The Subculture of Violence. Towards an Integrated Theory in Criminology*. London: Tavistock Publications.

Ziino, Nunzio

1911 *Latifondo e Latifondismo. Studio di Economià Rurale*. Palermo: Orazio Fiorenza Editore.

Other Sources and Documents

Archivio di Stato di Palermo. Gabinetto di Prefettura.

1893 Busta 130. Cat. 16. Fasc. 52 (Elenco capi influenti dei "Fasci" circondario Corleone).

1893a Busta 134. Cat. 20. Fasc. 154 (Concessione di terre).

1893b Busta 136. Cat. 16. Fasc. 61 (Visita Bernardino Verro).

1893c Busta 137. Cat. 16. Fasc. 15 (Visita Fascio dei lavoratori di Bisacquino; cenno biografico di Nunzio Giaimo e Vito Cascio Ferro; concessione di terre).

1894d Busta 136. Cat. 4. Fasc. 54 (I partiti municipali di ***; composizione, dissidi, e conciliazione).

Archivio di Stato di Palermo. Questura Archivio Generale.

Gabinetto di Prefettura.

1916 Busta 1637 (Associazione a delinquere interprovinciale).

Archivio di Stato di Palermo.

1919 Corte di Appello di Palermo. Sezione di accusa. Processo contro Paolo Grisafi *et al.*

1922 Corte Ordinaria di Assise di Palermo. Sentenza contro Paolo Grisafi *et al.*

1922 Corte Stra Ordinaria di Assise di Palermo. Sentenza contro Paolo Grisafi *et al.*

1922 Corte Stra Ordinaria di Assise di Palermo. Sentenza contro Paolo Grisafi.

PRIVATE PAPERS

n.d. Several original written and published documents of the 19th century regarding local landownership.

1863 Corte di Appello di Palermo. Sezione di Accusa. Processo contro Luca ***, Matteo ***, *et al.* Associazione di malfattori. (Handwritten manuscript, 15 pp.)

1866 Prospetto Bibliografico Documento. Palermo: Stamperia di Salvatore Meli.

1902 Tesi di laurea. No title. Handwritten notes on local agrarian conditions.

1921 Intensificazioni Culturali nei Latifondi di ***. (Handwritten manuscript and stray notes on "Baronessa.")

1928 Corte di Appello di Palermo. Sezione di Accusa. Sentenza. Processo contro 198 persone. Handwritten MS, 355 pp.

STATISTICAL SOURCES

Archivio Comunale:

    Catasto dei Terreni.

    Registro delle Deliberazioni.

    Ufficio Anagrafe.

1935 *Catasto Agrario, 1929.* Compartimento della Sicilia. Provincia di Palermo. Roma: Instituto Centrale di Statistica.

1947 *La Distribuzione della Proprietà Fondiaria in Italia.* Sicilia. Roma: Instituto Nazionale di Economia Agraria (INEA).

1955 *IX Censimento General della Popolazione.* 4–xi–1951. Vol. I. Dati Sommari per Comune. Fasc. 86. Provincia di Palermo. Roma: Instituto Centrale di Statistica.

1956 *Le Elezioni in Sicilia. Dati e Grafici dal 1946 al 1956.* Milano: Giuffrè Editore.

1966 *X Censimento Generale della Popolazione.* 15–x–1961. Vol. III. Dati Sommari per Comune. Fasc. 82. Provincia di Palermo. Roma: Instituto Centrale di Statistica.

BOOKS

1851 *Vocabolario Siciliano. Manuale Completo.* Nuova Compilazione de Giuseppe Biundi. Palermo: Stamperia Carini.

1965 *Vocabolario della Lingua Italiana.* Compilato da Nicola Zingarelli. Novissima Edizione. Bologna: Nicola Zanichelli Editore.

1964 *The Concise Oxford Dictionary of Current English.* Edited by H. W. Fowler and F. G. Fowler. Based on The Oxford Dictionary. Fifth Edition. Oxford: Clarendon Press.

1950 *Riforma Agraria in Sicilia.* Legge Approvata dalla Assemblea Regionale nella Seduta del 21–xi–1950. Palermo: A Cura dell' Ufficio Stampa della Regione Siciliana.

Index

abigeato (cattle rustling), 51, 130, 138, 142, 146, 147, 148–49, 151, 152, 156, 163, 188, 196, 197–198, 204, 239–43
absenteeism, 32, 47, 54, 59, 68, 90, 91, 168, 193
action-set, 109–10, 138, 148
Adams, Richard N., 7n., 100, 137n., 212
Adernò, *mafia* of, 131–32, 135–37, 145, 147, 148, 149–50, 156, 164, 165, 171, 178, 185, 186, 196, 241
adultery, 236, 237
agrarian reform, 34, 36, 37, 77–81, 83–84, 91, 142, 181, 191, 201n., 203, 208–09. *See also* counterreform
agro-towns, 20, 25, 31, 46–47, 54, 74, 200
Alongi, Giuseppe, 15, 172n., 207n.
Anonymous, 108, 110, 128n.
anonymous letter, 108, 242
aristocracy, 28, 29, 39, 89, 90, 186, 214; and delinquents, 100n., 101n. *See also manutengolismo*
artisans, 121, 124, 185, 194
associazione a delinquere, 142–45, 183, 188; defined, 144–45
autonomy, 89–90, 93. *See also* self-sufficiency

Bailey, F. G., 7n., 9n., 25n., 62n., 92, 198n., 220n.
banditry, *see* brigandage

banditry, social, 99–101, 133–34
bandits, xxviii, 6, 94, 96, 99–102, 109–11, 114–15, 128, 130, 131–33, 148–49, 192, 204–05, 233–35; as distinct from *mafiosi*, 94–96, 130, 235n. *See also* retainers
bands, armed, 94, 101n., 103–04, 128, 131–37, 190, 192, 197, 204–05; of Capraro, 108–10, 114; of Giuliano, 197, 204–05; of Grisafi, 131–37; of Labruzzo, 197, 204; of Luca, 103–14; d'Orgères, 101n.; of Santo Meli, 105
banquet meetings, 110, 149
Barnes, J. A., 137n.
Barth, Fredrik, 44, 62n.
Barzini, Luigi, xiv, xxv, 78, 125n.
Bendix, Reinhard, 28n., 213n.
Bisacquino, *mafia of*, 154–55, 156, 164
Bloch, Marc, 28n., 111n., 179, 180, 211n.
Blok, Anton, xxxi, xxxii, 31n., 47n., 79n., 99, 100, 180 n.
Bobek, Hans, 56, 64
Boissevain, Jeremy, 137n., 138n., 145n., 150n., 151, 180n., 203n., 204n., 215n.
Bourbon, centralization, 10n.; government, 38, 39, 90, 93, 94, 98, 103, 113n., 114, 116; Neapolitan, 29, 90, 91, 98, 114, 210n.; State, 10, 11, 38
Braga, Giorgio, 14

Brancato, Francesco, 23, 112n., 116n.
Braudel, Fernand, 97n.
Brenan, Gerald, 100n.
brigandage, 30, 76, 93, 94, 97, 98–99, 100n., 108–09, 115, 121, 128, 133, 183
brokerage, 25, 137, 153, 177, 178, 187, 214–15. *See also* power brokers
brokers, *see* brokerage; entrepreneurs; patronage; power brokers
Brown, Paula, 211n.
Buttazzoni, Guido, 58n., 72n., 73–74

caciquismo, 8, 160n.
Cahen, Claude, 27, 28n.
Campbell, J. K., 175, 176
campieri, 45, 55, 61, 62, 66, 69, 71, 77, 81, 106, 131, 135, 136, 139, 146, 147, 149, 152, 153, 154, 156, 159, 162, 163, 164, 165n., 166, 167, 168, 177, 182, 183, 184, 185, 195; decline, 216, 235, 236
Candida, Renato, 15, 145n.
capital investment, 67–68, 69, 73, 116, 128. *See also* rent capitalism
Capraro, 108–10. *See also* bands
Carabinieri, 105, 108n., 110, 127, 130, 142, 164, 185, 195, 200, 234, 241, 242
Caro Baroja, Julio, 49n.
Cassini, Alessandro, 127–28, 129; Alessandro, son of Giuseppe, 139, 157, 159, 162, 163, 164–165, 169, 171n., 174; Ferdinando, 157, 162; Giacomo, 128, 129, 240; Gioacchino, 129, 130, 162; Giovanni, 159, 160, 161, 162, 174; Giuseppe, 127–28, 129, 139, 148, 150, 156, 157, 158, 162, 164, 166, 169, 171, 185, 187; Ignazio, 129,

187, 188, 189; Melchiore, 187, 196, 202; Simone, 163, 164, 187, 188, 189, 234; Vincenzo, 128, 129, 130, 131, 162
cattle rustling, *see abigeato*
centralization, 28, 89, 91–93, 98, 213. *See also* encapsulation; state-formation
Chilanti, Felice, 207n.
Christian Democrats, 193, 200, 202, 203, 206, 207n., 208, 215
church domains, 37, 39–41, 50, 116–21
Cinanni, Paolo, 220n.
civili, 49, 91, 107, 112n., 114, 115 116, 169
civilizing process, 176n., 177n., 211n.
class conflict, 75, 92, 97, 112–13, 122, 127, 141, 186, 210
clientele, 75, 223, 226. *See also* patronage
cliques, xxviii, 131, 135–38, 145
coalitions, xxviii, 120, 122, 138, 148, 150, 197
Cobb, Richard, 100n., 101n.
Cockcroft, James D., xvi, xxv
Cofano, Edoardo, 136–39, 149, 150, 156, 165–71, 178, 182, 186, 196
Colajanni, Pompeo, 198n.
common use rights, 38–40, 54, 90, 118–19
communications, 22–26, 44–45, 59, 69, 89–90, 92, 126n., 189
Communism, 193, 200, 205
Communist Party, 77, 79, 194, 199, 201–03, 209
configurations, xxviii, xxx, 9–10, 12, 96, 99, 153
co-parenthood, 156, 159, 166, 167, 170, 181
corruption, 228–29
cosca (pl.: *cosche*), 137, 142 *et seq.*, 145, 147, 148, 150, 153, 154, 156, 157, 161–71, 174, 177, 179, 189, 234; defined, 137; in

conflict, 161–71; network, 142
et seq. See also mafia
counterreform, 208
Cutrera, Antonio, 15

D'Alessandro, Enzo, 98n., 108n., 128n., 185n.
Davis, J., 238n.
De Stefano, Francesco, 112n., 120n.
Dickinson, Robert E., 45, 54n., 70, 71n.
Diem, Aubrey, 18, 79n., 83, 209n.
Di Matteo, Salvo, 190, 191, 198n., 203n., 204n.
Dolci, Danilo, 15, 16, 160n., 206n., 207n., 210n.

Elias, Norbert, xxvii, xxix, xxxn., xxxii, 9n., 26n., 28n., 62n., 91, 97n., 137n., 176n., 198n., 211n., 213n., 229
elopement, 158
emigration, 24, 34, 51–52, 59, 68, 121, 127, 139, 141; and class solidarity, 127n.
emphyteusis, 31, 32, 40, 53, 106
encapsulation, 9, 12, 25, 90, 92.
See also centralization; state-formation
enclosures, 11, 33n., 38, 91
entrepreneurs, 26, 33, 44, 47, 54–55, 68, 131, 213, 214, 225; decline, 222. *See also* power brokers; *mafiosi*
estates, Ch. III, IV. *See also feudi; latifondi*
expropriation, 68, 77, 79, 97, 238
extortion, 142, 156, 174, 235, 241
extortion letters, 108, 234, 236

factions, 120, 121 *et seq.*
Fascism, xxvii, 12, 14, 34, 69, 72, 73, 74, 76, 81, 142, 147, 154, 159, 166, 182, 184, 186, 187, 188, 189, 190, 191, 195

Fasci Siciliani, 121 *et seq.*, 127n., 143, 205
Feder, Ernest, 208n.
Fèl, Edit, 48, 49n.
Ferro, Don Vito Cascio, 125, 126, 143–44, 146, 149, 154, 155, 156, 166–71, 173, 181, 186, 187, 194, 226
feudalism, 27, 28, 38, 62, 89, 90–91, 112n.
feudi, 29, 31, 32, 36, 37, 38, 39, 58, 148, 149, 188, 201, 225.
See also latifondi
field systems, 43–45, 59, 60, 64, 68–70, 71. *See also* land tenure; *latifondi*
Firth, Raymond, 135n.
Fortune, R. F., 171n.
Foster, George M., 12n., 13, 48, 49n.
Franchetti, Leopoldo, 15, 40n., 172n., 212n.
Frank, André Gunder, 9n., 76n.
Franklin, S. H., 64n., 79n., 84n., 220n.
Freeman, J. D., 150
Friedrich, Paul, 7n., 8n., 160n., 161, 175–76, 179
friendship, 45, 63, 71, 99, 128, 146, 150–51, 154, 155, 161, 162, 165, 170, 171, 180, 200, 217, 219, 226, 234–35, 237

gabella, 32, 33n., 81, 128; struggle for, 131 *et seq.*, 193, 221
gabelloti, 32–34, 38, 43, 47, 51–52, 53, 54, 55, 59–71, 77, 81, 82, 91, 93, 96, 98, 107, 108, 113, 115, 120, 122, 124, 126, 128, 131, 137, 149, 155n., 163, 168, 170, 177, 184, 195, 196, 197, 199, 203, 208, 225, 239, 240; as money-lender, 38; decline, 216. *See also* entrepreneurs; *mafiosi*
Gaetani D'Aragona, G., 78n., 79n.

Gaja, Filippo, 190, 191n., 204n., 205n.
Galtung, Johan, 121n., 220n.
Ganci, M., 121n.
Garufi, C. A., 30
Geertz, Clifford, 76n., 83
Genovese, Nicolò, 66
Genuardi, Luigi, 32, 33n.
Giuliano, 197, 204, 205. *See also* bands
government, 75, 89, 90, 91, 92, 116, 190, 191
Govone, Uberto, 108n., 109n., 110n.
Grieco, Ruggero, 187
Grisafi, 131–38, 149n., 150, 167. *See also* bands
Gullo (Land Act), 191, 195

hacienda, compared with *latifondo*, 55n., 74
Hall, John W., 28n.
henchmen, 29, 131, 143, 153, 173. *See also* retainers; *mafiosi*
Hess, Henner, 13n., 95, 126n.
history, and anthropology, xxviii–xxxi, 9, 10, 12, 13
Hobsbawm, E. J., 97n., 99–100, 101n., 102, 121n., 128, 134, 235n.
homicide, 15–16, 103–06, 107–12, 115, 129, 130, 132, 133, 134, 142, 143, 149, 156–57, 159, 160, 161 *et seq.*, 171, 173–76, 181, 188, 190, 197, 205, 206, 207, 210, 233–39
Honigmann, John J., 49n.
honor, 198, 211, 238; *see also rispettu*

inheritance, 117–18, 120
Italian State, 11, 12, 22, 23, 25, 39, 115, 116, 127n., 191, 209

Jaconi, Domenico, 59–60, 64, 131, 135; 138–39; Francesco, 60, 120, 122–23, 126, 129; Gio-
vanni, 108, 110–11; Giuseppe, 104, 123; Michele, 59, 64, 120, 131, 139; Nicola, 59, 64, 120, 131, 138–39; Pietro, 123, 126; Stefano, 112
jacqueries, 97, 121. *See also* peasant rebellions
Jannuzzi, Lino, 226n.
Johnson, Chalmers, 173n.

Kaplan, David, 12n.
kinship, 45, 135, 150, 156, 161, 162, 179, 180, 199, 223; kinsmen, 99, 103, 135, 137, 139, 219, 226

labor, attitudes toward, xxxi, 39, 47–50, 56–57, 91; itinerant character of, 46, 54, 67; *see also* peasants, occupational structure
Labruzzo, 197, 204. *See also* bands
La Mantia, Giuseppe, 32
land, fragmentation of, 43n., 80–81, 84; related to power, 37, 62n.; tenure, Ch. III, IV. *See also latifondi*
Landsberger, Henry A., 114n., 210n.
latifondi, xxviii, 31, 36–38, 41, 42, 43, 50–52, 54, Ch. IV, 93, 141, 186, 189, 191, 192–96, 198, 201; anachronistic features, 74, 83; decline, 76 *et seq.*, 83, 127, 208, 217; defined, 53–54; management and supervision, *see gabella, gabelloti, mafia, mafiosi*; occupation of, 190, 195, 201; persistence, 73 *et seq.*
latifondismo, 53 *et seq.*, 72, 79, 84, 182; defined, 53–54
latifondisti, 37, 42, 47, 53, 77–78, 81–82, 93, 139, 142, 186, 190, 192–97, 199, 200, 202, 204, 210, 213; and bandits, 109; and English culture, 191n., 192n. *See also* aristocracy; nobility

leadership, 114, 121, 124, 137, 143, 162, 174, 198n., 209
Livornese, Giuseppe, 60n., 65, 69, 165n., 196
Lorenzoni, Giovanni, 42, 51, 53, 56n.
Luca, 103–07, 112–15, 161. *See also* bands

Mack Smith, Denis, 11, 14n., 19, 28, 30, 39, 40n., 41, 56n., 72, 73, 89n., 91, 94, 97n., 98n., 113n., 114n., 115n., 182
mafia, defined, xiv, xxviii, 5–10, 227–28; origins, 10–12, 89 *et seq.;* repression of, 182–89; revival, 190 *et seq. See also cosca*
mafiosi, defined, xxvii–xxviii, 6–8; chiefs, 125n., 126n., 136, 143, 145, 152, 153, 154, 168, 170, 171, 186, 187, 188; decline, 216–17, 222, 230; relation with bandits, 94–95, 101, 109, 130, 136. *See also campieri*; entrepreneurs; *gabelloti*; power brokers
manutengolismo, 172n., 173n., 186. *See also* patronage
Marciani, Giovanni Enrico, 77n., 78n., 191, 201n.
Marino, Giuseppe Carlo, 15, 128n., 212n.
marriage, 39, 59, 117, 118, 129, 158, 161, 162, 196
Marx, Karl, 4
Matteo, 103, 106–08, 110–16, 118, 134, 161
Maxwell, Gavin, 183n., 197n.
Mayer, Adrian C., 110n., 137n.
McDonald, J. S., 121n., 127n.
mediators, *see* brokers; entrepreneurs
middlemen, defined, xxviii, 7–8, 9n., 25; decline, 216. *See also* brokers; entrepreneurs
migrant labor, xxx, 21, 24, 34, 35, 80, 84, 218–21, 225, 230

Mirabella, Adriano, 118, 184, 186, 194; Emilio, 41, 117–20; Giacomo, 118, 194, 199, 202, 239
Mitchell, J. Clyde, 137n.
Mitrany, David, 55n.
mobility, upward, 39, 47, 75, 91, 100, 214
Molè, Giovanni, 42, 72n.
Montalbano, Giuseppe, 204n.
Moore, Barrington, Jr., xxvi, 98n., 101n., 172n.
Mori, Cesare, 15, 132–36, 144, 146n., 160n., 182–86
Mosca, Gaetano, 15, 145n.
Moss, Leonard W., 49

Navarra Crimi, Gaetano, 54n.
networks, xxvii, xxviii, 71, 96, 99, 115, 128, 134–37, 140, 142, 143, 145, 147, 148, 156, 161, 179, 222, 225, 234; as an emic category, 134–35, 146–47
Newbigin, Marion I., 17
nicknames, 127–28, 179, 206n.
Niermeyer, J. F., 211n.
Nietzsche, Friedrich, 87
nobility, 39, 42, 89, 98, 191n., 192n. *See also* aristocracy; *latifondisti*
Novacco, Domenico, 13n., 15, 173n.

Olivieri, Aldo, 81, 203, 221; Aloisio, 150, 196; Pietro, 82, 221
omertà, 51, 211–12, 227
outlaws, *see* bandits
overseers, 61, 118, 195. *See also* stewards

Paine, Robert, 150n.
Pantaleone, Michele, 14n., 15, 125n., 143, 145n., 160n., 182, 183n., 191n., 197n., 206n., 207n., 210n., 217, 224n., 225n., 227n.

Parliamentary Commission (Anti-Mafia), 5n., 14n., 227–28
partnerships 60, 64, 67, 117, 128, 135–38, 168, 196, 236
Passerin D'Entrèves, Alexander, 213n.
pastoralists, xxviii, 44, 45, 60, 62, 63, 70, 82, 132, 147–50, 150n.
pastures, 42–45, 50, 51, 59, 70–73, 82, 106, 119, 148
patrinominal families, defined, 135n., 136n.; 60, 69, 161
patronage, 54, 62, 96, 151, 172, 177–78, 180, 184, 197, 199, 202, 203, 214, 224, 238. See also brokerage; brokers
peasant, cooperatives, 68, 77, 141, 190, 195, 201, 205, 207, 208n., 209, 238; entrepreneurs, see entrepreneurs; farming, decline, xxx, 84, 219–20, 230; leaders assassinated, 15–16, 77n., 205–207; rebellions, 42, 68, 76–77, 81, 97, 100, 114–15, 121, 122, 190, 193 et seq., 201, 203, 204, 209, 210
peasants, categories, 15, 47, 48, 60, 75, 80, 218–19; exploited, 52–57, 60–62, 65, 66, 68; occupational structure, 46, 60–61, 67, 75; proletarianization, 39, 90, 94, 98, 214
Pecorini, Giorgio, 200n.
Petacco, Arrigo, 143n.
physical force, see violence
Pitkin, Donald, 24n., 47, 49n.
Pitt-Rivers, Julian A., 49n., 100n., 151, 238n.
Pizzorno, Alessandro, 220n.
Poma, Rosario, 224n.
Pontieri, Ernesto, 28, 33n., 54, 95n.
population, 5, 29–35, 68, 90
power, basis, 37, 61–62, 62n., 198; local domains, 6, 46, 54, 89, 97, 98, 99, 100, 101, 136, 176, 191, 200, 209–14, 217, 228, 233–43;

rival, 187, 191, 209, 210n., 212; tactical, 113n., 199
power brokers, 7–8, 177, 191, 212. See also mafiosi
Prestianni, Nunzio, 61n., 71n., 73
priests, 20, 23, 66, 95, 105, 112–13, 165n., 166, 168, 196, 200, 238, 239
primogeniture, 38, 91
private armies, 11, 89, 142, 190
protection, 28, 46, 51, 55, 99–100, 101, 109n., 116, 146, 151–52, 154, 178, 181, 182, 192, 198, 203, 228; See also manutengolismo
public security, 51, 61, 91, 94, 130, 182, 187, 199–200, 210–211, 214–15
Pupillo-Barresi, A., 33n.

Raffiotta, Giovanni, 141n.
ransom, 151, 153, 157, 174
Redfield, Robert, 49n.
Reid, Ed, 143n.
Renda, Francesco, 34, 127n., 225n.
rent capitalism, 53 et seq.; defined, 56–57; 64, 68, 92, 214
retainers, 11, 93, 94, 96, 99–100, 141, 153, 177n., 186n., 194, 195, 198, 199, 204, 210
rispettu (respect), 62, 68, 69, 100, 146n., 147n., 152, 172–73, 198, 202, 211–12, 243; defined, 173n.
Rochefort, Renée, 79n., 192n., 195, 209n.
Romano, Salvatore Francesco, xxv, 15, 30, 100n., 125n., 127n., 141n., 192n., 206n., 225n.
Romeo, Rosario, 40n.

saints, 214n.
Salvioli, Giuseppe, 27n., 30, 32, 33n., 40n., 56n., 65n.
Sansone, V., 204n., 205n., 206n.
Sartorius von Waltershausen, A., 27n., 33n., 40n., 66n., 70, 73

Schneider, Jane, 52n., 76n., 110n., 148, 150n., 220n.
Schneider, Peter, 26n., 76n., 136n., 220n.
Sciascia, Leonardo, 224n.
Segni (Land Act), 191, 195
self-sufficiency, 23, 24, 26, 27, 29, 92–93, 98. *See also* autonomy; power
Separatism, 192, 204
Sereni, Emilio, 33n., 56n.
shepherds, *see* pastoralists
sibling bonds, 179
Silverman, Sydel F., 47, 49n., 61n.
Socialism, 121 *et seq.*, 204–08, 222–23
Sonnino, Sidney, 40n., 41, 56n., 66n.
Sorgi, Antonino, 77n., 195, 206n.
State, xxviii, 5, 12, 25, 26, 28, 29, 37, 38, 39, 40, 42, 46, 78, 91–96, 100, 116, 142, 153, 162, 172, 176, 177, 180, 184, 199, 211–215, 227–28; State-formation, 9, 26n., 28, 91, 162, 176n., 177n. *See also* centralization; encapsulation; Italian State
stato, 23, 29, 89. *See also* autonomy
stewards, 43, 44, 47, 69, 81–82. *See also* entrepreneurs; overseers
Stone, Lawrence, 177n.
strikes, 122, 124
suicide, 189

Tarrow, Sidney G., 75n., 77n., 79, 141n., 201n., 209, 224

Tilly, Charles, xiii–xxiv, 9n., 25
Tomasi Di Lampedusa, Giuseppe, 11n.
transport, *see* communications
tributes, 46, 151–22, 153–56, 168. *See also* extortion

usi civici, see common use rights
usury, 53, 55. *See also* rent capitalism

Van den Muyzenberg, Otto D., 100n.
vassalage, 27–28
Vassallo, Ippolita, 139n., 165–67, 169, 178
Van Velsen, J., 14n.
violence, xxviii, xxxi, 10–15, 61, 62, 75, 79n., 91–93, 100n., 116, 137, 139n., 141, 147, 151, 153, 160–61, 162, 171, 180–82, 191, 200, 202, 207, 210 *et seq.*, 233–43; decline, 224–25
Vöchting, Friedrich, 18, 43, 58n., 74, 78

Walter, Eugene Victor, 14n.
Weingrod, Alex, 9n., 25n., 220n.
Wertheim, W. F., 102, 229
Wolf, Eric R., xxxi, xxxii, 6n., 7, 49n., 55n., 70, 74, 75n., 95n., 100n., 113n., 114n., 136n., 150n., 151, 178n., 180n., 209
Wolfgang, Marvin E., 176n.

Ziino, Nunzio, 54n., 56n., 66n.